Author Wolf Arenberg
Adventure Crime

The Part of the most need Amber Room is Found, and on the end 8 people are kilt

Of the shaft Mühlenbach (mill creek) of the cooper and silver mine

Koblenz Round Germany EU an USA

Copyrigth by Engelbert Rausch

ISBN 9783946925231

1 Alarm in <monastery (Kloster) Arenberg and first dead

Alarm in the Dominican inside the Abbey Hotel, in Kloster (monastery) Arenberg hive of activity, the holiday season and the wonderful weather bring the sisters a full house. The monastery hotel is wonderful and offers every guest feel special. In addition the directly connected to the Holy Garden and the pilgrimage church St. Nicolaus. Walks in the beautiful little city from Arenberg and Immendorf make every guest joy. But also walks in the adjacent Westerwald and the Rhine and Mosel are easy to manage from here. There is a bus every day to the city of Koblenz. In the beautiful middle Rhine valley, then by lift or cable car to the fortress Ehrenbreitstein or just walking through the beautiful old town.

Many guests of the monastery hotel make good use of the many so-great offer. It also makes a group of men who came from northern Germany and southern Germany. The spokesman of the group comes from the vicinity of the monastery he is from the adjacent Westerwald a forest. These men walk very much and always in the same direction. Often in the beautiful Mühlental /Millcreek) in south of Arenberg located. There is also the old Disused mine pit on the millstream (Mühlenbach) in near of a small creek). The mine is these in 1960 completely shut down because the operation was no longer profitable because of the price decay of zinc lead and silver. From 1945 to 1947, the pit had already been shut down because of the war influences there was no more electricity there to control the water quantities. The pit is partially submerged, closure time in 1960 use exactly these men who now well in the hotel in Arenberg to Nazi treasures to bring safe there that were previously hidden in the Westerwald. There were no longer safe because of rain construction activities around the town Hachenburg. The man has so far not approached the salvage of artefacts married.

It was too dangerous to lift these treasures and sell. An offer of a rich American has now to put everything yet to recover from the sealed shaft. You have prepared well, near the Valley of the Mills, they have a barn rented by the owner of Sauer mill. A little forest out they have already begun a close connection tunnel to dig into the shaft. The men from the Westerwald is the former engineer from the pit and knew the area and pit excellently. You have the older gentlemen difficult told, they are now no two Meter more from the breakthrough in the tunnels. Laboriously Crawling they the small tunnel along and sluggish the sweat of their browse the earth in small quantities with buckets out. "Schneider, please explain to me how we should get through this little corridor the large parts of the Amber Room (Bernsteinzimmer)". „My dear Ulrich, which is not a problem, this tunnel is only the access to the bay so we unnoticed by everyone here still living people can take care of everything alone for the removal and prepare.

We must remain an observed, we can`t goes through the main gate at this time. We transport then everything from about the old sealed great gates. Well, as the other Outputs that we are only just opening.

For loading in to the container. If we must be loaded in few hours all have prepared everything. No one can get some of them with. " Ulrich wipes the sweat from his brow, No then I will believe so the times. What do you mean what amount has Hans negotiated with the Ami? ". ,, As far as I've noticed, we get about 50 million divided by the five of us are these 10 million each. Gerhard can say this very precisely. For this, but worth the drudgery se, is quite neat. Well, give it no more than two meters up into the bay." "When the whole shit is drunk, what then?". ,, Be not worry, I know the pit is already a long time and have chosen a place for loot of art which is "well above the water table. ,, Well then we hope this for us and our money. When we come to replace the others so that we come out of this hole.". ,,An hour then the other three are tuned to be third and create something more than the two of us ". ,, Well, hopefully, I have slowly fed up with what is behind this narrow tunnel ". Do not worry that it will not give anybody. Will be able to understand what we have dug up here and how we have all this done so unnoticed. The tunnel has a great advantage for us. No one is a little remark s we can go unnoticed out and in, until we can on ends left.

Through the main gate all days we load in Container. We make sure that the few residents around here will not be at home. " Shortly afterwards, the detachment also appear already and you are certain that you've made in the latest two days the breakthrough into the shaft. At evening in the people in hotel sit together, whispering advice, draw and already preparing theoretically salvaging the goods before. They are so deepened and obsessed with their intentions that they become loud and incautious in conversation. Sister Ulrike served them food and get long, very long ears. She feels by the secrecy.

These men have something urgent things to do. One day she gets up and follows carefully the five old men. Old men yes, but all seem in very good condition. Careful and let it leaves in its civil clothes dressed the monastery. She goes to the men careful after. As harmless hikers are the five on the way to the shaft. There they go the greatest distance through the forest, may sister Ulrike go unnoticed behind the old men. Soon the see in the Mills disappear in a barn, they have to wait, and the men are long time out of sight. It was not until an hour later they reappear with grave tool and in old dirty.

With her work clothes dressed. They sneak so funny dressed carefully through the forest. Still is from the astonished Non Ulrike. The men do not notice, like a cat creeping nun. Although they look a few times in order before getting into the tunnel but they do not notice Ulrike that ad here's cleverly hidden. Two of the men go around the bay area. Three of the men move into the narrow tunnel. Then Ulrike makes the decisive mistake. Her great curiosity drives her into the tiny tunnel. She wants to know where this tunnel leads, wants to know what the old plan. She wants to explore only the direction of the tunnel, but she ventures into it too far. The men they discover with great dismay, they have no choice they have to catch. You have to bring this curious woman silenced. Ulrike immediately comprehends her situation when she sees the faces of the men. She realizes with a shock that is not dug here for fun, she has discovered something they should never have discovered. She puts into reverse and tried. To speed the men crawling on, all four to escape. She has no way to turn around in this narrow part of the tunnel. The men have the advantage that they can crawl forward. And they have overtaken Ulrike just before the exit.

They would also not escape so the men in front of the exit of the tunnel have been waiting two other men on Ulrike. The touch of the alarm line, which has two long pointed out, there's something is not right s in the tunnel. Ulrike is pulled out and pushed then tied up immediately. ,, Now what you curious stupid woman we have to keep no choice but you silently and make". The men looked horrified, no one had planned murder. Then another so pretty sister evens a child of God. They immediately recognized the sister's pretty curious face. ,, You Ulrich bring the Lady in the barn and bound them neatly strong. It is may not move or scream. ,, Four more days, then we are done then the tunnel her grave and she remains missing for ever." "No, no Gerhard excites the engineer of the troops, murder is not at all." ,, OK, you've heard it, off you go you stupid goat then you remain our prisoners." An hour later is Ulrike packed and tied into a small package in the barn. It is more capable of any rational thought. Her heart beating wildly and are breathing is very difficult. It only gets air through the nose. Fortunately, you are quickly dying of the senses. The men make as planned, not knowing there. Is a three other men have long been on the trail.

Even for them, who watch everything, there is no other option than these silly and curious girls for ever disappear. They have inspected the tunnel already secretly, and know that in latest two days an achieved a breakthrough in the mine. They wonder very pleased that these five men at least as to the eighty years, these are creating ever. But the while waving translucent them legendary Kraft s to give. Turn put these five men does not mean the three men a lot. Since will come as it is for the three strangers it is crystal clear. For each of them waving 10 million € In addition, these five German men are war criminals have stolen Nazi art and hidden. One American and two Dutchmen, it is still a mystery how the five men, this could create treasures up to this point. The Amber Room is already searched for many decades and has never been found until now. Who would have guessed that it is in this small unknown mine, it's a mystery to them. You, the Customer men are American and are dealer and Billionair. Ground the five old men already in good time send them to hell. The three commissioned by the buyer who has a contract with the five men have long been prepared the removal of the Amber Room. To Rotterdam. Everything is still packed.

In place here in the bay in their containers. Containers those are already empty in the port of Koblenz. Were the relations of the Dutch transport Company, with the German customs this preparation will be completed very fast. The Container for sealing has been declared content and car spare parts. It was the same as their German friends planned, but they lacked the right relations. Everything is already on their part but started the containers are still in Frankfurt and customs clearance is not yet prepared. The Dutch truck for transportation of the containers in the port of Koblenz, are already on the way from Holland to Koblenz. A wheel engages with the three men already in the other, her client receives daily report. He probably wants to save a lot of money to the three received only 30 million instead of fifty million. He wants the Amber Room to his employer have ben, of course as cheap as possible. Of the two daily recover it, and he has to pay less to the 20 million. What men? Have the five German men. The five are completely not care. These men have also stolen this room and as so much too old for this world. The three strange men back off, for today they have seen enough. At the earliest.

It is in the next morning, it will again be exciting for them. They have a low profile for a few days ensconced in the small Hotel Trierer Hof in Koblenz city. There they do not drop a little. They behave very well and play the righteous nice men holidaying together in the beautiful Middle Rhine Valley. They also make themselves really cosy in the great old town of Koblenz. You are almost every evening in the wine village and then at the end in the old town of Koblenz pubs. Let it go very g well. The prospect of nearly 30 million euros, this is so easily earned it makes easy, loose and lively. Today they make an excursion by cable car to the fortress Ehrenbreitstein. It is always an experience for them to visit this fortress and to look up there over the city Koblenz. The confluence of the Rhine and Mosel River, on the great monument of the Kaisers Wilhelm I how seat of his mighty horse. Far away on the horizon you can see the mountains of the Eifel and the Hunsrück. For Dutch people, this is the right small mountain. Not more than 700 Meter height it is a very great for them again and again it experience. They are omitted, to work all nice things. The beer on the Rhine and Mosel is schmackelig and treat you self to some of them. To the Koblenz pubs.

World also offers great food for delicious beer from the Eifel and from Koblenz. In the monastery it is tonight as always, only the cute nun missing from the usual service at the hotel. The mother Superior is excited, never has sister Ulrike failed their service, in the evening it's always there even if it has, at the date. Today, Sister Superior is in trouble. But when Ulrike is not on site the next morning and has not spent the night in the monastery, it sounds an alarm in the missing spot in Koblenz. No one has even a clue about where Sister Ulrike is. She put on her private clothing is not in their order costumes go. No one knows anything about their paths they may have taken. She has not confided to anyone with her suspicion. The Mother Superior calls a secular friend of sister Ulrike, whose phone number it has. This friend is Commissioner for the crime police in Koblenz. Renate Völcker is surprised by the call, the mother superior of the convent never called her. "What is Mother Superior?" we are looking for since yesterday desperate sister Ulrike we all hope that it is with them. ,, No Mother Superior I have not seen Ulrike long time.

I have no idea, I'll be right Arenberg ". A little later, Renate is in the monastery at the Mother Superior, not far from the two women who now talk anxiously sit five men and food. Five satisfied older gentlemen. Denes not miss the excitement about the missing sister. You assume that new lady without cowl is by the police. You also hear there's the whole area to be searched from morning by helicopter. You hear the suspected policewoman say. ,, Mother Superior, tomorrow morning soon we start searching when we have so far heard from sister Ulrike ". The five men look in horror that they can use now. With the thermal imaging camera DISCOVER the helicopter the girl in the barn. ,, The small must still away, far away. If the nun is found and there can be no guarantee of our area her. The men no longer take the time to eat their food. To pick up on the way Gerhard car from Montabaur they have also been a possible location for the nun select. "Well, we did not take Gerhard with us and did not inaugurate, he would not have tolerated the murder. But they are all four to very safe; there is no alternative without compromising anything. This sister is now between you and her 5. 000.000.00 €

The man who had been with Gerhards car sits knows the little small city Kottenheim. Near of the city Mayen, where he's been often for climbing into the disused quarries from the north. ,, Men, where we let them jump off a cliff, there are always climbers they will find quickly. That is about 40 Km from the monastery and I know from one of the sister. That sister Ulrike likes to go climbing and often. She fortunately has the right clothes on." ,, You're good, my dear, from it we must still govern evening ". When lifting the old well packaged sister after their arrival in the parking lot of Kottenheimer Winfeldes from the trunk it is already choked excruciating. Morning at 10.00 it rings in the Bureau of Koblenz he police, the police from Mayen are there the corpse Fund known and asks for help. Because the victim or killed probably comes from Koblenz. Only the Pathology (Coroner) can also help in Koblenz ". The plan of the four old ex Nazis has risen, they have stopped their work and remain today in the monastery hotel. There learn quickly, as s they found the missing. Not in the area but far away in the Vordereifel. Gerhard is horrified and wants to stop the action. No men, I will have nothing to do with a murder. ,, Gerhard she just stifled us.

So we did not want her dead. It was an accident"."An accident, I will not take it from you". ,, What do you want, you have nothing to do and our plan has worked. The Helicopter is more fly over the area and explore this no search teams are searching the undergrowth and the forest. " But Gerd swallows the men are right and they go back to work. Still am same day the breakthrough them into the shaft. They cheer and have set up their emergency lighting in the tunnel still sufficient time. The batteries and lamps have brought them into the tunnel days before. She delighted to see them, they're there, and they have what they have been waiting all almost 60 years. They were all still Jung boys when they get the chance to let disappear valuables. They needed this really just to secure and these have only later in the shaft warehousing when it was finally closed 1960th now after so many years it's in the front of a large fortune. About they burdened the murder or manslaughter of the young woman little. Chief Inspector Gerd Schöder goes into the office of his Kommissarin Miss Renate Völcker. The works hard and call there with the criminal investigation department in Mayen, when she sees Gerd entering in her office.

She quickly finishes the conversation she has tears in her eyes and has a hard time speaking. It hurts her that her best girlfriend is going to be killed. ,, What's going on Renate? ". ,, The cops Mayen asked us for assistance. The Pathology is already on the route to Kottenheim". ,, As so Kottenheim, they were found there, they had crashed when climbing. I can, t understand. Why she is alone went to climb, then without a car. ?. ,, It's easy and very possible we has good bus connections there, to come to Mayen don't need you a car. She can also go directly to the train to Kottenheim and the rest run loose. The rest on foot is a trifle ". ,, Yes there you know your way, s, lives there now thine Marianne in your Eifel goat with his Dog Sally. "

,, Come Renate, you throw in your jacket, we go there directly, we also take Schmidtchen with the Austrian he is still expert for hills and is well acquainted with mountains and mountaineering off ". A little later the three are from the murder SOKO Koblenz in Kottenheim. The Cops from Mayen has already done good work and reported the Koblenz Commissioners and then leaves it to the Kottenheim Winfield the field. It's strange why climbs a m None Organs.

At five o'clock here around alone, the Police doc has established the time of death at about 5:00 PM. A nun who has always made her work dutiful and has never made any extra trips. We wait the abductions his results, may she find something else let's see if our Pathology sea was an accident. Whether these are indications for somebody else to find fault? ". In the meantime, is in the bay, the mountains he loss artefacts?. All the men have brought. Heavy hoists and chain hoists which they now attach to the scaffolding of the shaft. "Do these things still hold the weight of the individual parts?". "No fear, that goes without problems, which have been dry all the years here. Packed confessed how you are viewing all parts safely packaged." Kurt runs down into the shaft, which has a depth of nearly 450 meters. ,, To pass me just to represent her to the three that gave me none of you slipping down there it goes 450 meters down. " ,, Do not worry Gerhard, we are careful, we have reached the first parts. Please load the chains and ropes down so that we can ensure the first parts and prepare transportation needs. Their voices are quite proud and their mood is outstanding. Soon, they have managed 50 million. € will change the owner.

The three of the five men n are in a short tunnel approx. 10 meters below the two men, the decrease up the goods. You just have to overcome these 10 meters with the loads. Slowly the chains and ropes are wrapped around the first portions of the walls and these are in with the hand. And chain hoists evenly pulled up. There are comic noises when the ropes are tensioned and the ropes and chain hoists are moved by man power. But the air in the shaft is not the best, the sweat running down them all n from his forehead. Then because of work and the other for fear because crash s one of the parts into the shaft. Then the parts would at least be lost to them. The American, who is full of tension, can, t wait. He does not pay attention to the warnings of the Dutch he simply creeps into the tunnel. He must know what's going on there, too much depends on it. But he did not care about his life either. It has been discovered before it reaches the middle of the tunnel. The men watch the control lamp light up in the shaft. ,, some cattle are in the tunnel, Ulrich calls ". "I still see we can afford anything, not now where we have found everything." Both men are astonished when they suddenly look in the tunnel. The American also has no chance against the old man.

Who can crawl along, the Ami however, was soon at the end, and his companions came to his rescue. But Paul can hurt him more lethal as it reaches him. It was a deadly sting in the heart. Then the sun for Paul goes under. Lightning quickly the men create the dead; they leave in the trunk of the car and disappear. The other men in the bay looking to him to Paul who has disappeared and remains, his helping hand is now missing where it is important. Did he fall into the shaft when he went out? There remain open questions, even outside they can after a long Search no trace discover no trace of Paul. Even in the evening and the next morning he does not appear. The two Dutchmen sit in their car and have two bodies in the trunk. Where do they ask, we're going to Ehrenbreitstein and just throw them both into the Rhine". "You're crazy the danger is too big for us to see." "Come up in the direction of Montabaur, where we dispose of them in a secluded parking lot. There, the Crime police Montabaur are responsible and the Koblenz police have no idea of the new dead. The four men in the monastery hotel ordered the one room and say that her fifth husband was tired and took the train home. We take all his belongings in the car. Perhaps he will come back.

Tomorrow or morning we will see. He wants again see his old, the desire? ". The next morning, the four hopes there is Paul have found their way back. But no trace can be discovered by Paul. You have no idea that Paul approx. 10 km far away from them is in a parking lot and the man from America two more mails along a forest path. The Dutch is no matter when the two are found. Take the dead men everything from what to them is. Everything looks like robbery, and the police will be busy for a long time, and a connection with the dead in Kottenheim will be difficult. Meanwhile, the recovery of the works of art goes on for the now four men. It is only very slow progress, the parts are very heavy and difficult to handle. Even if the walls were divided into smaller elements. The heavy Part pieces to recover from the poor conditions in the shaft, which that is an act of violence for the four men. Homicide is busy at this time in full Stress and the murder in Kottenheim. They are still waiting because it is the results get from pathology. Anita the Pat how login comes personally from the Pathology (Coroner) he over to the Bureau. "People I've discovered something that could close to murder. The nun has traces of tight bondage on hands and feet.

She must have been already tied up for several days. The nun is also not died from the fall. The nun has been choked or suffocated pretty sure. " The three commissioners jumped. Now they can be officially engaged last. But they still have no idea where to start. First, they checked the sister's friends and the family. There was nothing where they could have started. "I'll go to the monastery tomorrow, I'll be there. Perhaps the dog is buried there. Renate asked all guests and sisters in the monastery, thus ensuring some disquiet in the monastery. They interviewed the four old men. No one noticed anything. Renate has a list of all the guests who have stayed at the hotel for the last 14 days. A great deal of work is waiting for them, all of them have to search through them and ask for all the data. With a briefcase full of work she goes straight home and studied all night. All data he possible ways suspects about them checked. Unfortunately she commits a great mistake. The five, now four, older tourists cling directly to their research. It completely overlooks how vigorous the old men still are and driven by greed accomplish performance. They want to bring in the harvest of the second world war. A war that was ruined their lives so early.

From this now old men. Anna who was the sister of the mother Superior. Even all the other sisters are shocked by the death of Sister Ulrike. Now it is also not to rule out that it was murder. Ulrike was tied for a long time before her death. Anna includes Ulrike every day in the official prayers with the sisters. Do not take it anymore so behind the beautiful walls of the monastery. She must get out she must be able to cry alone. She makes herself up and goes in the areas adjacent to the monastery sacred garden. This saint garden was created in the 18th century under the leadership of then-Pfarrer Kraus. This all happened only with the strong support of the citizens of Arenberg. All individual stations are lined with rubble from the volcanoes around. Cross paths and roads lead to Mother Mary and describe the Virgin Mary's life. There are every, were Jesus figures in small wonderful caves. A masterpiece of church and Arenberger citizens were the decisive role in this expansion of the sacred garden. Each viewer has to see this garden as he really is now. One should not sentimentalize this in his mind you have to see in him what he is. This garden is a monument from around 18.th. In this time everything was different in the Church and in the.

Of the people and in the depth anchor in faith. Anna, the head nurse sits down by the Jesus figure in the middle of the complex and regarded Jesus with moist eyes. "Oh Jesus, why did you take my dearest nun, she had the chance to take me over here, take over my position". She kneels down in front of the cloister of the grotto, cries and prays. Please dear God take them in your arms and make me because is doing well in the sky with you. She was always a faithful and industrious girl an able young woman. Why did you just have to tear them out of the blooming life. Why did you have to take her so early to me?. She weeps bitterly as she now travels through the sacred garden. At each Jesus Figure she stops and pauses for a short prayer. She goes through the suffering garden dedicated to the Jesus Mother Mary. Although she feels that you have exaggerated here with the suffering of the Mother of God. Yes, she suffered for Jesus her son. But what is it against the suffering of so many mothers in the world who have lost all their families and still lose. Do not have a child, but simply lost by a bomb anything and everything in their lives. But she also sees this garden than just a reminder of the Church in the life of Jesus the Son of God and his mother.

Anna migrates all stations and goes into the wonderful St. Nicolaus church. This church is a real pilgrimage church. With infinite effort, this was completely wallowed from inside with fragments from the volcanoes. Very colourful stones, with glass-like structures, have been processed with great diligence and effort. She loves this church and goes to the altar, the mother Marie altar, and has a candle for Sister Ulrike. ,, Dear Mother Mary, please help sister Ulrike the transition into your kingdom, please e make it convenient for them, there with her up there is going well with you. Unfortunately we humans have no idea what is up there. But we all want to come to you in the heaven. We all want to be children of God, please protect us, strangely also the people who never believed in you. Dear Mother of God, m oh please can we find it these criminals. " Crying, she goes out of the church and sees in passing that one of their guests he sad and reverent in church praying It is one of five older gentlemen who go so busily walking every day. The heavy door of the church falls shut behind her, she feels much better. She talked with Jesus, Mary and God. She speaks with him every day, they pray to him every day. But now in the emergency it is so important.

More importantly become for them. More than ever she feels closer to him. The road from the church to the convent she returned through the sacred garden with its many chapels and through the beautiful framed by trees Investment. You have to take this overloaded garden as it is and what it means. It was created at a time when the church still the only place was at the people in the Church and the Church the only protection against the ruling found. Now this garden still helps the distressed souls and gives people hold power and new strength. One feels his sorrows and his need not be left alone. In the end, it always helps re d s people praying here and be self build and here gather new strength. Even Anna found its way back to its former strength. She's back on her way to her mother's house and the hotel is waiting for them. There are many visitors here in this hotel, because they all find the peace and tranquillity necessary for their future lives here. In the evening, the mother superior gathered all her sisters and urges them to keep open on the ears at the hotel. It will also not help feeling that is involved in the death of Ulrike here from the hotel guests or at least one guest. The four old men treat yourself no rest, little by little mountains.

It well packed parts of the so sought ornate room from the bay. Actually thinking Gerhard often you reach the sacred garden transformed the place in this Arenberg was the only right one for the Amber Room It would have to stay here and find his final place in the sacred garden. In this Garden seems to be all full of precious stones, the sacred garden and in the church they are volcanic clunkers all painstakingly been walled up. ,, As we have many parts yet to recover, calls the man at the winch down? ". ,, Two days Bernd, then we have all of the parts above. " Interior for the shaft main gate already built up a huge mountain of wall parts in boxes packed on. It is good that these parts of the Amber Room are so well packaged. German workmanship thinks Gerhard. He has long planned their share, will distribute most of the money in Africa. He has learned in his time there, the needs of the people know. He can, t understand the country about the plight of refugees in the EU. It was for 50 years as foreseen it one day then come must do what should the poor devils else ?. They were robbed, enslaved and mistreated by the world. The alleged help of Western governments was always only help for their rulers and ruling here.

For the already wealthy the help of our governments has never been. Help for the people who would have desperately needed this help. Very many billions were by the Americans and Europeans burned in Africa. They were leaders stuck in the butt these billion immediately in to postponed their private assets in Europe or in the United States have. . Why because the world is ruled by capital, by the rich, against this a small portion of people no one can govern. Not even in Europe who were poorest and most are always the poor and they remain the candelabrum in the world. Nothing else thinks Gerhard is also the problem in Greece. Greece is an African Republic which lies in Europe, which the rich practice by their owners People r year tenth mercilessly. Was make them richer now all European citizens have for the debts of the Greeks and the refugees from Arabia and Africa rise .Debt and debt have caused our governments because they see rulers and proper it supported. Now that there is nothing to suck the rich Greeks bugger off to Switzerland and the United States. At their stolen the national wealth, no one comes close, because they find again the protection of the world from the other realms. This rich govern there in the US.

And in Europe, the world But here we have the cushion of democracy. Between rich and poor, it is also just a bubble, which those in power as required inflation or deflation can be. Gerhard has the experienced everything himself and has no bad conscience to salvage the Amber Room because of this here and to do with the money a good thing. Also become necessary murder of the nun touched him through but it was an accident. He will be able for it save thousands of lives. For him, this is a continuation of the war, it is his last chance. Those no longer look like hikers. Immediately stop the cycle and goes behind some bushes for cover. The men have tools for digging in their hands and dive in the bushes. The skirmishers hide their bicycle and follow the men carefully. It looks like these in wind ropes expose a hidden tunnel and then disappear into it. Again, the men feel so safe that they all must disappear in the tunnel through which they must creep without leaving a guard. The head nurse is amazed not bad; she's waiting for almost an hour and then followed the men in the tunnel. She makes the same mistake as Sister Ulrike. Only their position is even worse because the two Dutchmen have also observed everything. They have now brought.

Reinforcement and also crawling heavily armed behind the sister, it had to happen now. All preparations are completed by her side. But the other men now have their weapons in the tunnel; they will no longer have their goods catch now. The events are all at once. The nun is discovered by the older men. Rumble falls this at the end of the tunnel into the bay. Rudolph stands right on the end of the tunnel; she can just catch it and throws it directly to the ground.

Of course, he immediately recognizes the upper swimmers from the monastery and before she knows it, she is tied up and tied up. Men come, he calls his friends we have visit. One more damn nun visited us. The men get close from different directions and are armed. They are prepared for everything. But when they see the upper swimmers lying there tied up and tied, they take their fingers off the trigger. ,, So a shit, yet another sister from the convent, which is up there with the women going on." ,, Nice hands up guys they hear a cool man's voice from the tunnel and hear the several pistols and rifles are loaded. The old manor jump aside and chase a volley 9mm cartridges in the direction of the tunnel exit. I get his reward for the lost youth and the consequent botched life.

Bit by bit they pose difficulty the art which is worth gold from the bay. They have no idea because she they are being watched since the beginning of the work, this has already disappeared at the hands of these people r her Paul. You have no idea that the superrich and his henchmen will bring them even here the reward of their work. In Koblenz Bureau all the wires run hot to the zinc that detectives from Montabaur asking for the support of the Bureau of Koblenz. The President of the Presidium can hardly believe it. As long rest in Koblenz, now it's all about at once to murder. Three murders in the area of the jurist direction of Koblenz, homicide is sitting in his office, led by its Boss Gerd the first Hauptkommissar Gerd Schöder. An experienced and look good cop. ,, What they now intend to do sir commissioner "?. ,, Mr President, I will not shake the feeling these are the three murders together, that there is a connection between the murders. The monastery seems to me to be a centre point. A sister of the monastery was found dead. A guest of the monastery is dead and an American of which we not yet know much also murdered. Both of us have already identified and hope soon to know more.

The guest from the monastery is a harmless hiker an almost 80 year old with the like-minded wandering in the area. The American is guest in the Trier court in the city, which is the hotel in the theatre. This is or was also with two friends from Holland in the city on vacation. I do not see any clues at all, but we'll all have to go through. So I need at least five more people to share with my Commissioners. It will be a difficult work, but three dead, three murdered people that is hardly comprehensible. Something unusual is happening in our city and in the surrounding area and the monastery is apparent focus. We have already started recording the thread there. The Kommissar Völcker can say something; they took all the guests and staff under the microscope. " ,, Yes that's true, I have made to it to take all there because to the zinc guests under the microscope. I had only the five older hikers except but now after the also one of them was murdered I am looking for a connection. We have to monitor all those who are eligible. I have no idea what these people bring together. These three in the Trier court also appear in connection with stand this series of murders. " ,, Well Kommissar, I can already see there are extensive investigations be necessary.

I am still leaving people in Mayen and Montabaur. I ask her to be a special Kommissar for these murders. I will support them where I can. At to work, I want to be informed every night on the progress. " The four older gentlemen are struck by lightning when they hear of the murder of their friend. Strangely enough, an American has also perished. A man from the land of their order boar, ,, what do we do, there's something about lazy". ,, We have to go and the first close off the entrance to the tunnel. She must know there we have already recovered the Amber Room. I t may know that this is it here are any. What if leaves us our clients already control us, if he already knows how far we really are with the Amber Room. It's very strange, because has an American to do with the death of Paul. Let's go, before the police turn everything upside down. Above all, we have to get the weapons out of the barn; it looks like if we have this very necessary as ". Above all, my car must return to Hachenburg, with whom you have but the sister transported?. ". ,, Gerhard your car is already back at the station ICE.". A little later, the men have to carefully close the door entrance. They are very lucky that they acted so fast. The two Dutch are in the Harbour Koblenz busy.

To organize the transport for the Container which Just arrived from Holland into Koblenz, the two have no problems with her third husband was no longer alive. Also, there is already a lack them against the in a men. Now there are just two recent Dutch against four old men. They see the advantage with them. Not realizing that these old men are ready for anything, and neither God nor the devil fruits. They fear already I is not spoiled young men from Holland. You have thought about it and they realize there wants to save their clients money or want to play it safe. It seems to be so important that some deaths do not matter, that they have no value for him not suspect they the Amber Room. But they become the men to simmer the soup. You leave the Mühlental valley and will only check this once a day. They must await the invasion of the police. They avoid from now any contact with their clients. You are sure that she wants to do some mistake. But also the two Dutchmen suspect that is now a break. You know, there is they do not need the truck, and containers for some time. It is also clear to them that the police are now on their way. It was a very big mistake to remove her dead partner in the parking lot. You may have noticed.

How they are by some women, presumably police we observed. The one they did not address directly to their partner was a thinking mistake of the police. That has the impression for the two strengthened that one has them in mind. Enter the next day relaxed and happy and put their leisure days in Koblenz on. Not without still fast to control what is with the shaft is loose. They could not find it anymore, the entrance of the tunnel has disappeared. ,, Damn old also smelled a rat, which are proof; there is no trace of the tunnel. We even allowed us not so often move here we do not betray. We the police did not draw attention to the shaft. We will find again where the entrance of the tunnel is. The two men are glad that even the old bags have switched and have done their work. It is also clear to you that the stupid American has brought everything out of control. Too great money has never brought happiness. They have informed their client about everything. He was not happy with the events and now knows that it was a big mistake to want to save money. If it is that he also saves a lot of money. When the Dutch the five, now four elminate. How the two do this does not matter to him, but it must not endanger his intention.

The two Dutchmen must also wait as the matter continues. Also is clear that is the Koblenz police right now in turmoil. Three men dead in so few days the old gentlemen are also withdrawing, now they can risk anything. Nothing is allowed to draw anyone's attention to the Mühlenbach pit. Gerhard has set out once one day to rest at the hotel. The other three go to turn in the surrounding area; they have distracted the Rhine and Mosel. Just do not go into the mills. Gerhard stretches out in the hotel on his bad; he is not tired but somehow strangely restless. The stakes are high for all of them and there has been Tote and caught one of them is very bad for him. In particular, the unnecessary death of the nun is a burden on him. He did not credit his old friends, this fact brings some distance between Gerhard and the three other men, and there are murderers. They have survived everything, the last months of war. The transfer of the trucks, the later backup of the treasures in the pit Mühlenbach. He still hears the laude calling captain in his ears, as if it were today. You have three days and three nights stood behind the Flack Gun. You have volunteered as Flack helper to Berlin. They were only 3 months in business of this War.

34

They have been age only some T military training in Koblenz. From there they were taken directly to Berlin after the bomb attack. The handling of de r Flack taught and then distributed to the anti-aircraft guns. Every night, and often during the day, they were called out of the dungeon. They rarely had more than 5 hours of sleep. He Gerhard Maifelder has risen in a few weeks to sergeant and the flak was able to use. His assistants were even younger than him. He was just 17 years old but physically very strong. It was madness in last nights; hundreds of planes were in the sky. They could shoot as much as they wanted. Instead of less, there were more and more airplanes. It pops everywhere terrible a bomb carpet lies on Berlin.

The sirens of fire and ambulance cry nonstop. Next to him and behind him flowing individual anti-aircraft guns and its crew into the air. The killings in his battery are silencing more and more. Everything around him is in ruins, but his gun shoots yet, he was still chasing a shot after another in the sky. He does not need goals, meeting is hit or miss. He was surprised that his aides are still able to load his gun. All around them burned his gun, is already red hot. Someone is pulling shut him of his gun. You race s for their lives.

And are not 30 Mete a way than this gun into the air flowing Inviolate they reached her small self-built bunkers, which also them only the most necessary protection give. Cut it only still on their simple bunks. The crew of the Flak, five young men had only the bare essentials here. So far they have been spared a hit. All other gun crews who are also very young men, they all bore no longer in this world. Gerhard Maifelder it is not clear whether these not drawn the better lot have. Simply close, simply an end. They all volunteered. But what I here they could not, he guessed. But they also wanted to fight for the fatherland until the last second. But what now, their gun is in the bucket and their ammunition at the end. The still small remainder of perhaps another night, they could badly throw after the hated airplanes. He was sad when he realized is that for them now is break only once. The guys If his four behind he lance or off and but want to disappear now. But the roar of an unfamiliar captain Rated Most of them phones planning. He come with their upper Feldwebel (sergeant) jumped into your hole. The commander officer turns immediately to his small Officer ,, Gerhard, here it's all over, we have in this area any more flak and no more Munition.

But the captain has an order for you. " ,, Yes, "said the captain of the self and not older than 30 years; ,, I have brings out an important mission for you to you from Berlin. A special commando Maifelder you're coming from the Westerwald. We have three loaded trucks, on the outskirts of Berlin. Civilian trucks these must be brought to safety in the Eifel. You shall bring them there. Three of you still have the military driving license for trucks, two travels as a companion and keep in contact with us with the radio devices but which can only be used when we report. Get out of the truck. You must go straight the Russians are approaching Berlin inexorably. The cargo is important documents which must be brought to safety. You have papers which give you free passage through every control and barrier ". One hour to reach by jeep traveling through the rubble of Berlin until the truck. They are instructed and agree the route with the main man. ,, So now there is again or what dent royal to eat and rations. In each truck, a box of Chokakola, a delicious kind of Choco to give the driver power, you have to drive as fast and as far as you can. Reserve tanks are under the truck, s, it has over the Eifel region rich ". The guys do not worry. For now concerning their cargo.

They keep the new job very seriously. You were with the importance of the order of the Armed Forces leadership to them so as s trusts and entrusted. At least Gerhard comes like that closer to home approach. Then there's Wolfgang and Siegfried of Mannheim, the come their home also much closer. Only Helmut and Rudolf from Emden are, do not come quite as close to home zoom but away from Berlin and far away from the attacking Russians but also a little bit closer to Emden is far from Berlin. But she scientific also because the invasion has already succeeded in France and there will be a race between the Russians and Americans. Is also between them and the Americans, he was rather in the Eifel. You or the enemy that is still completely open. You are close to Frankfurt when the news come the Russians have reached Berlin. The Connecting with wireless device is discontinued since that time, the connection between you and Berlin are capped. Gerhard s pulls in to control his home in the Westerwald, Hachenburg and wait what will happen no other option than once. The boys all feel as this millennium after so few years near the end. On the outskirts of Frankfurt ha b s it passes the last military control.

More and more soldiers come from the Western Front to come to meet them. All do not know where, the German army is in the dissolution. The guys really manage to take the truck to Hachenburg. At the edge of Hachenburg Gerhard knows a farm on this bring them once the truck in a huge barn under. The farmer a relative of Gerhard is surprised to see his nephew again. It supplies the guys with civilian clothes and retains this for a few days with him. But the news does not bring anything good from Berlin and also from the Western Front. The leader has shot him, she has left cowardly. The Americans have conquered the important bridge of Remagen. The allies flow into the German Reich. From the south from the west and the Russians are victorious after their Berlin conquest. The guys stay near Hachenburg until everything has settled. They have loaded the old temporary containers from the trucks with the help of four huge front loaders. The Container are difficult secured and the documents which are attached to them. They now open for the first time are works of art of the East listed. No one dared the time being to open this container. The Lkw.s was later sold to a vehicle entrepreneur in Frankfurt. Deutsche Wehrmacht.

The claims an Log could no longer stay. Neither claim to the goods still on the LK W, s. so then separate the Jung people an Is it in the country a little quieter. The containers were well hidden under the hay. But no one was looking ever go to this because no one but the boy and the farmer knew. The captain, an Adjust ant of Goering and the Sergeant are in the defence of the madman and the even crazier Goring's life. So it is not prove respect this transports. The guys become always smaller financial support from the proceeds of truck sales. Nobody dared to open the containers for decades. One was just afraid of it, one had a slight idea. The one slightly damaged container allowed an insight into its interior. I` m be all the containers were opened for the first time in 1956, at a single corner. They gasped, out of the box looked them against the wall parts which no other conclusion access passage in these containers, the Amber Room is looking well packaged. One from the family of Gerhard is an engineer in the ore and silver and lead mine. I` m Mills at Arenberg / Koblenz he brought Gerhard after his studies as a young mining engineer under there. 960, this shaft was closed because it became uneconomical. He should fill up with water.

Only as a water reserv for the small city of Arzheim and other places. A company from Hachenburg, also from the relationship by Gerhard was commissioned sure to close this slot. Most miners came from the Westerwald. So this was a unique opportunity to let the Amber Room disappear valid. The whole world is looking long time for the Amber Room. But nobody would guess it in this unknown pit. They wanted to wait and see just how things develop in Germany. All involved agree that this should be their reward for that shit war. Since 1961 everything now is lumbering in this closed slot in Arenberg. Now 2014 are once again all and located at the gateway in upper headframe. It is now ready for transport. Sold for 50 million € to an American billionaire who wants to set this up as his favourite- room. The room must be smuggled out of the country and smuggled into America. This means for all they involved will be very custody. But this has now led to the delays and has already cost three lives. Three murders are still a mystery for the Koblenz Crime police. The first chief Kommissar is once again sitting together with his special commission. They evaluate the part what they have already identified. In the end, it is not much. They checked all the people.

All guests at the monastery Hotel, all guests in the Koblenz Hotel Trierer Hof, you have the detectives attached to the two Dutchmen. Check for such since the paths of the four remaining old men in nuns Hotel. But all seem to just want to relax and enjoy all the Rhine and the Mosel area. „ Men love Commissioners, it can`t be. We have three dead who seem to have no connection with each other. We have no reason to believe why a nun is dead. We have no idea why a harmless old gentleman of a guest at the monastery was murdered. Even more strange is the death of the American People. The only thing that connects them is the fact that they are in Koblenz or were. What strikes me is that both groups the two Dutchmen and the older men seem not large impressed with the death of their partner. They enjoy their holidays further as if nothing had happened. The hiking and enjoying our Mosel and the Mittelrheintal (middle Rhine Vallay) to the fullest, the only connection of all three people is that Monastery. But only to the extent that the two dead men were found on the same route, in the forest parking spaces between the monastery and city of Montabaur. The nun was found in Kottenheim that fits less to the foundations of the two men."

,, Guest Commissioner Schmidtchen from Austria in Koblenz has its say. Yes it's true, we have remarkably little. But the place where the nun might still be been chosen to us from other region lure from the area around the monastery. I think there must be a connection. The disposal of the two men has happened hastily, one has not the time to distribute these corps better. Because we acted so quickly here these two men were killed in the vicinity of the monastery and had to be disposed of immediately. The problem is somewhere between the monastery and Montabaur, ,, everyone agreed that comments on. They waited for the clerk's; Renate Völcker is still on the way from Kottenheim to them. She has the results of the Mayen Commissioners and, of course, was once again at the site of the corpse. There they ran into their natural adversary in the struggle for their boss, the Eifel goat with her dog. This Eifel goat's Marianne and is the long time girlfriend of her first main commissioner Gerd. She also fell in love with this quiet but so successful chief commissioner. Renate has already chosen this long as the father of her daughter. Gerd can handle it so well with her girl.

That it is a pleasure to watch them. ,, Na Marianne it's nice to meet you here. " ,, Marianne know how wonderful can cheat Renate this regard. She has noticed for a long time that it is, and behind her Gerd ago they did not see omits to give her a swipe. ,, trampling you our crime scene broken ". ,, Well if this is the crime scene would have had to shut off her this, but I see far and wide nothing. " ,, Watch your dog on that destroyed the nothing here. " ,, The mutt makes your work, look what the dog has found." Marianne extends the Commissioner a chain with a large cross. " Where did you find the chain," ,, Now Renate is again matter-of-fact and overthrows the small private tears. Over there on the small hidden car park, please show me the place, which could be important. " They keep ample clearance from this place and Renate immediately calls the detection service to secure all traces. Here one could have taken the nun out of the car. She might have lost her chain. The discovery service safely the traces of the car, which is very difficult because Marianne does not know the exact location of the chain because Sally her dog this has brought. Marianne just knows Sally has come from this little.

Hidden parking lot with the chain, the men look for everything thoroughly and seem to have secured by the tracks on his profil. You have to search for the most thorough search also the exact location of the chain. This was only possible because it has remained dry for the last few days. There is a small very small track; the men in Koblenz are waiting for Renate and the result of Mayen's commissioners. Also these are very happy with the results, it could bring them something further when they find the associated car. Of course, the men also thank Sally and Marianne, without those two they would never have had this track. Renate struggles need to do is to thank through to Marianne. The Special Commission in Koblenz is delighted with the report of the Commissioner Volcker. The vehicles of all current guests are checked immediately at the Trierer Hof and the Klosterhotel. Without result, the main suspects the two Dutchmen and the four older gentlemen have no car they could check. All rental car companies in and around Koblenz are under construction. Nearly 1000 cars then the cars of the companies in Montabaur were checked. It would take a few more days if they came to a conclusion. Gerd Schöder.

goes to the monastery with his commissioner. You want there to the back at the monastery remaining older man speak. With Gerhard Maifelder so is the name of the man who comes from the Westerwald and actually does not have far home. Then they have to talk to the sisters and, above all, the nurse. Gerhard shrieks from his reflections, it knocks on his room door. "Yes, if it's not the devil," he shouts loudly and somewhat annoyed. Gerd Schöder pushing on the latch and opens the door and enters, with its Commissioner Renate in tow. ,, Good day Mr. Maifelder it, I'm Commissioner Schöder and my company is my colleague Commissioner Völcker. Please excuse the error but we have to talk to you again ". ,, Their I have already told all my colleagues, I and my friends we know nothing, and know the murdered sister only two evenings she has served us. " ,, If you noticed on those evenings not alter the sister and possibly other guests in the hotel? ". ,, No Commissioner, we did not even have any, even the smallest conversation with the nurse. If they asked me if I know what this looks like, I could not answer their question. Also with the other people here in the hotel and we had very little contact. We five came here because.

We start our hikes from here ". ,, Today, Mr. Maifelder but they are not with their colleagues on the go." ,, knowledge they Commissioner, I am with 78 years the oldest. And I need some rest; I always wander just two days, the third day I am recovering. The path through the sacred garden and the walk into this wonderful church is always enough for me. I find here the right distance from my Freund Paul who was so brutally murdered. We still can, t believe it. We make these meetings every 5 years. We are old anti-aircraft mates and have not lost sight of us since 1945. But it's getting more and more difficult with us. But as they see the other three are back on tour ". ,, Where are the people today, "asks Gerd Schöder. He knows for sure, but he wants to hear whether Maifelder tells him the truth. ,, My friends wanted today to Braubach on the castle Marksburg and castle Lahneck in Lahnstein. Both castles I know enough, because I live near here, in Hachenburg. Tomorrow we will return together to the other side of the Rhine, in the castle Stolzenfels. This is so interesting because this palace of Kaiser Wilhelm was extended to us. " ,, It's beautiful, Mr. Maifelder it, it is really worth, but please think about whether was something suspicious.

Here in this hotel before the sister was killed. All the threads seem to converge in this hotel. We can`t avoid the impression that the murders. Of her sister and American friend are somewhere and somehow connected ". ,, I cannot imagine Commissioner says Maifelder which now ends at Renate Völcker a pretty young Commissioner thinks Gerhard. ,, Commissioner I could not imagine what connection could there be between the two of me. Even our friends Paul, not long know the sister and the Americans. If I had known such a pretty sister, would not have concealed this from my friends. " ,, Thank you, "says the chief inspector, thank you for that information. How long do they intend to stay here?.`` ,, We wanted to stay for the weekend and want soon back to home. But now it can take longer. We are waiting for the children and the wife of the murdered our friend and want this eventual still to Bremen accompany to attend Paul's funeral. " ,, Well, Mr. Maifelder it, they tell their colleagues that they also should think thoroughly again. We will come over again. We ask them all again because is they remain at our disposal at the hotel. Please plan your excursion for the afternoon; we will need some time for a final discussion. Mr. Maifelder neither.

He nor one, has one of her friends a car here?.".,,
No, Commissioner, we all met in Montabaur at the
station and are common to Arenberg took the bus.
" I am also driven by car from Hachenburg to the
ICE train station and then went with my friends to
this point by bus. " ,, Then again see Mr. Maifelder
it, they remember the stand she and her friends
about tomorrow morning available." Gerd, closes
with these words the door behind her. ,, Dear
colleague, Renate, unfortunately, there was
nothing for us to know about you. Even the walk
to the Marksburg and castle Lahneck, our people
confirmed observe these men. They have not
made any conspicuous observation. Damn it's
been noticeable because they are all so
unobtrusively. " ,, Come Gerd we go to the cafes
of the hotel and are now trying to learn about the
sisters and the mother superior. Someone must
have seen something. One of the sisters must
know where wanted the sister to their r private
clothes. That's certainly not common because s
just assume this s in jeans. I can, t imagine there's
Ulrike wanted to climb alone. Then she had me
ask, we were often climbing together to
Kottenheim, but as I said always together. There
must have been another reason.

Why they not their climbing clothes. On hand and did not inform me. " ,, It is quite strange as in this case, Renate, but we are still going on, even the tire tracks we have not yet identified. This could bring us further. The detection service is still there. The tires are noticeably wide; they try to get over the tires to the vehicle type. That would be a success story. It's bad, three dead and we're still clueless. " Tonight I have to go back to the police presidency, I hope that the discussions with the Superior and the sisters continue." These conversations also run in the sand, nobody in the hotel has noticed anything suspicious. Lead as the two commissioners go home they are not a bit smarter in this case. ,, I have an idea Renate; I go to my old friend Mani, who has here in Arenberg, a beer pub in the old style. Just as there is otherwise no longer one of these, you'll like the pub. Which is really old-fashioned and has if I remember correctly a museum status as a pub at least he has such a sign on his house. This is one of the few Bar still I just can from the sale of alcohol. But it is also getting worse, the sales amount go back every year. " ,, Then into your pub I have an appetite for a good beer. Gerd travels in an arc back to Arenberg into it, past.

Visit the church and then the right Pfarrer Kraus road down. It stops just across the street side of the pub / Klönsack called the hot box. You are Luck Mani just opened his pub. Gerd and Mani welcome and Gerd ask him Renate before his Commissioner. The looks around in wonder at the simple but nice old pub, you're probably not on duty here Gerd." ,, No Mani, at least not with you, here I am private. But I have some official questions for you. Because you still the only real pub in this place have. All around have disappeared all pubs. If we here in Arenberg will even drink a beer, it is only for you. " ,, What do you want to know Gerd ". ,, Did you recently five elderly gentlemen here with you, strangers ?. ,, I'm not here every day, but I remember the most Wednesday were the saving box empty up there at the table five elderly men sat never been here. " ,, The men are exactly that matters to me . When the resurface once call me immediately " . ,, OK Gerd I'm doing, the two beer of course, go on the house, I have to go urgently. If you want to have a drink Kathrin is there, he points to the over slim pretty operator behind the counter. ,, Ok, a beer we still remain. Renate now sits down with Gerd at the bar. ,, You're right, a wonderful old pub.

Far for me to walk, but together we could ever go back here. Has your old friend Mani noticed something?. He has a notice anything, but he knew that the five old men were here. If you know this pub they will probably show up here again. Then he should call me with a lot of beer in your stomach start to a few like to talk. Ulrike my love, please do e your blouse again. You know I speak in this regard only to my friend. "Yes I know you disgust on your Eifel goat you jump on. But what about me, you do not like me. " ,, I mean love Renate, I am for years with Marianne together and that will not change so quickly. If I tell you humble, you're a great colleague, you look dazzling. You have a great daughter. But you're my best mate and I will not change. Colleagues were always taboo for me, because this causes problems at work. " Do you Renate that's what I just said, these five men , now unfortunately only four could also beer so talk nonsense to one or more glasses as you just after only one beer. " ,, boss, you have to try, maybe I do have it again at some point a little luck there with . " ,, Renate my love, we have not you noticed in recent years, I can, t help you there's nothing like the two of us. " Renate buttoned her blouse, she is not mad.

But she is sure that they will try again and again, but only very carefully and not as flashy as straight. After the second small beer they go home, it is now also closing time. Everything else can wait till tomorrow early. ,, Gerd we have something forgot, the Mother Superior. " ,, Dear Renate, we have not forgotten I had the opportunity to talk to her as you had to in the herb garden. It was an interesting conversation, but the Mother Superior could not say much more than the others. But I have a feeling she suspects something, and they will call us in the days when she checked her idea. "The mother superior actually has a clue, more than a hunch. She has found something in the room of Sister Ulrike has simply overlooked the police. A small cheat sheet on a map from wind mills it was also easy to miss perhaps had no meaning. But for the Mother Superior it was a small very tiny clue. She looked this evening the card again and again; they found it not out what it odd about feel. But she wanted this track, this tiny track when it was a watch. Two days later come the police as I said at the monastery hotel and asked again the four older men. But even this survey has revealed nothing, nothing at all. One could say then confidently, as s it's here on the wrong.   53

Track are also the survey and the observation have absolutely not disclosed any. Gerd give the extra men back to their units. The Soko halved so again. As between them were denied the four old and the two men become active again after the police tranquillity again it. They were but just again worked more carefully, more carefully than before. After she had two days of absolute rest, the four reopened the tunnel entrance and begin can order the freight prepare?. It lacks only the forklifts and trucks with the containers. Everything has yet matched are and happen in a day. You ha b s not s organized in Frankfurt in Koblenz but everything. In two hours could also be from there all in Arenberg. You`re planning via Frankfurt while the Dutch have everything planned over Koblenz. Two containers to the ship, the other container by truck, and the Dutch men have shared the risk. While the commissioners continue desperately against a wall start is what the men on the dark side more quickly now. Only the track of the chain with the cross showed up for the Commissioners successful track. The tires are part of an old heavy American car; probably this led to the dead Americans. An old Cadillac is equipped with these special tires. That could.

Only mean there has been moved to the Kottenheimer climbing walls with the car of the Amis. Ulrike year car then disappeared mysteriously. It is also clear meanwhile least two men had contact to Ulrike. Which from the rocks have down drop, one man alone they could not provide here so high. Now they only had to find the vehicle that Ulrike has transported, but this is unfortunately disappeared and remained so well. But on American came more and more into Vizier of Commissioners. But unfortunately, and this has now been also killed. The commissioner`s twist and turn as they wanted even the tiny new tracks give them no result. At least no any quick result the newspaper has now smelled and makes big reports and speculated itself wild. Here in Koblenz worked thankfully still the police apparatus. None of the investigations has penetrated from here to the outside. Thus, the newspaper reports to have happened in Mayen and Montabaur focused. That was good for all, for art thieves and for robber he of art thieves and the police investigation. The Mother Superior has expanded its idea and has the pin n infected needle terrain map in the Mills discreetly inspected. But with her nun's habit would never only take.

For one day is not so simple. Where the pin needle stuck it found the old shaft with its two winding towers in nature. There they would look tomorrow today it would have been too dangerous. It is already getting dark. The next day they organized the service in the monastery and he and your electric bike on the road. As she drives through the hairpin she looks suddenly in the forest their four guests. This is the start of a wild shooting that lasts for several hours. The Dutch are now in the majority marvel which also can shoot well at the courage of the old masters. The nun is between them and trembles with fear, it is a miracle that she is not hit by any bullet. "Give to men," cries one of the Dutchmen. We know what you have here, we share. Give it to you and everything will be fine, it's enough for us all". The old know that these men would never share. It continues with the wild n shootout, first as Helmut and Siegfried lying dead in the tunnel is Gerhard on. Rudolf also throws his weapon away and surrenders. Of the five old men now remained only two. But the Dutch have lost a man by dead and two are seriously injured. "Get rid of the stupid nun and take her there into the small room.

You also go in ".The men Gerhard and Rudolf also be carefully tied up and tied into handy packages. Only then do the Dutch devote themselves. To the commodity now it is certain that the amber room belongs to them alone. 3 0,000,000 € are the reward for so many deaths. ,, The remaining two organize all in here in the bay. They open the gates the goods must today still out here. The call the trucks and forklifts come to the bay entrance. Then go to the nearby houses, where people still live, I tell them let them know that we have bought equipment from the bay and this pick now. I have the necessary fake papers with me for 3 containers full of machine parts for a mining museum in Holland. This will reassure the people who are still left in the breaks. Get going, now it has to go fast. The truck with the containers and the trucks are on rolling on. From Koblenz they need only half an hour from the port. This time is used by a Dutchman to tell the few neighbours. There are only three remaining here. When the trucks are rolling, the gates are already open and the forklift trucks transport the crates into the containers in wind ropes. It takes less than two hours because everything is cleared out of the bay and the trucks are already.

On their way to the port of Koblenz a container is already on the road over the highway directly to Rotterdam. All containers have already Customs seals. Get so they can`t be opened by German customs. I n all papers are given as charge used industrial parts. The well is locked back and no one can see what has happened here over two hours more. Only traces of the trucks have remained, a dead one 2 almost dead and three tethered lie in the shaft closer to death than to life. Only a miracle can save them. In the monastery there is great excitement now the sister Superior missing. But this only falls on the evening because the head nurse has logged up at 20.00. The Soko Koblenz is already in the monastery at 9 pm and asks all staff and guests. At the same time, Commissioner Völcker and Commissioner Schmidtchen are in the Hotel Trierer Hof in the city of Koblenz. The two Dutchmen have already struck out in the morning. Planned as booked they have packed their bags and are no longer tangible. At least not in Germany anymore this makes a survey more difficult in any case. The owner's wife could not say much about it, she had a reception at this morning. She could only say that.

The men had it in a hurry and all have paid in cash the two commissioners searched the rooms and there and not see anything. All hotels in Koblenz have been checked in the meantime. Now here are suspicious guests. The Koblenz detectives still sitting on the Dry n. There is no idea of what happened here, they do not know that there are still three more dead and there are three people tied closer than the life of death. Their own severely injured comrades have also left the rest of the Dutch back in the pit to die. Gerhard is the first of his KO-like sleep is awake, Rudolf and the upper swimmers can, t move. Also do not noticeable as they are back to their senses. Gerhard know there`s s they have to die here if he can, t get free. They are locked in a stuffy n small side room. Cry s will do no good here, no one will hear them. They would only waste a lot of energy. From the dream of the amber room, from the dream of big money the dream of the good life in the world. Now only the naked survival counts, he tried to lose the shackles, he has the muscles tense in shackles, but a lot of freedom has not brought this to him. But a little bit, the ropes do not tighten as much as the other two. He feels as is this knows awake us. A he feels about also that these.

Have two very great pains, it is certainly in it for her Freedom and their survival. The nun moans loudly and thus arouses Rudolf, so Gerhard has to endure groan of both. The seriously injured Dutchman lying on her doorstep, they have only minutes or hours. The moan of his friends sees Gerhard as a good addition to who moans is not yet dead. Outside it starts to flash and thunder and then rain terribly. With the roof is small sale part of water. Gerhard is tedious drinks there and then laying on his stomach the water from the small trickle. Unfortunately, he can, t offer anything to his fellow prisoners. He looks for a subject on which he may wear out his bonds. In his cowboy stitching, there have always been such items but not here in this room.   Gerhard cannot see anything be smockable. He now needs the darkness with giant steps come survive until the next morning. Fortunately, he can slowly creep and comfort the others. In the monastery hotel hell is going on now, too, the old men are no longer surfaced. These have not been checked out, the children of a murdered friends s arrived at the hotel. They are appalled that these men now all are missing. You also want to wait for the next morning and then with the search of the men and the head nurse begin.   60

Yet they have not the slightest idea what she's all so mixed in excitement. What may have been the reason for these three murders?. The commissioners regulate the search party inform all police station s with respect to the nun and the four men. Not all hope that this will be available here more happy at the door. For the sought this night is terrible, Gerhard can his fellow prisoners not help. He has the opportunity had something to drink, he can only move a little also. But this is better than the state where the other two are. All right was the head nurse packaged and gag. Gerhard crawls to her and makes her heart. Sister, we'll make it, but I can only continue working when it gets light again. Please do not worry, we just need some patience. They had good luck sister none of the innumerable spheres it has taken. " ,, sister m to a Freund Rudolf getting worse and worse, he groans so strange is crawl to him now. By s c hew how he is doing. Rudolf is seriously injured, has a shot in the chest. But Gerhard can give him consolation, otherwise he can, t does anything. Only tomorrow my friend Rudolf, only tomorrow will I try to get rid of my fetters again. Rudolf groans only briefly, to the sign that he understood Gerhard. Gerhard is now looking for a place to sleep.   61

At the entrance door, he will have sleep very much. With the first sun rays it creeps in through the door into the slot and looks for the floor and walls for an object from. Order to cut his bonds or can solve. His hands were tied to his back. The feet also tied with thick old knitting. The shackles on her feet call i to have suffered a little therefore Gerhard begin with the shackles. Chopping on the wall gives him the opportunity to do so. He crawls over there and pull on your back and has feet one with the shackles in the hook. He pulls and pulls and soon succeeds, the ropes disintegrate literally. He can stand up soon and go to the tool they have used for tunnel construction. There he sees are the fatally injured Dutchman, they seem to be already dead. It has let them die easily here. Gerd it is clear there is the same with all of them before. He puts his tied hands on the sharp face of the spade and rubs his hands on it. Until he was so painful, the cords cut can. He shakes his arms free and is happy because he can help his sister and his Freund Rudolf. They are both awake and have noticed the activities of Gerhard and are building themselves up inside. **Chapter 2 Shots in the old manhole** Soon he will be able to help them. Gerhard looking for a knife.

He knows they had a knife, but unfortunately he does not find it. With a piece lid of a tin can he found in a corner he hacks at the ropes of the Mother Superior. First, he frees the nurse's mother from her handkerchief around her mouth, so that she can breathe again. This is really good, even if the air is not very good. This air is still better than no air. The Sister Superior is recovering very quickly. In a few minutes he freed them completely. ,, Do they already Gerhard, they free their injured comrades. Which deals with seemingly no good, then I'll get right on to the injured. " Gerhard bends over Rudolph, who is breathing very hard, Gerd felt as s has this great pain. Very carefully Gerhard cuts it out of its packaging. Rudolf feel the help is so weak that he can, t support Gerd. Gerd's been easier than Rudolfs Kopf is already free and this difficult to found air. Then Gerhard working on the embroidery with which one has packed Rudolf. A little later the Mother Superior and removed with Gerhard's help with his blood-soaked o over clothing. Rudolf has a lot of pain. He groans like a wounded animal. Gerhard pushes a piece of wood between his teeth. On this he can bite his pain away. At least it makes the pain more bearable for the injured.

The Mother Superior finds the wound, but cannot do anything right now; the wound in the chest has already stopped bleeding. You turn Rudolf now on the Side, the ball or balls must still in his body taken s. ,, We cannot do much here Gerhard, we have to get help quickly." " We cannot get through the tunnel, the guys have destroyed it. They wanted to let us get stuck in the tunnel." ,, What are wrong Gerhard six deaths and almost three of us still here. What is so valuable that so many people risk their lives?, be it killed mercilessly ". "Sister Superior, I'll tell you everything when we're out here. Through the tunnel is nothing more, the Dutch have blown up before they have searched with the containers the distance. But let's get out of here; we are here shortly for the main gate in the shaft. We only have the chance to save us if we this can open door from the inside. " It is already late afternoon, the Soko Koblenz is active, and two police units look for the sister. Of course, you have no idea where that might be. With her electric bike she is quite mobile. In the radio is constantly called after her. But there is no trace; all data and results of the previously ongoing investigation are discussed with the inspections Mayen and Montabaur.

In Montabaur, the Cadillac is particularly noticeable. This does not have to be the American's car. Here in the Westerwald there are many fans of old American cars. Immediately makes someone on the way and rattles all Car traders. ,, That would be a trail, "said Hauptkommissar Schöder to Schmidtchen, ,, Think you Schmidtchen feel with can be, the sooner we learn the do better it is. " "Sure, boss, we are always the result of the Americans the nun has killed, but if there are still others involved in it, we have complete new approaches. I'll take Renate, it'll be better. I already have such a thought; I will follow with Renate's help. I am now sure the car comes from the Westerwald and I am sure that this knowledge can be the key to everything ". "Then take your socks and bring me the key".

,, OK, here is searched with several hundred men to the Mother Superior and the four old men. I can do nothing further. Interpol takes care of the two Dutchmen, their personal information with us and the hotel were wrong. They used fake badges; they do not make it when everything is clean. The motorways and border crossings are alerted, they are looking for them. So slowly develops a picture, there is only the occasion.

For this wild action which allows 3 dead. No one knows about the police as there are now six dead and two are seriously injured. In California in Sacramento man sits the already difficult planning the renovation of his house. His home in San Francisco, two architects are with him, they do not know what their client with the huge room wants. With very high ceilings and a room completely without outside window but with a super good air conditioning. This room gives you puzzles. But the landlord did not tell them anything. He is keeping this secret very strictly. "How far have you been with the conversion?". "We still need four weeks then everything is ready". "Is the air conditioning system ready for the house?". "Yes, they could get started in the super room immediately. What do they want to do on the walls and the floor; there is still all the raw concrete and screed? ". "This is already OK that will be something special coming from Europe". ,, As called ring at the same time the Dutch in Rotterdam by, the landlord learns that everything has been running and the containers are loaded. A container is already on its way to the port of Rotterdam to be then shipped over England.

The other two containers are on a Rhine ship Move, should actually already be in Holland. We check the shipping company today. I think that in two T recite everything on the ship to San Francisco can be loaded." "OK, what about my husband from San Francisco, whom I sent you?" ,, He is suffering r accident in the work in the mine, he will not come back. " The Ami at the other end swallows a moment. "But also good my friends, one less knows the answer". It does not bother the man at all that the dead man has given it; even the death of his countryman does not touch him. He is only interested in the room he wants as quickly as possible. ,, The money for you, a discount is already in an account in Switzerland. It is free if I have the Bill of Have loading from Rotterdam. What about the five Germans who offered me the room? " "We've also put them all down for security reasons. They, too, can not reveal anything more." "Outstanding men i praise myself for such prudent work. I have a lot in mind for the future. You will not want to stop. " "We are ready for every evil deed if this only brings enough money", "ok, call me when the containers are loaded". "All right sir, we will not forget that. So the works of criminals run

Faster and more successful than the work at police headquarters in Koblenz the police still floating in to uncertain. Yet they still do not know what it is all about here. The first chief commissioner, Schöder, is on his way to the Vordereifel. He wants to re-examine the site where the corpse, all alone with Sally the dog his girlfriend Marianne. Who is always called Eifelziege (Eifel goat) by jealousy from his commissioner. On his way to Kottenheim, Gerd passes directly to the Commissioner's apartment. The calls to the daughter of the Commissioner, Monika. ,, Hi, Monika you want to go with me to Kottenheim "?. "Sure, when?" "Immediately, I m stand ready down". ,, I'm coming". While Monika to come hurrying down Gerd Renate calls and tells her he takes her daughter to Kottenheim. You want to share with Sally area the climbing walls roam again. ,, I have a feeling that a lot can be discovered even here that there are outstanding ". "Yes, yes, Gerd, love always attracts you to your Eifelziege?". ,, you my love Renate to Eifel goat but a stupid cows dim witted. " Gerd interrupts the conversation because Monica is coming. Three quarters of an hour later, the two are a regular Marianne in the garden and Sally raged around with Monika. The two are a heart and a soul.

,, Want to Marianne; I want to search again with Sally and Monika all the climbing area. I can, t shake the feeling that there are not even more to pick. The chain you have found was a great start. But I miss some of the men they've dragged through the rocks." "I wish you three good luck; I wait here and bake an apple cake for you". ,, Oh Yes, Marianne, your apple pie is always so delicious. " "Gerd grabs the rope from Sally and both storm behind him. In the pit site, he then takes Sally to the leash and gives her the order to look for her. Immediately know the Border Coli bitch it is now important and she has to work. Playful work, which makes them great pleasure, the knows that they pay attention to unusual smells must. Also Monika puts the Detective work in the blood. They scour through the entire area of the pit for meters, and they will find it. Monika discovers a jacket hanging in the tree and difficult to see. "My gods, we all overlooked, where she hangs they could have heard one of the men who have pushed the nun down here." Gerd has to climb onto the tree to recover the jacket. This must be the jacket of one of the gangsters. "My darling that was great, he tells Monika, you were a very big help.

The jacket must have fallen from the rock in the tree. Me and Sally we just took care of the ground. Great absolutely great Monika, can we go to Marian, which has yet determined already finished the apple pie. " Yes we can, ,, the sweetheart we deserve, go off quickly after Kottenheim ". ,, We're still here in Kottenheim?.".''Yes, you're right, that's all part of Kottenheim. Then off to Marianne, we deserve the cake ". At Marianne, he examines the jacket and he notes to his astonishment that this jacket must belong to one of the old men. Inside is a tank of paper with such a tank capacity as it can hold a Cadillac just a huge American. If it was not from a truck but there is not the super gasoline eats or booze in tank size this truck. The first chief commissioner is now clear. As already suspected in the beginning, the three men from the Trier court and the five men from the monastery somehow belong together. Gerd immediately calls Schmidtchen and shares this with what he now found. "Shit," says Schmidtchen. "If we had found that earlier we would have known more. That fits all together, the dead nun, the jacket now. The fuel receipt and the Cadillac, " ,, we have stayed here the fourth Cadi l lac dealer inspected but our car was not there.

But the tire width is at almost every Čadillac since. You'll be amazed there are 15 peace`s of Čadillac owners in the Westerwald. One is thereby in our new theory fits and to your Tankrecive. A Cadillac belongs to Gerhard Maifelder he and I'll eat my hat if the Čadillac is not the wanted man and the jacket by Gerhard Maifelder he is not. " ,, Ok, break your search for the car from the search for the old men n has been running at full speed. Sure depends, all this with the death of three people and the disappearance of the four men and the Mother Superior. After the delicious apple pie, Gerd does not spend much time in Kottenheim. Monika remains for two days at Marianne. Monika still would have to this vote with her mother, this is not right, Monika her daughter she would like for the girlfriend of the man for himself. But when her daughter so much it she then but agreed because this is on holiday and little time. The search teams have initially said the search for the men and the nun from. Tomorrow they all want once the new findings for it. Maybe they could after that restricts the search area. They still had no idea where they'd have to touch s. meanwhile, however, had Interpol good news for you.

In the shaft of the mine mill Bach the first sun rays illuminate a little bit, the interiors of the chute tower. Through the few small windows comes just so much light that Gerhard can orientate something, the nun tries to help. It comes to an aftermath that costs a lot of time. You have the time. Only the wounded did not. Gerhard hears the cry of Sister Chef, he runs back to the shaft. He has the sister so much warned. Not to go so close to the bay. Sister give eight, there is at least 200 meters down. The total depth of the well is 450 meters; the rest is likely to be water?, I have no idea how high the water is. Gerhard took another stone and showed the sister how high the water is. After rapid thud of the stone, it could be only one 50 meters deep. Hopefully the sister has not crashed;, Gerhard has only heard the scream but not the clapping. This means that the Mother Superior still stuck somewhere up here. Gerhard hears the sister's silent whimpering. This is upside down overthrown and has remained attached to their habit. The dear God must have had his fingers in the game. There is only one protruding hook in the whole shaft. It is precisely this that has caught the cowl. Gerhard gets panic, no, not a sister can die by her fault.

He has become cautious, and looks at the situation of his sister extensively. This is so shocked that she is no longer able to speak. Gerhard looks for the remains of the cords and binds them together. So sure he hit himself from the left leg and at the end of the scaffold. Anchored six feet from the shaft centre. At the Second rope he fastened it can down there too. The rope is just enough down to r sister.   This, however, does not answer his questions. She does not get her mouth open. An infernal fear ties her throat. Gerhard recognize quickly what hangs there for a tiny hook the sister. Half-rusted reinforcement rods it has collected, the iron is no longer than 10 centimetres from the concrete out. At any moment can break the rusty iron, or dress it with which they depend tearing at the iron. Gerhard also lurches headlong to her down. Pull the second rope in a loop around the left foot. He has secured so only once before the crash. She can crash, though the iron breaking or tearing the skirt. It can be for this backup again headlong to her head under her. The nurse's mother looked at him with wide-eyed eyes. The blood has already risen to her head. "Sister, he is not afraid, they must get up, and they have the strength to do so. I'll stay here next to them.

They have to stand up against me and then climb up to me. The sister understands what he wants from her. With its weak support they can easily raise their s torso. Slowly she puts on Gerhard's body upward. Gerhard is threatened with the effort to lose consciousness. But the sister moans and groans and torments him very much. But she already has both feet in Gerhard's soft tissues, but there is no other option. The nurse can sense this only because Gerhard is crying. Very slowly, she transfers her weight back onto the rope and relieves Gerhard of her weight. Slowly, the nun is able to pull him up on the rope. Gerhard now prays aloud that keeps this rope, it was not a good rope more but something else did not exist. They hold the air for a moment and pray together a father. It sounds odd in this pit from everywhere the prayer comes back as an echo. God seems to have understood them; they have new powers after prayer. The sister climbing up already painfully over the concrete edge of the shaft and Gerhard is close behind her. He, too, has made it to the top with his greatest and most recent effort. Can happen to them nothing but create Gerhard must still the last meter. Gerhard falls literally on the nun and they remain together.

Are exhausted almost 30 minutes. They both know that here only the love god had his hand to save his nun in the game. "Dear God, could not you have watched before she fell down?" Sister Superior smiles when she hears these words. ,, The Love God remains its principle FAITHFUL we should live our lives by the sweat of our brow and deserve. We really did this today. We can be glad that we still have our lives ". ,, D as we can really sister, now something to do with it on we Rudolf keeps his life. " The commissioners have also finished your meeting; they have come very close to the matter. You now know with great certainty that this is something valuable. To do something quite mysterious; it is not yet possible to assess why the company is active in the USA and Holland. What does the five men who live in the hotel and what connects them with the three men from the Trier court. It must be a secret that is here in the immediate vicinity of the monastery. Gerd takes a piece of paper and draws a ring of 5 kilometres around the monastery. You are looking for this ring with Google. You will find a distinctive building on it. The old disused mine, the mill brook pit in windmills. "This can be the focal point". "What do you think of Gerd?"

"When I add our new realization, this pit makes sense. The five men know each other from the military service in Berlin. They were the last years artillery men`s for the leader. " "That can hardly be, since they were almost still children". ,, Yes that's true but that's why they are so now all been about eighty years. I think in the shaft is booty art." "But why do they raise them now, after so many years." They will tell us, if only a single one is left. " Gerd, is suddenly quite certain, everything fits together at once. Several hundreds and the SEK immediately burst out. Three ambulances and the fire department are also on the go. There are riots in the small tranquil Arenberg and Mills. The bicycle the head nurse is found and then the survivors, injured and dead in the shaft. The two Dutchmen have failed with their bullet wounds. Now, over the events, everything is at once clear as for SOKO. Only the objects of desire are encouraged so many lives have not in Germany. Now the police apparatus is running at full speed. Gerhard goes directly to the underground prison and Rudolf to the prison hospital in Wittlich. Wait after they have testified everything trial. The Soko working the two old the murder of the nun to prove what will not be easy.

Rudolf can`t testify that Gerhard was completely uninvolved in the death of the nun before his death in Wittlich. He says the Gerhard murder would not have been tolerated and would rather have given up. Since he has had to deal with his friends, they needed the money very necessary. They had to bring the nun away from the shaft and Gerhard`s car look from Montabaur get where he had parked it. The other murders go all to the cap of the Dutch money and the principal of the Billionaire their motivation is guilty of the United States. The matter is international, the FBI and Interpol come to Arenberg. Such an elevation had never been to Arenberg. For yet the search begins now until after the art theft. All believe in fact it is the Amber Room. Russian experts also there have announced. The Koblenz Soko has pulled out all the stops, that was too much, so much dead as a riot in Koblenz. The first police chief confers with his troops without the officials from Interpol and the FBI. Only the closest people are privy to the things that the first police chief has taken to yet to catch even the murderers, and the spoil NAZI GOODs. You still do not know, because chase is the famous Amber Room. ,, Well folks, now we have Interpol and the FBI on board.

Only by our finte we have managed to keep at it. Because everything is us slipped out of the hands before we even knew what was happening. But we have returned us to our action the initiative. The freight forwarder has appeared to happiness ". ,, This was mainly your performance boss ", the Commissioner Völcker interjects. ,, No, no the idea, yes, but we pushed through them together. Only the Interpol not pity the individual containers from the truck could get transportation. But it is presumably only a matter of time to fish also this container from the vast amounts of container out which are driven cross Europe. And these containers must have the pond. Unless you distribute the content or several?, But after the action of SOKO Koblenz there is certainly among murderers and thy have a big emergency. The news from the USA was cruel to them. The customer was so angry and they now sent its own people to strengthen them. Guys who can herself to quickly deal with the weapons, it is clear the two Dutchmen if they will not make it, they will inevitably follow the other dead men they have conveyed to the happy hunting grounds. You know, there is they must be on guard from now on.

You have the three men from the United States picked up in Shipol from the airport and the first talks in the hotel are not encouraging. Ron, the spokesman of the three men engaged the Dutch in the hotel lobby directly, even verbally with words. ,, You are the biggest idiot on this globe. How is it possible, since is her the wrong container you take in Koblenz container port you and taken away. It's not to grasp. How stupid can you be, we can`t explain this at all, of course, we had to act really fast. You have to we have set aside an extra, who then reversed again in the port the container. Only in this way can it be that we then labelled the wrong container in a hurry. But then our containers have to be definitely in Koblenz. This could also mean that we now have a huge advantage. " ,, Why advantage, "the Americans asked back, but clearly, one now most certainly, since we've recovered valuable parts from the bay and they have shipped in containers. Which are now looking for the wrong containers and we can use the other two containers at rest pick up and loaded. No one knows that we have the wrong container, only the carrier in Holland and is silent, the other container on the truck. ?, what about the".

,, That we have trucked directly via Rotterdam to England. The then goes container of England much safer in the United States. Only to the east coast and then by train to San Francisco, across the continent. " ,, If this is so, then we still have every chance and the boss will see you the error. Then the whole thing may still be something good. " The man from Boston informs its clients via secure e. mails on the circumstances and everything is still in the lot is. This can also breathe the client and breathe. The seed that Gerd has sown goes to full. They now expect the men from Holland in Koblenz in the container terminal. The FBI men now come to the meeting to Soko into Koblenz Bureau. They explain the commissioners attending the Soko, which the two containers now found on the MS Antwerpen. This ship brings the containers directly to San Francisco. ,, We have wired the container and then can pursue this to its destination; we will probably find the client. That's cruel what happened here, we can tomorrow to see the pit", ,, yes, we pick you up tomorrow at the Hotel Arenberg and go with you there. It is not far from the hotel. There are more than four mails. ,, OK, as it could to the windfall come these idiots have confused the containers.

They go so brutal and clever before and make than such a mistake. " ,, Yes, Ronny the rush it was, we have also implemented with our speed so much is pressurized and then luckily were the containers at the port , so there's then labelled the wrong the Dutch and sealed have. You have agricultural machinery parts that should go to San Francisco confused with your stolen goods." . This fact allows us now again access to everything. Only the individual containers were transported by truck, we must still find. Is Interpol tracking them down?, there is nothing more to discuss and make all the well-deserved leisure time. Gerd, the first chief inspector brings the men from the FBI straight to the Hotel, he chose the monastery Hotel for them. He knows from their papers, the s they are devout Catholics. They will have their joy in the monastery hotel, the sacred gardens and the Sanctuary. He turns directly after leaving the village Ehrenbreitstein into the mills. Gerd himself lives in Ehrenbreitstein and can the Americans his house on the hill from the bottom of the street her show. The Americans are no longer a surprise out as they go through the mills. Here they do not have so beautiful and splendid expected vineyards.

,, Yes Men, in this small valley so beautiful we have 3 wineries and 7 long ago abandoned mills. ,, A great dell says Ronny, who also speaks German. He explains his colleagues also nod approvingly. I'm driving from the other side of Arenberg. Arenberg is a district of Koblenz, is actually a great independent village. Behind Arenberg, behind your hotel it then goes to Immendorf. Immendorf is the last place a district of the city of Koblenz in front of the Westerwald. Here we turn now; here are the largest of the old mills, the grain Mühle. Right, it then goes to another city from Koblenz to Arzheim. We now go left through the woods to Arenberg. Gerd stops after approx. one mails on, here gentlemen, here is the old shaft. Here the valuables were hidden. Meanwhile we know how these came here. They rise briefly and take the shaft in a glance. ,, Sure, this bay is naturally gorgeous hidden". ,, If men from the hotel, tomorrow more of it and I have to sleep, it was terrible week for all of us. Waiting for me also my girlfriend, she cooked me some excelent food. They drive through Arenberg, when Gerd explains the situation of Arenberg. On the main street are the necessary shops.

A very great Italians who makes an excellent Pizza for the way, the restaurant is called Roter Hahn (red rooster) and is ready as old as the monastery and the monastery church. It used to be the main connection for horse-drawn carriages in the world. Here the horses were changed and the coachmen quartered. " ,, Gerd, s chon great so it Koblenz, today we were already at the German Corner and in the fortress. " ,, Well, then you've already seen some, if the case is completed, I will show you a lot more if you can, t extend something. " ,, If it does not allow the case, we will definitely be back here, with our wives. We've never been to OLD Germany and we think it's fantastic. " Gerd brings the men into the hotel and the nurse who was strongly involved in this case and has shown much courage to explain their whole story to their American guests. Thus, Gerd saves much time. He must go home now Marianne his girlfriend has finished the meal. Gerd is always happy when she comes to her with her dog. It will be a long night for him and he smiles before he falls asleep mischievously over his tricky proceed. The next morning Schmidtchen is with the Americans in the shaft, the Amis look at everything and marvel at the good condition of the shaft.

Then Schmidtchen goes which is also a strong feeling Christ through the Holy garden and into the church. The Americans are thrilled and feed their chips in the cameras until overflowing. Gerd has him placed an order with the Americans as long as possible to keep him till her in office was. This is not a deal for Schmidtchen the Charming Austrians. Gerd had something to clarify in the harbour. The harbour master was exchanged for security reasons. One of his people took over this job. ,, Ernst was in his younger years Skipper, was at the water and shipping Arts Office in Koblenz. He has also helped to make this container port. Nobody knows as well as Ernst. The real port captain, and the substitute port captains, is always in touch with each other to eliminate mistakes. ,, From tomorrow Ernst, you're the harbour master here, so we expect that appear in the next two days the Dutch here, possibly with reinforcement. The old harbour captain is in Egypt on the Red Sea on vacation and you represent him here for so long ". ,, Well, yeah Gerd ". What should I do next? " They'll ask you for the two containers. I and the harbour captain have already marked this for you. We have made them as identical as the other two containers which were delivered to the USA.

But they must not look at them at all, for then our plan bursts ". ,, What if they use force. " ,, Two more people we are here this morning to your support, disguised as dockers and are only in the background to your support. Renate my Commissioner's office as a typist and Wolfgang up with the crane operator in the cabin, you knows both of them very well. " ,, Yes, good people, and where I live, I do not want to jeopardize my family. " Also,, because we thought dear colleague, do you live as long as the Trierer Hof ". ,, OK if there is a decent breakfast there, then it's OK. " ,, That there are my dear, remember you are from Cologne and doing only vacation replacement ". ,, All right Gerd, then let's see what is going to do here. " ,, Be careful, it seems to be to tremendous asset in the contents in the containers. You're afraid of nothing, be vigilant, and always keep in touch with your people here, and of course with me. I have to worry about the FBI, but they need only a permanent occupation. Schmidtchen busy the three shows them all the crime scenes and will surely come to you in the harbour. Something dominated the Austrians like no other of m a troop. The ensnared the Americans so that she will not understand really."

They are used in the US, but they should also only ask about the conditions. They should find out what is supposed to be so valuable in the containers here, of course. Yet it knows no one from the police force, although one suspects it but no one knows anything for certain. Ernst takes his new job very conscientiously and then instructs his police colleagues on their jobs one. They still consider their wireless connections and can only wait for the length which will come as n that because hopefully get away with it raises the plan by Gerd. The three Americans are on their way to Koblenz by car with the two Dutchmen. Of course, they do not go to the Trierer Hof, where they know the Dutch. They have also again under a false name with false papers in Mercury in Koblenz first filed class hotel. They are all happy again, and they can rock the thing easily and loosely. The next morning they are early in the harbour and want to talk to the harbour master. They are astonished and are visibly disappointed when they meet the substitute they have not seen before. ,, You're not the harbour master? ". ,, Yes, I am the port most r, for the next four weeks, the harbour master is in his well-deserved annual leave for 4 weeks.

My name is Ernst Müller; I represent him for these four weeks. But do not worry I have been here many a time I know my way around here, how can I help you? ". ,, We happened to their harbour master a mishap, we have confused two containers, two containers that should go via Rotterdam to San Francisco. Unfortunately these were confused by the harbour master and we sent the wrong ones. Here the FOB papers for the inland waterway vessel and here for the sea-going vessel. Only it is not our car spare parts but agricultural machinery parts are destined for San Francisco," ,, that is a thing that happens to the harbour master?. Then let's see where these containers are, they come to the office. Hello, ,, Renate welcomes the Commissioner Renate Völcker, his police colleague. The harbours man has made crap and delivered the wrong containers to a customer in San Francisco. " ,, That's a big thing, this is never happened. The containers are all numbered, they have the numbers ". The Dutchman presented to the harbour master spares the FOB papers ". The outputs them to continue Renate, see the numbers looks and takes the list of containers in the computer go through. ,, There, there we have it, actually.

Yes, this is possible because s were ultimately confused them. They are now in the middle of the big stack. We can do this only tomorrow remove. Come tomorrow at noon again and then we have this stand below and look again at the papers on the containers. The containers are on the next ship to Rotterdam, they were lucky, the shipping company has announced the acquisition we moved ill there are problems with the ship give the transport is scheduled for 3 days ". The men breathe heavily, Renate and Ernst look at them. Then, well we are at noon tomorrow again in the evening, the men from Boston give their report by e-mail to the end customer. This is also glad that everything is still good. He orders them to refrain from shipping, but also to send the containers via England for security reasons. While also Schmidtchen is the FBI people with all the history in and around the monastery hotel entertaining, they asked Schmidtchen about the five old men who did everything they could, and also lived here in the hotel. ,, These five men were indeed in 1944 actually still children when you i n the position anti air craft by Berlin came. It is inconceivable how these guys for all of us stood to Hitler. How can one with 16 to 18 years get the idea to go to the antiaircraft gun to Berlin?.   88

These guys were already come with many different Hitler Youth in Koblenz together. They came from all over Germany and were prepared here for their deployment. A whole company is here in Arenberg in the elementary school. That was the beginning of 1944. Just this school here in Arenberg was destroyed by a bomb with a direct hit. 16 Young men were killed instantly; the survivors and the few uninjured were then distributed. Most of the boys have been ordered to Berlin. Because these guys were trained here in Koblenz at the anti aircraft gun. These guys have shortly before the fall of the thousand years Empire get the job Valuable war goods to safety. Then, when the Nazis realized there's the Russians are unstoppable. The Flack guns around Berlin were mostly destroyed or as were no more ammunition. The Jung men were then sent to the west with three trucks full of Nazi art or know the devil what is in the containers. We still do not know exactly. Then they can hide everything to 1960 in the Westerwald. They have not come to the Eifel, and from there the Amis have already approached them. In 1960 the mine mills creek was then closed forever, of the five men was engaged in it.

They then stored everything for the next 50 years here in the bay. Until one understood it must sell the goods to the USA. Unfortunately, to this day, we still have no idea what is the value. " A sister here out of the house and four of the old men, the former four Hitler Youth are dead. The fifth is still in jail. The sister-in-law has certainly told them their story. " Yes, ,, she has, it's a crazy story. " While the men i m of the hotel cafe to sit. Get the two Dutch and the Boston 2 and the leader from Arkinson n in. You are looking for the fifth man of the force, want to know from him whether everything has been taken out of the well or whether there are items there that they need to recover?. Curl up on the most distant table of the Cafe, convenient, they want to remain undisturbed. But sometimes life is crazy. Accidents often make the most impossible possible. The Mother Superior represents precisely the Sister which is otherwise service for the responsible. She sees immediately because s three Americans sit s here at the table. She also correctly classifies the other two men as a Dutchman. But only when they place the order in a bit bumpy German she is sure. The Mother Superior is only really taken aback when she will ask an elderly men.

After of approx, it was strange, she could only tell them because four men dead and one does not live here for weeks. ,, We know the men of the past; we want man like to talk these gentlemen Maifelder. Do they want the address of him, thus they would be very elves? ". ,, Because I have a look that takes something I have to do once my service here. When my colleague is here again I have time ". ,, That's okay sister, we wait. The four men look at a grin. ,, That was easier than we thought, if we have the address, we have enough time for this. The well is to try to be your own. Surely this is also observed by the police. We go there purely if the two right containers are finally gone and are safe. If something calm has returned and here again, but now we can make the old bag identified. So what turn 5 grandfather still such a thing about 50 million. They were anxious to improve their pension. The Mother Superior is a right detective, she immediately felt because s is not suitable s something with these men. It calls Schmidtchen inconspicuously into the Kitchen the same simultaneous bakery and shares this with her suspicions. Schmidtchen immediately reports this to his boss.

,, Commissioner, Gerd, i be at the Klostercafe with the FBI men, i think just the two Dutchmen who have the old men killed and stole the container with three other Americans come in. " ,, It's possible Schmidtchen, we expect the men here in Koblenz. But that's strange they come to the monastery. But if you are looking for the old man, then they can do this only there. We had to leave the old Maifelder free. He has a permanent residence and will be available to us for the other investigations. " ,, I'm going inconspicuously for types over and watch them at me, I know the two Dutchmen from our search images. I make a secret video of the table. I can, t believe how outrageous these guys are when they are. " ,, In them are still these three Americans, oddly we suddenly here in Koblenz have "so many Americans. ,, The Mother Superior bring the men from the FBI the order, they say them I'm prevents they have to wait a bit until I get back. Gerd I'll call you later, I think I'm exchanging the job. I now make on headwaiter, ok Schmidtchen that you can, please register as soon as possible. " The mother superior and Schmidtchen switch roles.

The five men are very puzzled as served them Schmidtchen the coffee and cake. Please, my master, the nurse, must find something for a guest. I'm home here and sometimes help out. " Schmidtchen can play the service men wonderfully, he wraps the men around his finger and they are fast in conversation. They also succeed so well because they want to be mutually exclusive. ,, If they help out here more often make sure they can even the old men who were here. " ,, But yes, the nice gentlemen I know very well, we have quite often at night still tickets played. But there were crazy hikers who were on the road every day. I want to be as fit as I am at age. " Unfortunately, four of them were shot, they say that they were involved in a cultural theft of Hitler, all we know about them. " ,, What is there is not anything that Ron says the Americans from Arkinson in his bad German. Something crazy here in this quiet Arenberg, who thinks of something. I am very sorry for the old ones. " ,, Ah, they're from the US, that's fine, I know the United States is also quite good. " ,, Then another good appetite gentlemen, they can taste the cake. I think the right of use will be here again.

"All right, ,, the Lord, it was pleasant." ,,
Schmidtchen away like a real Austrian head waiter.
But he goes directly into the garden and informs
Gerd of his encounter.

 Schmidtchen is one hundred percent sure that the
Dutch here with reinforcements from the USA sit.
,, That's odd, but it fits into the picture, of course
we do not know why they seek contact with the
last survivor old. ,, They want to question the poor
guy and then also make him quit. The men may
never know where Gerhard from and where he is.
" While Schmidtchen converses outside phone
with Gerd, something happened in the cafe. There,
shots are fired. The five men stormed out and the
other three Americans by the FBI wild shooting
behind them.

Chapter 3 FBI in Arenberg

 Gerd, ,, you have to come here is the hell is going
on. " The FBI chasing our suspects, have no idea
what happened here ". ,, stop the Americans, I
come with a special police". ,,OK". No sooner said
pulling Schmidtchen his gun and cocked it while
after the others run. But the FBI men and the
fleeing are a hundred yards from him and can
hardly catch up.

He only hears the wild shooting in the holy garden. The men fled from there in the direction Immendorf. The next village but also borders as Arenberg directly to the Convent of the other side. God thinks Schmidtchen, Commissioner Schmidtchen; they do not want to go to the village. He must stop the FBI people. They want to get these people alive and get caught with the container theft, do not shoot here in the wild. In ricochet hits Schmidtchen arms, he did not notice this. ,, My God are that fast, I would rather have done more sports. " Schmidtchen can, t not keep up with the men. The Wild Hunt goes through the village until the men left in a dirty farmer road in open field and a small valley, run the opens up before them. Schmidtchen breathes when he sees that no citizens are more at risk. At least no people have so far been damaged, it is initially gone well. The FBI people lie behind a wooden pile at the exit. In the open field they can, t follow the gangsters shoot damn good guys. Schmidtchen poses next to the officials from the FBI. ,, My God Men's what happened, why these ill-considered shooting. These are our people, these are the Dutch who have killed our old ones and are waiting for them in the port. " ,, which is a thing.

That we come here to Germany and find one of the most wanted men of Arizona. These are notorious killers, we can, t let them run," ,, we jeopardizing the whole operation with the Nazi Guy what we want to do. " ,, I call my boss Gerd that is to decide the intended cut them from the other side the way. Up there is a police academy, the guys he has to put in March. Those who come to meet them will not be able to escape. " The FBI officials have stopped the ball bakery, ,, going on " Schmidtchen can be delete not slow the FBI officials show rushing behind the five men without intelligence. The Soko chief of the first chief commissioner is shaken by this development of things. He knows also no advice they need to make the men closed for Jail. While Gerd informed the police school and people in march setting. M eight Also, the SEC set out for Urbar / Arenberg. The fleeing have also a little break choose PREPAYMENT. ,, Fucking shit, now I have thought in Germany, I have my peace, because I meet here at the FBI of here probably Christian holiday with the nuns makes. So a fucking craps, as here we come out of the hole out again?. So many millions before the eyes and then here in this hole, no, that does not go ". They are on the Columbus Bridge.

One new wooden bridge that crosses the creek times, ,, Los men into the creek and back to Immendorf, this is our only chance. The brook has so deeply buried that we could pass the insane FBI men unseen". In fact, the creek flows through a very narrow deep it bed. A bed that he him has drug in many thousands of years. Our followers can't not see us in it. The men actually manage through the ditch unseen at the FBI and climb to Schmidtchen past back to Immendorf. By bus which stops just in Immendorf they drive into town and are initially escape. The police combing still everything in the area, but the men remain disappeared inexplicable way. The dogs used no trace later. The men are immediately prompted to ring a ring. These are by this time somewhat disillusioned and annoyed at their Hotel beds the Mercury Hotel. You ha ben no eye for the Beautiful view of the Rhine and the fortress Ehrenbreitstein. ,, Ron can, t believe it, because he has come with his false passport so good America out and so clean into Europe. Since such a stupid FBI tourist in a convent Hotel in Germany recognizes him. ,, We have no choice men, we need the container steal from the port. " ,, I have long been organized says the clever Dutch. Tomorrow is our low loader.

There, a forklift for the containers. A he of low loader excess length and the can accommodate a container and the giant stacker. We break the Saturday, that's tomorrow there one if we have chosen the morning container and sealed. Within an hour we have done then." But ,, As we arrive on Saturday through the gate." ,, Quite simply the powerful 25 tons truck is our key to the gate, which raises the gate just off the hinges and push it aside. " ,, First of all, my dear, we have to search for us to survive, the FBI man will set out all the stops to find. The Germans have no choice but to have to look for us, but mostly for me. " ,, The Dutch can, t believe it, how can send them such vulnerable people the Americans. They do not remember that they are five times the murderer as well and are just as sought by the police, Interpol and the FBI. They are all five heavy very heavy guys; criminals include the life sentence behind bars. ,, I have everything "organizes, Jan says of Veen. We will be picked up in an hour. Put all your things together " ,, Where to go in January? ". ,, way from Koblenz, on to Bonn, there is no one look for us in the next few days and we are in 40 minutes in Koblenz harbour. We can make this route also by boat, it takes longer but it is safer.   98

My people from Duisburg bring us a boat fast boat to Bonn. We are safer on the water than on the road ". ,, When the police show up at the hotel and ask for Americans and Dutch are those already provided all five in Bonn in their new hotel under another name and with new Dutch passports. Also from the Americans out of Dutch have now become new papers. They have brought them from Holland new Dutch passports, very good product which has its price. With so much capital in the back everything is just possible.

In Koblenz, Arenberg and Immendorf the hell is going on, the police still combing through everything, as the sought are long gone. On Saturday is the region quiet again, but not to the police. In high profile murderers have slipped through their fingers although they have immediately and responded well. ,, We have no chance and e re we must appeal to their containers thefts, if possible all together. They will not show up again until Monday, because they are now forewarned. They will send other people to identify the containers. Unfortunately, ,, they were already this morning there; the containers are identified and are.

To be picked up on Monday by a shipping company in Rotterdam. I have put you the paper on the desk. " ,, He is good, I was not at the desk, the events here have overtaken everything. I still can, t not grasp that meet FBI people who visit us on the most wanted criminals of Arizona and jeopardize the project enormously it. It is incredible what sometimes happens in this world. But she did the Koblenz Soko well. ,, Why Schmidtchen you let these gangsters hunt, that was completely unnecessary. " ,, Well said my dear but I was just out there and talked to you. That must have gone with the America so fast that I had no possibilities to slow down. You heard yourself; the shootings went off directly, just as I talked to you. I could only run after one has yet me. Probably a Querschläger (ricochet shot) through the jacket. " ,, Have you copped it," ,, is not worth mentioning, only a tiny scar. But I have a broken Jacket, what is now Gerd, the men are now warned and even escape. They will pass us back to Immendorf. Presumably they escaped through the deep trench of times Bach these are quite clever men. " White, ,, the depth where the plug now at least once away and disappeared, but they must definitely go back to their containers.

This is still our only asset. " ,, We will put them all, all no one will escape us. " But the most important thing is to catch the client. " But even these murderers can, t escape us to me it's just a mystery what they wanted, nor of the only surviving of the five men. I said definitely in the hospital Wittlich decision; the man gets a special surveillance ". I think he is free? ". ,, he is yes released from the underground prison but he's volunteered for a few days in Wittlich, he can go at any time. With regard to the goods at issue here, we still have no idea. " The FBI people can it still can, t not believes they have not caught the most sought after man of Arizona, they have it stop It completely ruined. You must believe the consoling words of Gerd. The FBI headquarters can also not understand and understand how the men have come to Germany. They send reinforcement to Rotterdam. The Special Commission expects until Monday so as it continues. But that is a mistake, a very big mistake. Criminals and crimes have no break and no weekend. The police did not rest but a monitoring container. This happens if you underestimate your opponent. At Saturday before the ban on Lorries rushing approach the two low-loader, already on Saturday.

Very early in Kesselheim in and have their own site no 300 meters more to the gate of the terminal. The two civilian investigators who keep the gate from their vehicle in the eye are long that you passed through the gas into the car really deeply sleep. The loader hum approach his wheel loader is driven by low loader down and has nu lifted the gate off its hinges in, the vehicles drive AFEN in Container. Everything is prepared so that it takes less than 30 minutes are loaded to the container with the giant forklift and the door is hung on again. There is something wrong but you can hardly see it. The trucks vanish with their cargo in the outskirts of Kesselheim. Until then completely unheated disappear in the Ruhr. The transport can be tracked later up to the exit Krefeld on the 57. The two officers in their vehicle in Kesselheim only are awakened by their detachment. Unfortunately 8 hours too late the Soko is informed. Then there is no trace of the two NPP, a huge collapse for the SOKO Koblenz. The only one who is not worried, strangely, the first Hauptkommissar Gerd Schöder. The FBI people turned on the road and greatly abused by their superiors from the US, there one could not understand how one could let the sought escape be.

Gerd Schöder sits with his men and Renate in the Klönsack in Arenberg. He wanted to keep the FBI people out of this affair of SOKO Koblenz. Only two Dutch Interpol police men out of Amsterdam are with you.,, Madam, "said Gerd applies to men and Renate. You are safe amazed das we sit here in the little pub and I am calm. It looks and large Gora for us not so sad as it seems at first glance. We really all that the FBI people mess under control, I have you not yet opened, I wanted to avoid us back into the craft, just as they have made it up here already in the hotel. ,, To have nothing to pay, I have with Interpol Amsterdam Also because two Dutchmen pull the threads here. We really want the buyer but we want to see all these men behind bars. They should not be able to leave Europe at first. We want to condemn them first and then the Amis can have the men. Please gentlemen of Interpol they say what they have to say. ,, Gerd turns to his friend's bar owner Mani. ,, Do you have the door ". ,, Yes Gerd here comes in no mouse, I'm going now. Call me on the phone when you're done. You know where the drinks are. " Thus, the detectives are alone and the Interpol official begins. ,, You know that we are involved right from the very beginning we looks.

Thanks to Gerd not as bad as all think, We actually have everything under control. We know exactly where the men are, we know who they are. We know exactly where they and where the containers are. " A whisper goes through the pub in Arenberg. So that no one expected, since she left her boss completely in the dark. They have made all the worries about the progress of things. Concerns about a development which they have screwed up, we do not only know the whereabouts of the five men in Holland. We also know their new passports, all five are now Dutchman ". They do not take a step without being observed. We let the container to England ship and always keep this in mind. Of course, these are also buggy these, too, can, t not escape us, at any point of the earth, we can locate them. " The information gathered here breathe through satisfied, they think t s all been. Since s they have lost this fight. No, her boss Gerd, has the whole thing in the safest towels. We are still looking for a solution as we want the five trigger-happy men arrested as inconspicuous as possible. They should and may Holland rely more on no case. " We are still working on the solution, the arrest must be done so that can, t not find their clients why the men were arrested.   104

,, We will then, of course , but only our FBI friends informed, we need this in the US. I think then the Yanks also be delivered so the L ow finally the FBI also be satisfied is. Because of course we want to be there when the game comes to an end. Because we still do not know what is really in the containers. " About all, we naturally want to know who is responsible for this actions of today, the complete mill stream is tested bay. There one suspects still objects. The Dutch Interpol man answering his cell phone and grinning when he hears the news. ,, men, here we go. " The containers begin to move towards Holland. " Gerd informed Mani he can have back his pub again. It was very good, because s they have crumbled over here. The stupid FBI people are not, they have long since noticed that all people SOKO forget have. And since the action in Arenberger Monastery hotel far from everything hold has. You know, of course, they have reacted wrong and have the overall action greatly damaged. But they could not hold back when they discovered the sought in their hotel. Little did they know that these same people are involved in the container theft?. Three civilian vehicles leaving Koblenz towards Holland, the FBI men are with in Gerd's car. Gerd she inaugurates. 105

While driving in the ongoing things, the men will again begin to spoil. ,, shit, then we have our headquarters to early informed and have turned us is a huge rebuke ". ,, Well, men's certainly to real ". ,, Yes, we have great shit built, but they saved our ass, Thanks first chief inspector, you might have names for euro police officer, that's some. First police chief, Commissioner, Chief Commissioner. Wachtmeister and so on, you have to really study to understand it. " ,, Because you are right, but we know our business. " ,, , No doubt Mr. first chief inspector, you did it to her German commissioners ". The mobile phone of the first main Commissioner interrupts the conversation. The Inter Pool People turn. Have Gerd, the truck passed the Dutch border. The five men follow the truck in a small distance. We also have these without control from Germany to Holland,." ,, that's good, we settled till our people agree. " ,, So my Lord turns Gerd it to the FBI. We and Interpol have everything under control. The truck with the containers and the five criminals have just crossed the German / happened Dutch border. " ,, you let them so easily across the border? ". ,, Yes, my friends from the FBI, we are interested in the perpetrators to catch in the US ". These five men will never leave.   106

The united Europe ". But then it's all at risk in the US ". ,, No we're not, they are initially only arrested because of their false passports and this customer goes to the final buyer in Sacramento or San Francisco. The will use only new men and is perhaps glad he is going these men. ". The wanted men from Arkansas we will deliver, that's clear. " With renewed courage and renewed vigour the Americans are now in the process again. You can grind out your saddle again. You want to be at least in the arrest of five there. A short time later they get the information that the loader on a construction yard standing near the ferry terminal and the wheel loader is discharged. The low-loader is hydraulically shortened again and is now ready and prepared. For loading in Rotterdam on the ferry to England, the two Dutch and the men from Arkinson are meanwhile quite sure which one are them not on the track. They are free and act freed, they get out of their car and examine again the low loader and container. Very satisfied back off again as the low loader roll in the next stage, the transition to England they will create. The loader start moving and stands than for some hours before the ferry. The Remanufacturing walks briskly from s Tatten and.

The loader disappear into the belly of the ferry. Interpol has since formed the people`s inches. The five men, two Dutch and the men from Arkenson have parked their vehicle. Of course, they take their containers to England. Its 50 million not let her out of sight. They also check their weapons; they want to be ready for anything. When then everything goes much faster than they believed. The passports are issued to control and are waiting for the examination of the papers they surrounded by civilian Interpol men. Disguised as passengers, very soon the five are disarmed and pushed aside. This is the so trigger-happy types, the biggest problem, to arrest without a firefight with these five men. ,, Gentlemen, unfortunately we have to arrest them for the time being, their passports are all fake. Then they have illegal weapons with them, which is banned here in the Netherlands. All five disappear into police vehicles and come in a secure barred building. You still grinning, no idea, since s there forever for all of them will. This was just her last appearance in freedom. You already know how dangerous these men are at Inter pool. In particular, it will give them nine murders prove. Was for a more times mean life imprisonment. The loader.

Is your freight on the road n oh England and then a few weeks later at the Port of San Francisco. Things take their course and Gerd with its Commissioner on the Rev to Koblenz. For them pause is long arrived to the ship in San Francisco or until the even has been found-lost container. The other two containers are still at sea, but these are in five days in San Francisco to be. There, the people from the FBI have everything in hand. They are exploring all possibilities of already to the end customer approach to come. But they will probably still have to wait to have arrived the other two containers in San Francisco. But they will not defeat the first to be wrong container out of sight, it has recommended. Gerd them, he wants this, really right who later returned to Germany. Of course, the FBI has no idea that this return is already under way. They will also this neither this huge hall go. But for that they have not had the approval of the responsible scientist. Depending on what is possibly the content, it could be used for d s contents are dangerous. So all remain involved no other choice than once to wait until the containers are all available. The Soko Koblenz is back from Holland back in Koblenz and lost in the paper work. All are happy.

With how everything so far has expired, the five men from the US and Holland are once stored safely. The only surviving who can explain the matter fully and knows what is in the containers located is only Gerhard Maifelder. The old Mann Gerhard Maifelder one has lost sight and from memory. One has the initially afraid to the old man. But this fear is unnecessary, there is nothing to him happens. But this is already with large own plans again in Montabaur, near his hometown but still near Arenberg. Arenberg Koblenz and the problems in Muehlental keep the police for a completely closed case. Except for the following investigation that have now shifted to UK and the United States. The police investigation in the bay have shown there's nothing anymore in this absolutely It is officially stated that all again to protect the water is the retention basin closed we can see the ground. Only the former engineer know there it is not true. Just in case, he has time some itself seven smaller pieces borrow safely in the shaft. After this catastrophic development, it turned out that this emergency solution was golden. Gerhard knows how bad the whole thing has gone. He has lost four of his best and oldest friends. But they took it knowingly accepted.

But such a bad output they have never expected in no mind game. But that is precisely why he does not want to give up. Also for these pieces, which are still hidden in the pit, he already has customers. These things are not as extensive as the Amber Room and not complicated. For the removal of the images a second man and a small transporter is enough. There are great treasures, there are pictures that are in demand and are conveniently packaged. Narrow widely sought of course, even the world; it took so long until he found someone who buys these images. Gerhard has quartered himself in Montabaur, with a younger friend whom he trusted. He needs to stay in cover, he is sought and, of course, put up for investigation, he does not that the warrant has long since lifted s. He does not know that he in the meantime by the testimony of his is totally acquitted in Wittlich who died in prison friend Rudolf of the murder of the nun. It runs because of the art theft investigation against him yet but these are for the time being deferred until all investigation is over. He lives first with his friend and is safe there. Gerhard sits in his reading corner in the living room of his friend and reconsiders its position. He mourns for his friends. "Manfred, it was just shit.

So many years we waited until we dared to sell the amber room. Also just to America, Manfred his young friend, young in quotes". Manfred is also already retired, but a good 20 years younger than his 62 years Gerhard with. He is with his 62 years also n still fit. They know the common hobby of the sail fly. "My God Gerhard, how was it possible that this thing so out of control?. There was a giant vortex in the region Koblenz, in the particular in Arenberg. Now everything is gone, is not you s been more than four dead friends. They were killed by the gangsters from Holland. For this you have a Dominican sister on his conscience. Was it this VALUE? ". "If we had known this exit before, we would have had the amber room stuck in the shaft. But in life one never anticipates anything. Little did we know, there`s This Stupid Americans US People behind. In the sum of 50 million they have become weak. " ,, Now what Gerhard, how can we get the little treasures your last out of the bay. I was now a few days, a day in the mills valley bay. There is no movement there, everything is locked up again and locked this is good for us; there is a way to approach this last little things without much effort to come. " "Why did not you use this route before and dug the tunnel.

This approach is too narrow for the great tools we needed, but for the few small images ranging access. Of course these pictures should remain my secret. Exactly in this walled access are since 196 0 pictures. Super airtight packaged. I think everyone is still undamaged. None of the images is greater than O.7 x o. 8m ". These pictures of me personally were immured in the air shaft was no longer needed. " ,, Then you still have chances but yet to come to some money." Manfred, ,, get from the proceeds as promised 10% ". 10% of nearly 5 million, which also secures your requirement." ,, Are you sure with the sale, which is not such an idiot as the Americans. Also for 2 million it is worth for some humans to kill. Here, people are killed for 5 € ". "I get the first 50,000 acres, which I asked for as a movement allowance". "How does your plan look like, how do we get these pictures out and how does the transfer look like?" "We wait until we have the 50,000 tomorrow, so you buy a box van, without windows, and car is neat and is possible without any label. But please can, t cost more than 20,000. I'll make posters with which we then glue the car later when we have the images safe ". ,, This means that we still have 3 days fresh air, I drive afterwards go and think.

For a good car out, then everything goes faster, which should not be that hard. " Three days later the new company run. Gerhard has come up again died rushes newly steep. He has taken his beard trimmed hair and glasses with plain glass glasses on his nose. He looks like the old gentleman professor who kindly enjoys his retirement. No one would have thought of connecting him. With robbery and manslaughter, they lie in the forest of Arenberg and look at the environment with binoculars. Today, everything is calm around the manhole. "There Manfred, there the mound, we must dig. In the hill is a flap through which we enter the shaft. We want to check it all today. We want to tackle everything calmly and safely. You quickly realize there are not at home the few inhabitants of the old surrounding houses to the since. Only then do they cautiously make their way to the hill, which is a little out of the way and facing the forest. At least the side at the loudly Gerhard the Input into the shaft the men are working cautiously toward the hill, and begin immediately to push the iron rod into the hill. Very quickly they have discovered the hidden door. At the sound of the iron and of the resistance they have very quickly found the door. Cautiously, they should be.   114

Applied to the grass. They want to close the site as carefully. You have uncovered the flap very quickly. "One gets tight; the output is smaller than I thought. But cross it might just work so pass me your ruler, so it will go just 0. 7x 0.8 ". ,, How do we get the thing only once on?, in huge old Castle, the flap closes with an even more stable latch. "Shit, we have to think of something. This looks very stable ". Manfred was the locksmith before his retired life, everything looks thoroughly. "Yeah, my dear, that's not all that simple. We can, t not make so much wheel here and do not get a burner here to simply weld the whole. Unfortunately, that goes with the on Never cut with a hand saw, too. That would be the easiest and fastest, but is not. ,, We still need some time; I will build a small lifting device in my workshop. We put this then this tab and I press a Hydraulic everything from the rock out. " It will make little wheel and we have a slightly larger hole, it can arrive to centimetres. We can also afterwards with some Rakofix again properly sealing machine eat anything. ,, Manfred pulls back his small meter from his pants and wrote down some extent. "Yes Gerhard, a good locksmith, always has something with him. But hopefully we get your photos from this narrow hole out? "   115

. "It has to go even if it is scarce; the course is also not much wider than this hatch". "There you want to creep in, it never goes." "That's what I've also put the pictures in the aisle". "But then you were still young and beautiful, do not worry, suits me again today my communion closes". "Whatever you are Catholic, you can, t go wrong here in Arenberg. That God has directly punished you ". The dear God always keeps an eye on the holy Arenberg". "Why my dear, how come you now to the dear God". ,, I declare same if we take you through Arenberg, if you want we can also go briefly into the Wall ". No,, a dear that will not do, it could recognize me someone; we have lived there in the monastery for weeks. " The two cover everything properly again from, no one is being able to detect whether someone has dug on the hill. "You see, it looks like new again. I'm still a thread so we know later whether someone was at the place". "Here nobody comes to Manfred but it cans hurt where you get a thread now". "Yes, my dear, a good locksmith." "Yes, yes I know it's good". Hopefully we'll get the thing up? ". "No fear my dear, with a bang the thing will fly up". ,, How long do you need to build this thing? ". "With my great drawing and notes, one day.

"Well, then I'll stay this one day in Koblenz, I'll meet there with my buyer." "This is good but dangerous for you, you know you here". "Only in the monastery, otherwise I have changed very well; I have to take the risk". "Well then I drive. I leave you my spare mobile phone here and use as long as my other mobile phone. Where should I drop you? ". "Right here in Arenberg, I absolutely must go to the sacred garden; my nerves have this visit urgently necessary. Then I make an appointment with the buyer." "OK Gerhard do as you think, but sign up tomorrow with me". They carefully retreat and reach without anybody to meet their car. Manfred sets Gerhard as desired at the Holy Garden, Well then, have fun, do you really think Jesus helps you K warm". "No, but I have a conversation because of my lost buddies". "Well then tomorrow you little saint". Gerhard is making his way through the Holy Garden. He is not a strict believer, but a visit to the Sacred Garden gives him amazingly always something. He sees the Sacred Garden than to what it is for him. He lived for a long time in Arabia in Islam, there are no pictures of God, and those of Mohammed are also very little to see. But when he is standing before Jesus, he does not naturally pray. This Jesus.

Is vicarious for God here and this figure is simply the prayer bearer. He does not praise the figure, if it were not so in this garden. But this garden has something special for him. He is here with his God and all that belongs to it alone. Here feel be closer to him, as if he were in a church but here he feels it closer. "Hi Jesus, I need to talk to you. Do not think that I am old and stupid, even if I have built so much shit in the last months. But you know all the money I got, I just kept the smallest part for myself. I would have given everything to your poorest children here and in Africa. You know those are not proverbs! ". Please also pay attention to my four friends who were murdered for this money. Even the little money now that I get I will if you want it and allows also that I will donate 90%. Or even to Africa. You dear God, I know that I've only risked it all to others. With the death of his sister, I have no idea how this happens is I'll never know. Was it one of my friends or the killer from Holland.?. I do not know and the police do not. Gerhard goes on after his intense dialogue. It relieves him and helps him to cope with everything. "Yes I'm sure oh God, it helps me to be here and talk to you. He comes into the garden. Of Mother Mary, into the garden of pain.

When he was here for the first time, he was annoyed with the excommunication of the Mother of God by emphasizing her pain. "Now, dear Mother of God, Mother of the Son of God. Now I see the many beautiful still images different. You are the substitute for the many mothers who suffered a hundred times more pain than you. Those who have suffered a hundredfold in pain during the wars and struggles, but you are the mother of all these mothers and therefore the Mother of Sorrows. YOu remind me what to suffer and women can bear. Expulsion, death, rape, the death of their children and their husbands, "I ask you Mother Mary protect all women on this so rude earth".   Help me also, or the day after tomorrow I manage for my family and friends in Africa to get the money tomorrow. I lost all the big money and my friends, the more I ask you to stand by me. " Gerhard now goes past the monastery of the Dominicans, at the mother house of the Dominican nuns in the direction of Arenberg. Because he meets with his buyer, he sees this today for the first time personally. Meet at the Pizza for their Roter Hahn (red rooster). Gerhard considered yet whether he should make a trip to church, but time no longer.

Allows. In the large dining room is only a table occupied, with a man. Gerhard considered what he was supposed to do; he did not know the man's name. But since only one is in the restaurant and the time fits, he goes directly to this. Good day the Lord? They are my buyers? ". "Yes, my dear I am the buyer, they sit down. Do you want something to eat? ". "Yes, I can handle; I've been on my feet since this morning." "That's good, what should it be?". ,, I do not need a map, spaghetti ones pretty sharp and have a beer. " The top stands directly next to him and thanks for the order. "When can I take the pictures?", ,, my partner is to build the device for opening the door I have this naturally hedged. It can happen tomorrow or at the latest overt tomorrow ". "Here my mobile number, when they have the pictures we arrange a meeting place. I check the images and they get the money. " Where can we handle this without being disturbed in the apartment my partner in Montabaur ". "Give me the address so we can get there. Actually we would prefer to do it in the hotel after the bad experiences we did. " "This should not be easy if we carry these 10 pictures through the hotel". "I know something better.

For the two of us; we do it in the underground car park of the hotel". "Well, we keep both in mind. I am storing her phone number and signing up to them tomorrow. " "That's OK, where do they live?". "I live here with the nuns, a nice hotel". "OK, I live in Koblenz at the hotel and I'll get in touch with you when we're ready." With these words Gerhard stops and goes by bus to Koblenz in the city and stays in the Trierer Hof. Still in the night he is called by Manfred. "My dear Gerhard starting tomorrow, can you be up at 8.00 in Arenberg? ". "Yes, I can drive from 6 am onwards the first bus to Arenberg. Then I take the bin at 7.15 then around 7.4 0 up against the Red Rooster at the station Silver Street ". "Ok, my dear, this is good until tomorrow morning".

The next morning, Gerhard already checked out by 6 .00 from the hotel. This goes quite quickly, the lady at the front desk is clever and does everything quickly. Outside it's still fresh and Gerhard has to put on his jacket. Traffic in Koblenz is slowly gaining momentum. He's just 100 yards from Trier Hof at the stop as the nine no, already turns the corner of the central square. Apart from him there are only two other.

Persons at the stop directly at the Koblenz Forum, opposite the town city hall. The journey goes over the Rheinbrücke, (Rhine Bridge) in Ehrenbreitstein turn to the direction Montabaur. He can still see the Ehrenbreitstein fortress and the cable car, which is only getting started at 9:30 am. To the left is the small cogwheel railway which also leads up to the fortress and the local youth hostel. Does all Gerhard made he wants to enjoy when he has collected his money and brought it to Africa. To his friends the poorest of the poor people, the bus stops almost every 800 meters. People get off one another. He gets off at the Silberstraße stop in Arenberg. From here the bus leaves for Immendorf. The last district of Koblenz in front of the Westerwald, the right, he already sees the black VW van. Manfred is waiting impatiently, though Gerhard has arrived on time. "That was time; I've been here for half an hour." "Na prima, then you have seen so many people. I told you I her come by bus at 7:40, look at the clock, now it is just

"You know five minutes ahead of time, the soldier is punctuality." ,, Yes, but not if you take the bus and has such a project, invisibility as far as possible ". Manfred.

Gives gas and runs the Silberstraße quite high, he too knows himself in the meantime. Up to the end of Silberstraße he comes directly to the road they way leads to the bay into windmills. You have already selected a favourable parking space the days before. The black car can`t be seen from the street. Manfred now packing his iron design from which he wants to brock the door, he pinches the one foot under the flange which fortunately has enough space. Is where the hydraulic press at the top flange and the cylinder pumping high?. When the cylinder gets pressure it gets harder with the pumps. But slowly pulling it self the anchors with the screws from the stone. Manfred must once again help because the screws are longer than he thought. With the small crowbar Gerhard levers gradually the screws from the stone. It fall closure of Sporty from the anchorage, you can conveniently open the door. ,,Now my dear Gerhard comes the moment of truth, the images are still there where did you put them. " "They will still be there, because I have checked the wall to the shaft, this is still undisturbed". Since Gerhard is the lesser one, there is no question that he has to go in to get the pictures. He has put a lamp on his forehead so he has.

His hands free to transport the pictures. Gerhard has to overcome only about 9 meters to get to the images. In a completely stooping, crawling. He must now through this narrow passage stuffy the images are still exactly where he has parked 1960th He starts with the biggest picture, it makes him big problems to bring this through the narrow shaft. If necessary, they have to take this picture out of the frame ". But with a lot of back and forth movements and rotations they get it out of the narrow door. Now he takes one picture after another out of the narrow tunnel. Manfred takes the pictures enthusiastically. "I really did not believe Gerhard, who is here after so many years still the pictures. Nobody has any idea of what we hold in our hands ". ,, Gerhard just want to climb out of the door, since it gets a blow to the head, it falls unconscious back into the tunnel, the hydraulic jacks and the apparatus falls behind him at his feet. Manfred closes the tunnel reinserts the dowels again with Rakofix. "Yes, my friend Gerhard, now you are in heaven with your war comrades. You've grown old enough; you do not need the money anymore. I still have at least 30 years to live and I want to live well ". Manfred quickly loads the pictures.

Into the transporter and disappears. As he drives out of the woods to the street, his breath stops before him a patrol car coming from the direction Koblenz down. He still needed it. He stops and lets the guys, who are looking at him. Fortunately, Manfred is already on the forest path which leads directly to the road.Really Manfred wanted to turn right and then turn left in the direction Ehrenbreitstein in the direction from which the patrol car has come. He has no desire to follow the patrol car. But these men are also vigilant. "What was Erwin, where did he come from?" A Limburger number, I have written this down for all cases. The Soko Koblenz had caused three times a day a cart drive past the shaft and controlled. But since nothing was reported by local residents and even the fence and the gate are in order. Have you no longer of great importance given to the matter. Manfred could escape with the pictures, his plan was fully developed. When Gerhard said he wants to meet with the buyer in Arenberg he has switched. This was his chance to get to the millions. He followed Gerhard secretly and then followed Gerhard's buyer to the nunnery. There he then got room number and the name out. He white there's.

This now waiting with the money on Gerhard. A Dutchman, a certain Wolfgang Nussbaum around. Manfred do not dither, Gerhard can`t get in the way him. He takes his cell phone and calls the monastery. He is directly connected to his desire to Mr. Nussbaum. ,, Hello Mr. Nussbaum, I am a colleague and friend of Gerhard. I m have passed the pictures to you and to them this behalf. The old man has not the nerve more for the handover. " ,, I ask how should have the address from him.". ,, We have to do this in Montabaur or Limburg? " "Then in Limburg, I can foresee the pictures". "OK, I can go to the Sacred Garden at her hotel, and then we can meet there. I then have a picture with me ". "OK, so I agree, what do I recognize them. "I'm almost 1.90 big and have a picture in my hand as I said". "When will I be able to do it in 20 minutes"? "OK I'm in the garden in twenty minutes". "The two meet in the garden and will quickly agree." While Manfred sells the pictures, Gerhard comes to the narrow tunnel. He is not dead, but his skull groans. The meeting place, Damn crap, these pictures this cargo from Berlin brought me only misfortune. All my friends are dead and a young friend also wanted to murder me. It's Gerhard by the minute better; he has an iron Herten.

Skull to happiness, his lamp, which hung around his fore head. He found immediately. He is looking for the hydraulic lifter and the device Manfred has built. With difficulty he straightens himself up. In fact, Manfred has the door completely closed. No half things were always Manfred's motto. Gerhard stands with all his strength he can muster against the iron door. "This dog that cursed, who has walled me up. But I do not want to die in this hole. The air here is enough for just a few hours. Gerhard the small frame snaps with which they are drawn from outside the closure on. The same must succeed can also I him now. Laboriously over and he turns the tool he is only there to hold for the hydraulic jacks, where the saddle the door are anchored. "No matter what side I get the door on". Gerhard is using the hydraulics and this packs immediately. With all his strength he uses the pump; it does not take long before he is at the end of his strength. The rod the extension of the lever he studied in the tunnel. This is not to be found because unfortunately it has not fallen into the shaft. Sweat forms on his forehead, which he does not soon open at least the flap can stifle in this tunnel. In the tunnel he once created himself to lead fresh air into the shaft.

Now he himself needs this fresh air very urgently. "He thinks, pulls his belt out of his pants, and makes him a loop. The belt depends on the short lever of the hydraulic pump and stands up in the loop with the foot inside. Clamps with his shoulders and pushes, set again and press. As it happens, there is a short dry bang and the door jumps open. With his shoulders, he can push them out of the shaft. He needed almost an hour to recover before the tunnel in the grass. He has exaggerated himself, but he lives. Once again, he struck a whip. But especial s He will give his friend Manfred ". Gerhard sorted felt itself off and then his pockets, everything is still in place and in order. Even his money is still there, in anticipation of the five million and hoping because s he's now done his friend, has Manfred dispensed drop everything in the bay the old there. Manfred is on his way to Ehrenbreitstein, at the Mühlenbach he has the opportunity to clean himself and his clothes and then dry in the sun. This burns today mercilessly down; Gerhard falls hard then to make the long way through the valley. Today he has no eyes for the beauties of the Mill Valley. He is met by a patrol car, one greets briefly and casually, and this car is past.

The second car of the three daily police car, Gerhard still looks like this stops at the gate to his shaft and controls everything. Because of the heat Gerhard has rolled up his pants and the shirt. He tied the jacket around his stomach. He looks like a harmless crazy old hiker. For the cops have him stop, for a poor old I droughty still wanders happily in this heat. He comes at the saddle mill past her camp, which the Dutch have taken from them. But happily it is Gerhard did not feel like it. He senses what happened, he felt it the Manfred followed him when he met his clients. But he did not trust him. They have been comrades in gliding for nearly 20 years. It is good that is Gerhard for his age so well on foot. Despite his injury to the head and his headache Gerhard manages to get it quickly to Ehrenbreitstein. Once there, he quitted his hunger. A delicious kebab with salad and a bottle of water help him. Then he buys a new phone pre payd phone and is available in the kebab shop from the store. Already after eating and the recovery period he can already use it. He calls to his buyer, which the buy his pictures hold. This is encouraged by his call, very nice that they still register Gerhard. I was a bit worried whether everything was so true.

We have done everything, it has worked very well and I am satisfied with the goods ". ,, Then everything's OK, I just wanted to hear if everything went well, I rise on occasion again. " Gerhard is now in the picture, it is now well that his ex boyfriend now believes he is dead. He pays and drives with the next bus from Ehrenbreitstein to Montabaur. He knows where Manfred is now, he is sure that he is there. He gets off at the ICE train station in Montabaur. He first finds a hotel and then dresses himself completely again. With a fancy summer hat and a new large sunglass, even his kinship would no longer know him.

Freshly cut, he now makes his way to the house of Manfred. This has locked everything and sits in the living room and bursts into his money. Not a single idea it his long-time Freund Gerhard. No feelings hurt him because of the murder of his friend. What interests him is only the one in which he digs with both hands, that's what counts. From today on, he has a life like a lord. Gerhard sees the black van before Manfred's doorstep, he is sure that he is sitting in his living room and groping in the money. He has no idea of murder; he only wants one, his money.

For his people in Africa, whom he has promised so long help, "what do not come to the house unintentionally. He has a key to this house, because he lived here for a few days. He has it all planned Discussed with Manfred. Now he is requirerment patience eventually Manfred has to leave the house again. Gerhard waiting patiently, there are almost 3 hours. Since Manfred has not cook at all can get hunger and has left his house reluctantly. He has the money into s Brought hiding in the attic back. There he had already established a hiding place at times when he was still married. There kept things that his wife did not necessarily have to see, every money. He turns off the case with the five Millio nen. The only one of this hidden place, but Gerhard rotting now in the shaft. Joyfully whistling leaving Manfred's house, hunger drives him. Food is his greatest passion. Gerhard observes the yard like the van leaves and goes to the city. Without thinking too much, Gerhard goes directly into the house. To lucky Gerhard has no time to change. He did not have to accept his old friend Gerhard again. Gerhard immediately know where to look, the money, the door to the hiding place is now though but closed with a kick he has entered.

This door and discovered the money suitcase jointly purchased. Five million already weigh a lot. Gerhard opens the case and takes two handfuls and distributes them in the room by Manfred. Actually, he would have earned a penny. That's about a hundred thousand estimated Gerhard. Then he sets out with the suitcase on the road through the settlement. While he wanders restlessly then he ordered from the way a taxi and goes to his hotel. A little later, he is the man of the digs with both hands on the money. It is such a wonderful feeling to be able to help his friends in Africa soon. But first he will disappear without a trace until all cleared up. You will soon find out that he has nothing to do with the murder of his sister. It will drop the charges. The Amber Room will make all happy investigators so that will think more of him none. He has no idea that he is already free but this caution does him good, too. He now has the time to plan his trip to Africa via Italy. 3 months later, he is with much of his money in Egypt and in Ethiopia and Sudan. But most of her things get turbulent again. No one thought he wasted more of his old buddy Manfred. He would have liked, of course, saw his stupid face as the wolverine has come home.

Meanwhile, the SOKO Koblenz is active again. San Francisco is strange figures moving on the container terminal. German English and Dutch unnoticed by the FBI they work there and do their JOB. The Federal Criminal Police in Wiesbaden has intervened in this matter. Before everything has spread further forms the Soko Koblenz with the Dutch partners of Inter pool and the British Scotland Yard new course is set in international cooperation. The President of the BKA Wiesbaden is in Koblenz, has long conversations with the president of the police headquarters in Koblenz. The matter to the alleged NAZI art and the five murders have the presents of the German BKA / LKA. (small Germany FBI) made it necessary, with the Soko Koblenz are now working all too closely. The development and the importance of the goods have forced them to. The first chief inspector of Soko is called to this meeting added. They greet each other quite friendly; all three are officials who respect each other very seasoned police. ,, Now Mr. Schöder, what's going on with the Nazi art in Koblenz. It was already a big surprise that these hidden in Koblenz where so insignificant mine are. Or were hidden rather, what my dear Mr. Schöder is in the containers.

The six have drawn murders by him, we know where the containers are, but we do not know exactly what is in the containers. Before we could see this at all they were already on their way to San Francisco. Since the FBI keeps his hands on these containers. " ,, What is the area with the new two containers on the way to the US, these have still in hand. " ,, This we had in hand, they were stolen from the container port in Koblenz. Through a wild action of the Dutch ". ,, man Schöder, they would still have to be warned, you would still need to know with for smart people who have something to do. What kind of ruthless criminals. " ,, I can only say that we have everything right now under control, but I would still not provide information before everything is fine is at least is fine for us. We work hard. Two of our people and two of INTERPO old Amsterdam and London Scotland Yard are for this project now in the United States. Our aim is to get everything back and secure and above all to find the end customer. " Can give them early minutely in 8 days a lockable end report, we are contacting all involved from Europe not agreed s to let escape to the outside. It's bad enough that Pres see everything has taken. We secure from only that, we need, as I said these 8 days quit time.

We can, t not allow us to draw attention to our actions the FBI. " So Commissioner, they can, t even tell her superiors. Please but well we trust them any actions that get us into trouble with the FBI. " ,, Certainly Mr President, the men from the FBI complain are when they realize that we have run over, but more they can, t do that. Because we can deliver from Arizona them to end customers and the other gangsters ". ,, Well, let's wait until they have brought the matter progressed so far that they can also inform their superior."

At the same time the men of Europe are slowing the FBI. They were denied the access to the container. Now they have in mind that they never see these containers back in Europe. But in these containers is European art. This they want to bring back to Europe and lead not long years of negotiations to these goods. In this way, they are soon once the company Mearsk have to give them access to these containers freely. The company Maersk has these containers transported and its bearing these containers now. The harbour master and loadmaster Maersk is after long discussion with it Boss. But they needed the pressure from Scotland Yard and Interpol to Koblenz.

With the boat to hols, two containers are identical preparatory how the two stored containers that have come from Koblenz. It is these containers right next which come from Koblenz. Sees each of these containers, which is immediately noticeable that these four containers are completely identical. ,, D as is "managed, says John of Scotland Yard. Now comes the most difficult, we have to implement the welded measuring instruments carefully. These measuring points to monitor the two containers via radio link with the FBI office. It was so clever it is not easy to stick to the container but this to weld; fortunately from the outside an expert from Germany will solve this problem. Kurt does not know what it is but it is pointed out that all procced very carefully must Than must see the other containers of dissolved probes again welding are that all may only last for a very few minutes. It must so be well done that you even later may notice that these doses were implemented ". ,, Henning, the notice something the FBI that we implement the load cells ". ,, I can you with great these things burn safety without something is happening. But if I implement them because I do not how sensitive they are."

Kurt of skilled craftsmen gets up and puts himself under the already raised container and does very carefully because the instruments to solve there are two measuring points. He considers this fast in his hands. Here, ,, men, now what "?. ,, We have to dare and to bridge a meter. Give me the two probes, climb among the other containers, then I'll give you those things, breaking in. " ,, OK". In no time, Kurt is below and prepared container and immediately in the right position. " ,, Give these things here, I'm ready. " ,, All parties standing around the containers hold their breath. How well these probes, they will report the meter movement?. Kurt needed only 20 minutes to the probes to weld again. Now still nothing, no one appears the FBI is moving. Of course, they have prepared for this operation a Matching excuse and apology. Two hours later, everything is done. Carefully remove the container to be replaced. The course Master of Mearsk puts the alleged original containers that are first come immediately back to the offloading terminal for the next container ship to Hamburg and makes this transport preparation for the walk back up to Koblenz. The next day, the ship should have with the two containers at sea to be.

That allegedly is wrong containers ready in port for the transfer. The FBI will marvel at the charge, and will not know for now what is in the containers. In addition, they believe, because the actual proper containers still in the day will come. They are of it convinced that in these two anyway not the NAZI GOODS is. All you wait for four days on the actual container. When that arrives and is unloaded from the giant container crane, the FBI again in the port and also secures these containers. The FBI does not notice that you have switched the other container. These two are already on the high seas on the way back to Koblenz. Gerd is glad them this Miss. succeeded in teamwork in European common Police business. The FBI is working at great speed to find the end customer. To the triggering of a Dutchman are not we constantly and a man from Arkinson. The two were selected from because they had shown not the least to do directly in the murders with the murders in Germany. But the second man is the most wanted of Arkinson was directly then other shipped to the FBI to fulfil a wish. Quickly this became clear during interrogations. The three were flown under heavy guard to America. These three would not lose the FBI.

The man from Arkinson anyway was immediately taken to a maximum security prison. The other two are now vaccinated to lure the end user out of his hiding place. ,, So men, now you can compete, your million are gone. But you can make a long prison sentence get around if you as a key witness with an Cooperating.". The two men are glad to escape the Europeans for the time being. But here in the United States, prison is not even a snooze. Only the man from Arkinson know a bit more, but has not been more than the FBI has even come by. ,, I know is that the end user lives in San Francisco and in Bear Vallay something new builds in which he wants to bring art treasures. I do not even know how the guy is called, we have a phone number, and it is a pre payd no. Here in the US. We have not logged in yet, we have logged in with us. Calling there now, just say that you have the right goods from Germany to San Francisco now. Then wait us from what it is going on. " The chosen one chooses, only a third time a man's voice is heard. ,, Well, that is the time, I thought you can, t make what is now ". ,, We now have the right goods at the port of San Francisco, where and how do we handle the business. " ,, Call me tomorrow at the same time, I will explain it to you.

" So the conversation is over and the FBI is cheering, they are very close. The next day, at the same time is actually back to someone's turn. The voice on it is a different man yesterday. ,, Now what guys; we make you the language because now I'm even on the phone. Where is the commodity and when can we exchange Coal against goods? " The man from Arkinson reads his specifications from the FBI note, the containers both of them standing in the harbour at Maersk. ,, It's all right, how should that occur. " We'll be at the harbour at 2:00 pm tomorrow; we'll call you when we're ready. What men, what about the third container, where is this?. ,, That's unfortunately gone back to Flissen instead to England. Which also comes in about 2 weeks, all right, then tomorrow in container ports we only take two." ,, Why the FBI asks why tomorrow, waiting for weeks to the goods and has at one time until morning. What if that also has connections in the port, now he knows where the container can stand and this may bring himself without paying. But we do not even know if this is the right buyer. What if he has advanced one, someone who wants to mix with at the high art and the giant money?. "

,, The inspector is his boss turns to. ,, That would not be so bad, then it is good that we have separated the four containers ". The claw us the old the wrong container, the containment it are all linked and they were us then lead directly to the buyer. " You're right, not a bad IDEA, we are waiting tonight on whether and happened as. It happened something in the harbour.

Than they could expect before, without intrusion. legally two low loaders come to the farm and within 40 minutes both containers are loaded and on their way to their new owners. Carefully follows a whole FBI team. Far behind them the Mobile special police command to immediately intervene. Even further away are four officials from Europe. They only want to see from a distance what will happen there. They have special cameras to this e noted also in the picture as evidence of their activities here in the US in California. The manager is there and everything is settled and approved. The trip goes out of the port area; the drivers are solved by radio. The FBI men no longer need their lenders; they are safely kept in the San Francisco City Penitentiary. Two helicopters are ready for use.

It is expected the possibility, since the two containers can be separated. A large distance is followed by some civilian vehicles, which of course have the containers always in their laptops. You will not be surprised; the trip goes to Dillon Beach, north of Francisco. The Lk W, turn off the highway and take a smaller road which then lead directly to Dillon Beach. You go into a large empty lot, turn there and stay in front of a small hut cess engineer. The FBI people are quick zoom and unbolt everything from. No mouse could escape more of this property. The truck drivers get off their huge tractors. From the small house on this property comes a man who is seemingly the buyer. Slowly he strolls up to the two containers and the driver of the trailer. ,, T he was so great people, had not expected you. Come out men he calls out to the little house turned out, come and open the containers. With many tools the men moved in and solve all seals. The heavy container doors we are pushed. With police sirens the FBI t now at large. ,, All hands up, you're all under arrest in the name of the law. Hands up, one of the men said the usual saying. Quickly, all the men in the dust of the campsite are naturally in handcuffs.

,, So people then let's see, the FBI people open the container, amazed them. In the first container they unpack, only scrap. In the second container only scrap. That you knows container to have come wrong, the men from the FBI knew that this but the wrong containers, the buyer could not have imagined. He was sure there stole the NAZI art in previous function containers. But it takes shock and anger to themselves for men. Also in this end of the second containers is only scrap, grin men from Europe consider everything from a safe distance and still filming. They have succeeded; they all know that the right material is on its way back to Europe. They are crumbling again as inconspicuously as they have come.

The FBI men collect the men of the buyer. The disappointment is great. At the FBI, as they realize there is the alleged buyer is also just any so wild straw man. Furious, she then leave the empty yard with the two containers which are filled with junk. The line of the FBI, complains loudly at the BKA and LKA, with the threat of charging all costs to the German authorities for the purge. In Koblenz is again a meeting announced. This time it smells so badly.

For the first chief commissions, we should be, with the nun We have now six dead. Then nothing behind it, only   two empty containers which are filled with scrap. This can, t be that 5 people maybe had to leave 6 their lives. What's wrong with the Koblenz Kripo (crime police). The Koblenz CID has snubbed course with colleagues from the Netherlands and England the FBI. But this is just a security measure. Only a few FBI people from San Francisco knew that in the containers only scrap is. Now in all four containers, the Germans of course, did not, as this valuable art in the US. Of course, a little revenge for it, since s has not allowed the containers and the follow-up in the US and requests to participate in the investigation as s as had been promised. You are with your investigation much further than the FBI; they are the true buyer on the heels. Of course this is terribly shocked when he hears the FBI's access. But he can, t help himself, too, when he hears that the containers were just scrap metal. He had this already guessed, because he knows, as these containers were delivered incorrectly. That's why he was so cautious and named a Strawman and the wrong goal. First he wanted to look and then take the goods somewhere else.

He had expected that it could happen. For they have often tried to deceive him with art. That's why he sent the Dutch and then the three from Arizona. It has been shown that his mistress was entitled. So he had once again proved how good his nose is. He is, despite this s accident, as he sees it happy to have worn them no harm. Of course he would have liked to now have personally the Amber Room itself. But this again should not be, this NAZI art, especially the lost one is a dangerous issue. The men from Europe are the big business men on his heels, have already come very close to him. All it over is known for all sorts of forbidden and not forbidden art. This man seated hurt and slightly injured, wounded in his dignity in his heavy chair in the living room and ponders to himself. His thoughts are with Adolf Hitler, he knows there this Amber Room, and he must have it. Even if it has not worked out now, the more he wants it. He knows the men from Europe; of course, you know that such a fanatic never gives up. You do it the next day for an appointment to get with him. The technician who puts the probes must believe in it. He is a technician, but first of all a cop. Send them directly to the front to multi billioaire him, the poor guy. He has to make.

The appointment with the rich Chris Hendricks. ,,
He ringing behaved and asked about his desire. ,, I
am here on behalf of a Dutchman and a man from
Arizona, to say which arrive the correct delivery
from Germany. " ,, One moment please the Lord,
they are from Germany ". ,, Yes, of course, they
tell him it's urgent. A few seconds later the
chambermaid came back. ,, Please the Lord my
Lord and Master can ask. ,, Kurt is loudly greeted
and dubbed with you idiots, you crooks and so
much more. Kurt knows there` s must be angry
the man to collect such a setback for absolutely
nothing, for two charges car scrap. These charges
have already cost him a few million. In proportion
to its total assets, these 2 million can hardly be
expressed as a percentage. ,, Sorry sir, they surely
silly three looked as if they have learned from the
scrap. But we knew long ago that the FBI was
involved by the stupidity of their people.
Therefore, we had to trick accordingly, we have
done well, or not. The FBI is frustrated and we now
have free rein. ",, OK. Ok, where is the Amber
Room now?. ,, That will be difficult now, they
wanted us kidding too. You have just sent us the
Dutch, then they have the Gangster sent from
Arizona and they have.

Not let the container steal Francisco us. To our lucky the wrong container, did they have to pay ever before had anyone s honest. " ,,The money is not lacking, we forget the experienced how we can handle now, they understand that I now after the two containers scrap miss'suspiciously.".,,Ha, ha, Kurt must be short laugh, they send us killer on the neck, steal the container and are suspicious of us ??. We have the goods perfectly safe in our hands. We ta deceive honest in the next days. You can think about it and we think about how it should go. We will then contact you again. Ah here because they are so suspicious, Images of loading containers in Germany. Everything was great and packed with only the packaging, we have really opened so as not to endanger their s. All this has located 6 0 years in a bay but how they look at the photo. All still in full splendour, due to the good packaging. " In fact, these images are real, from the time of loading the picture. In Arenberg / Mills bay with a glimpse into the container. These pictures convince the buyer, and then we clarify OK to be completed in a few days as anything. Of course it is dearer to me when we do it all in the US could end" ,, Goods has long California in they understand that they can, t see them.

Beforehand by the brilliant performance of tonight." My people will soon discuss the process with them, " ,, one more question Kurt Müller so was her name. How did they come to me as a buyer, Nobody knew that. " ,, This can and my dear I do not tell them, they take it as a sign of our life".. You have this really all hired super clever, you can see what is emerging for smart mixes when Europeans together work. They should do this much more often, they can do it. Kurt says goodbye and they arrange to meet them on the phone this take the next few days contact. The two Germans have to return home, the visa has expired and it is not necessary to extend this visa. It is also hard enough to settle the payment and expenses in his department. For this he also needed the footage for his house's own presidential possible ways for the BKA, because this president was not satisfied with the explanation that Gerd has delivery. When Kurt and Werner from California are back in Koblenz immediately made up the entire SOKO. You're listening intently to the report of the two men. They also have the experience to see the opening of the two containers in the sight of FBI life.

No wonder they have so pissed reacts here, ,, my God, I have done both presidents to the screw. I accepted them because it is the whole. Things alone tell them when you get back and the containers are returned. I hope only in the two containers is more than just scrap. What happened to the remainder of the three kill container?. ,, The dear Gerd was found still by no s in the United States. I think about also will resurface. " What Gerhard, the old men?, we have interrogated all involved, he has absolutely nothing to do with the death of the Dominican sister. We have lifted the arrest warrant; he is no longer officially sought. Wanted but for new interrogations. But e r disappeared from the earth. " ,, He is no longer so important who knows any more than we what is really in the containers. Because of the picture with the small cut it could be the Bernsteinzimmer ". "What the amber room, here in the Mühlenbach? That would be the hammer". ,, What do our friends from the FBI, they are very angry that we allegedly so rasped ". They want to charge your government for all costs. " ,, they may like to do. " I had told them, because these are the wrong container. I do not understand their excitement.

,, But we have them also left a successful criminal investigation to reconciliation. They now only have to use it properly. Watch the movie you have probably all filmed in the US?". "Sure, this country is no different. In this case, I am only talking to the end buyer. We found him and linked him the way he wanted to link us all. Because of his guilt, the four men and the sister have died. We gave the FBI the continuation in the hand. If they are clever than can grab the man. But I have a bad feeling. I think these buyers is not the real thing, this man Chris Hendricks did not behave like someone with something art can start the. I spoke directly to him, who seems to me to be only one station. I do not think that the real buyer would ever rake me sp. With a Concerned at the business crooks ". , Exactly my dear Kurt, I do not think even I also believe that this is the final purchaser ". "No idea why the FBI can think that". Two days later comes out of the container port in Koblenz. The message because have arrived from San Francisco the two containers. Gerd calls the special meeting with the two presidents he had threatened. All leading police forces from Koblenz, the LKA Mainz and the BKA are present. Gerd has to tell the whole story. The whole point was then our fault that.

I give to the we have from our safe hands that have two containers steal let I had no choice, we immediately spread the message because is are the wrong container. On its way to Francisco after that, all the bandits really react. We can then steal the next identical reclaimed container for them. They have brought out Saturday with brute force on our goal was to get the right containers back from the United States back. Store the wrong container there. Al though the right secured by the FBI w ere we managed to reverse the polarity of these containers and securing loaded to the two containers with scrap to staple. It was a good work and we thank Kurt great success. The two right container, we implemented and sent directly back to Koblenz back. These gentlemen have arrived there today in our container port. We have our containers back and we can all go after there and see what's really in the containers is ". ,, Then my Commissioners that is in the new containers. " ,, Here again only industrial waste but better packaged with a deception set in the container, then those have to entice the buyer out of his hole only purpose ". ,, Then later than experienced the FBI we have the real goods brought back, again have legally stolen them from San Francisco. "

,, Why Mr. President, they have never experienced, then we have just all been wrong. " Unfortunately, we can, t bring the four older men and the sister. To live, at this time we could not intervene in the events because we had no idea of the whole action." ,, What about the proper containers, "ask the president". ,, OK, I just got the message that they are ready to be opened. I have determined that this may happen only when we are all on site ". "Then to the container port". It takes about 1 hour until are all in expectancy. Everything is quite style as the first container door opens. Of course they do not see more than packaged goods. Only the first parts of the front are worn out and very carefully open from employees. A murmur goes through the mouth of all men and women who are here. What they see is for sure a piece from the amber room. ,, people calling the BKA President. This is mind boggling if we really have the Amber Room here, it would not be grasped. We can, t afford to unpack here. Pack and close everything quickly. These containers are strictly guarded from now on. Until we know how it goes with it ". Carefully and reverently, they reintroduce the piece with the magnificent amber.

" It is the right thing to do this, the President of the BKA takes Gerd Schöder in his arm. ,, Hi Gerd, hi Gerd Schöder the first time that was and is a strong piece. The criminal investigation department Koblenz. Is completely out of control, you probably have made history for Germany. Soon the assembly will be dissolved. Gerd goes to the office and call immediately his friend at the FBI in the United States. The first to terrify him because of the impudence to bring the containers back, so you cleverly put it down. First chief commissioner you thought we do not notice it, so stupid is the FBI; unfortunately we have noticed it too late. It has blown us tidy the march. ,, My dear calm down, I was hoping you this never noted I still have a Boon for you. But anticipated, in the real containers are parts of the so long sought for Bernstein. The first part in the container looks directly like this. "., My God Gerd when I give the more you get entry ban for life in the USA ". ,, That's why I brought back all this. " ,, As your alarm with the confusion was only deception, you have deliberately demonstrated. Then in the other two new containers is also just junk? ". ,, Yes, but beautiful packaging, really packed. We want to catch but the buyer, the client for this confusion. "

It must know no one, since s also scrap is in these containers. Retrieved I have this art again because it's just about German art, not American. We did this get out first as everything was already on the high seas. We would have taken years to get our treasures back if we had ever got back the containers with contents. " ,, You're right Gerd, but you say you've also important INFO for us. " Yes we were so free and have established in the US for you the right buyer, who despite his own hundred million also the container has claws leave. Clap has out of your hands. This man has to answer 6 dead also h ere with us. " ,, How you managed her to convict him? ". "Tomorrow I'll overpower you over a secured line a video, an evidence, then we'll talk and talk. " ,, OK Gerd, do it right if it is possible for you, then I have it now, I'm still in the office. ",, I think this man of which I you the video of the man is sending everything arranged for another. The only in-between, which makes the dirty work for a larger depends. I will send you all the data and you can initiate the reconciliation with the SOKO and the FBI ". My connection is absolutely secure, you do not believe that you can crack the Internet at the FBI. " ,, Good to your responsibilities.

But please give me a call when you receive. ,, OK that's the way we do it". Then good night my dear, I am now going home. How many hours difference in time do we have? ". ,, OK then until morning, there are 8 to 9 hours. " ,, Then we do it but now, you are still in the office. " Yes but on the way, but send it please otherwise we may have problems tomorrow ". ,, Okay I send it and wait your call back ". Gerd puts the stick into his computer and sends the video. 10 minutes later Ronny recalls enthusiastically. My God Gerd, so we get the guy ". Then until morning, when this works, you are forgiven. " Manfred is back and experience the biggest surprise of his life. Manfred's back home, he was at the hairdresser and has to eat something No one in Montabaur has such a good mood as Manfred Kuhlmann. Of course, his first path leads to his money-box. His good humour flies abruptly. Money is scattered throughout the room. He's ripping his hair, what the hell is going on. He opens the door of the hiding occurred. The safe brown suitcase I around the coal is completely gone. What was the use of the supposedly safe suitcase if he could not secure it? ,, Bloody hell, what's going on here, nobody knows or knows the hideout except Gerhard.

But Gerhard's dead, is not it? How is her then out of this tunnel come to end.". Manfred gathers together the money, which has always been here, has about left him € 100,000. He did not quite put it on the dry. Manfred hammers his head, now. All his plans, everything is in a bucket. ,, I go get the 5 million, far the thief can, t be ". The guy can not the police, but first I must check whether this Gerhard he Thief or whether there are accomplices. " He rummages in no time the round turned money in a small bag and surprises them in the kitchen cabinet, not exactly sure. Then he grabs his telescope and makes his way to the windmills. He parked in front of the fork in the forest and is unobtrusive as possible through the forest to the back of the bay. With the telescope he looks up the hill with the door in de m air shaft. Of course, the door is open and you have not even bothered to close it again. What then, has Gerhard been freed or freed him. But the guy was lying there dead in the tunnel. Has not been a peep from him. So there are still his liberators in the game. Manfred goes along; it is immediately clear, since s there if it's so, these people have the 5 million. Then it will be difficult for him to get back the money.

Then they have definitely done Gerhard. But how can it all be, how can it be that somebody knows. If they were monitored at m picking up the pictures, thousand questions swirling through his mind, he has no idea, because it is the biggest mistake was to appear again. Because it really gives someone the decision white, the man knew there's there anything else to get here. ,, A good friend of the Dutch, a thug from Belgium has initiated him Gerry before they were detained at the border with England because of stupid passes. Has the buddy from Holland Gerry the Belgians asked careful to keep air slot in mind. Unfortunately, Gerry has come too late for 3 days. He has discovered the open entrance and the Tunnel been investigated itself. Unfortunately this is empty, now the guy arrives here. ,, What examined the here remains Gerry cover. But he sees that the man Manfred Kuhlmann is badly shaken. Gerry stays behind Manfred to his car. It takes longer for Manfred to sort out. This gives Gerry the opportunity to get his vehicle, which is a little further down. He hurries, for he must follow the man. Gerry is also a well-known criminal in the Benelux area. But you could never snap him. He is a very cautious.

Clever and ruffled fellow. Fortunately, he has already become familiar with the environment. My buddy Hendrik was right. He suspects that things are still hidden here. There's someone behind her previous function things. He now puts himself with his car so in the curve that he can observe. In which direction the black box car drives. It will not be long, because the box is car in motion in the direction of Arenberg. In Arenberg, he then turns off to Montabaur. Manfred did not fall on the following him a car with a Belgian license plates. Only when it rings late at night at his doorstep, he is amazed when he looks into the barrel of a gun. ,, Good evening my friend, read us go in or do you want in the door be shot. " Manfred automatically goes back a step and the stranger follows him with the gun in his hand. The door snaps shut behind him. ,, He takes the gun down, but not sets out of hand. " Mr. Manfred Kuhlmann, they are called yet. I am convinced that we both have the same looking at things from this air slot ". ,, Since they are and I too late Manfred says quickly, things are in the US ". ,, Yes, I know, but not what was hidden in this small air tunnel. I was inside and saw the traces of crates and the wall to the shaft was also undamaged.

That tells me that someone was faster than me. " ,,
Yes, I also think the same "Manfred answers. Gerry
now puts the weapon back into his shoulder. ,,
Then my dear, we are partners, you know more. "
Manfred switches immediately, even for two ha b
s they find greater opportunities the money, ,, ok,
I'm Manfred, I know who has the money. But I
have no idea where he is this bastard." He does
not say that he has been stolen from the money.
He has done for his best mate. But this must have
somehow managed. They sit together all evening
and ponder what they can do, how they can get
back to the money. For five million it is worth a lot
to do, especially since this money is tax-free. They
have no idea that this money is not removed mails
of you and with the owner at least the current
owners. Together in the hotel rooms outsourced.
Ownership is something and properly, the current
owner of the millions is there better. It is still
uncertain how long this is. Where there is so much
money, there are also many interested parties. The
current owner also about ponders how he these
millions as he can get large parts of it to Africa.
How he should manage to come to Africa himself.
He rents his room initially for 10 days. He closes
the case.

Which is particularly safe very carefully. This can only be opened with a key and a combination. He puts this suitcase in the closet. But he is still a few thousand in his pocket. He need this, he then takes a taxi to Frankfurt. The money is not lacking him yes. It's driving him too dangerous with the ICE from Montabaur. In Frankfurt, he goes to his old buddy of good relations in the underworld has. ,, Bernhard, I need a new passport, what does this cost ". ,, If it is to be good, it costs about 5,000 €. " ,, There is no question that you can start. Here you have 6000.- € 6000.- € he counts Bernhard the back. The thousand or everything that goes on the passport costs for you. " ,, OK when you need to pass. " ,, quickly as possible". ,, How long are you staying in Frankfurt, only a few days?, " here's my phone number. Call me if you have something going on. Here is the copy of my ID which unfortunately is not original ". ,, Looks good but that is not also your passport can make. " ,, No, unfortunately he can, t. " ,, Come old buddy, let's to chow down and talk about old times. " ,, Do you still have the restaurant with attached girl house ". ,, Yes both I have some to eat, drink and fuck that fits well together yet. Just so is my relations to come to the underworld.

And to your new passport." ,, I still have a problem; I have in Luxembourg money that needs sent to Africa. You are able to control this transfer. I am willing you give 15% of the amount. " ,, How much money is it? ". ,, I want 4 million for a transfer to an Africa Bank." . ,, Gerhard, has attacked you banks or is the wrong money?.",, No my dear, this is not a counterfeit money that is honest money, I sold old pictures. " ,, Do I believe you, my dear, even as over I'll let you know. I think I've got someone a lot of money in Cairo and this would have liked here. Of course, discreetly and without tax office for the money should be here a gift. Also, I can tell you in a few days how and where this can take place. Gerhard then does not last long on in Frankfurt. He leaves his cell phone number. For Bernhard and sits back into the taxi and then again on his Money back at the hotel. The thing is burning Gerhard in the truest sense of the word under the butt. Would that be a hammer if he could just swap it and he might have in Cairo about the transfer here in Germany. Manfred and Gerry sit there and make calls in Koblenz, Montabaur. Limburg, Frankfurt from Gerhard to find all the hotels. They are with her efforts doing succeed because they do not know.

The new name of Gerhard. Also in Hachenburg in actual n Location of Gerhard they have no luck. Gerhard has not seen for many months. It was also not surprised because Gerhard often for months in Africa. ,, A beautiful shit Gerry, how are we to find the guy. " ,, Yes it is difficult, maybe he really is already in Africa ". ,, That will. Not be possible, then he needs a new passport, then I no knows his passport has expired and he can extend this bad. Then the money that can`t be, but out of sight. " ,, You are absolutely right Manfred, let's consider what we would do in this situation ". ,, I would have gone in his place to Limburg or directly to Frankfurt. Koblenz and Montabaur I exclude. That's too far away from Frankfurt and very close to me. He must assume that I will look for him. Fortunately, he has left me to the centre. ",, That will not be easy, who seems to have to be very clever. ?. I think we should accommodated us in Limburg, I also feel the guy is there because of the proximity to Frankfurt. " Those two men leave Montabaur and give Gerhard ignorant security. Three days later, Gerhard gets the call that his passport is ready. Long he wonders whether he can recover his money alone. But also take is not, he has no choice.

But he takes in case some 10 thousand Euros with. He also suspects, there's got his mater Bernhard appetite and is now demanding safe more for the pass. He ordered a taxi to the hotel again, this time by another company and drives a taxi to Frankfurt. His passport is super unusual and indistinguishable from a real one. Of course. This now as previously expected cost significantly more. But Gerhard is happy his departure, nothing stands in the way. With the friends of Bernhard of monetary exchange is still unclear. He leaves this course in the belief that this money in Luxembourg at a bank. The men do not get any ideas. Because that also Manfred examined the money is clear to him.

Chapter   2   In the USA
the matter will continue.

In the US, the FBI everything is in full swing, it is looking forward to finally come to the backers. Ronny head of the FBI San Francisco prepares all the containers are prepared the same way as the others are unfortunately only loaded with scrap. They could convince the customer that they now have the right container with the Amber Room. Only the FBI knows that the original containers are already backing in Germany.

Gerd but he assured that in these containers all real packed is. It has been the packaging boxes in the order perceived by genial containers. The first parts in the container sent the created Amber Room. These are directly forward stowed at the container port where. Also, the scrap is in this time. In the same package, a package that you used 60 years ago, you want this time open the container and the buyers can look inside. After the problem with the last delivery, such a desire is the buyer already evident. Ronny calls Gerd, on, e s ringing long and pervasive in Ehrenbreitstein one at the home of Gerd. Ronny keeps forgetting the big time difference of almost 9 hours. But Gerd is still awake and takes almost the last yodel of the phone for the phone. So long he wants to change this wrong ringtone. ,, Schöder, he moans sleepily into the phone. " ,, Hi Gerd, here is Ronny from the USA, sorry I always forget the time difference. Gerd, I just want to know if you want to be there when we make the end users arrested. " . ,, Nice of you Ronny I'll call you tomorrow, must clarify this with the Bureau. But I still think a holiday in the US that is too expensive for our department. " ,, I leave tomorrow our boss with your boss speak, that perhaps is something.

Because my boss by the FBI want you are about. "
,, OK Ronny , then I wait what then does in my office. " Gerd hangs up and turns back to its Marianne which again is for a short visit to Gerd in Koblenz. Sally Marianne's dog turns to this disorder back to the side and goes back to sleep.

Two days later, Gerd sitting on the plane to San Francisco. The Bureau has to be in allows for the transfer of authority to it. The containers again see original so like the previous two are back to happiness by Gerd tricks in Germany. The new container that simulated secured and is well guarded back in the container port of Mearsk. From a safe distance to my neighbouring Terminal, these containers are also not lost sight of. The villa of the end user in San Francisco is also ready and takeover Ready for the Amber Room. The third missing container has surfaced and is for the end user for such since still unattainable in Holland in Flissen. There are people who are employees of the advanced buyer while ensuring that container. He wants this Amber Room it brings him good 20 million. He has done everything he wants this room for its clients. But Inter pool does not sleep and has long constituted the containers and observed this also in secret.

Gerd is set by telephone after landing in San Francisco thereof, that they have everything under control in Flissen. He' rather Gerd be now in Flissen Holland than here in San Francisco. A he is confident about his team with whom he also telephoned immediately even gotten this. It is of course clear. Also these containers to the planned replacement and arrest the workers back to Koblenz got. The real buyer has no idea the distrust just be the acquisition of the Amber Room for him was impossible. There is something typical a distrust Americans happened and overreaction from preventing the shops and successes. The men still supposed unknown buyer propel themselves even for a few days on the premises of Mearsk in San Francisco around. To prepare the handover of the Container. After the last disaster they are this Mal cautious. You open the container after they have studied this thoroughly. But already the first showpieces behind the steely door to show them, because it is right that content. They shall immediately inform the buyer from making some photos and seal the container properly again. Of course, under the watchful eye of the FBI. It then takes another two days until these two Container be picked.

The FBI and Gerd Schöder follow this transport. A helicopter is in use, they LEVERAGING this time attaching no stations. Then the men are now the container pick are professionals, of course, they check the container. The heavy low loaders and tractors are hired and the riders are free enlisted.

You do not know what kind of cargo they transport there. Quick is the journey of the low-loader from San Francisco out. The very nice coast to Bear Valley, a peninsula, the trucks turn after almost 2 hours into a side road. The prosecution is now more difficult because this is a lonely narrow side street. ,, Ronny directs his people through radio and the helicopter kept a low flying over the route and sends the images to the pursuit car of the FBI. You can see in these pictures the track and also the end of this road on a magnificent individual Villas. With a fantastic view of the sea, just the rigth worthy place for an Amber Room, there, a crane truck awaits the vehicles of the containers then raises over the wall into the grounds. The trucks come back you will stop this only when they returned to their storage place. You have to pay for wear they can`t contact anyone before the action is completed. ,, What do you do now Ronny?, "

. let's see, Gerd, the containers can, t leave. Now we need patience. I will first of all put our people into a trot. The guys are right here, we'll stay here for cover. Disguised as a fishermen who want to go fishing with a tourist from Germany. " ,, Ah, I understand, then to me as a tourist in them run property and explore the cause." ,,Yes I thought so, because a German is hardly noticeable. " ,, Or even more so my dear Ronny. Just because the containers come from Germany. Since no one is looking for a relationship, but thou shalt not get caught you to. Otherwise my men near you and hear everything. You will naturally wire to FBI Art ". The car with the fishing team has now arrived. The car is proper to made legally and from a distance already a recognize ls anglers car. Gerd are now three comical men in fishing clothes in the car and drive along the road. No one 100 meters from the secluded villa away they park and look over the sea. A little steep and rock from here the way down to the water. But they also recognize, as s they can s come close from below almost unseen to the villa. They drag their equipment down to the water. You have already noticed you observed them from the grounds of the villa with the telescope.

,, So a shit says one of the men casually squatting on the wall of the property. I told the driveway from the main road must always be closed when the truck, s in this street into it went. Now we have the stupid fishing, I go after once r below and see my boys on. I must also clarify this here is absolutely private premises ". ,, When actually comes the boss "?. ,, He comes when. I give him the sign that everything is OK. He comes when we open the container ". Ronny is in the process to determine the owner of this house at his office. He was not astonished badly, because this one respected company of San Francisco. But the buyer they know is a multi- millionaire from San Francisco. You have to keep all the peace and to wait what is coming. The employee who has just viewed the arrival of the angler with is already down with them at the beach. ,, Hi master, "he welcomes this friendly. ,, you certainly overlook that they are here on a private beach, unfortunately I have to ask them to get out of here again. " ,, Well, my dear, that everybody can say when they set up no signs we can, t see that too and we do not believe them easily. " ,, That they do not have me believe when they are still in here for two hours.

She will have to remove the police. Till they leave this section of the beach as soon as possible. " ,, How far to their alleged plot is enough? ". ,, The entire beach as far as you can see part of our company. So they move away please the extent of this land that they can no longer see each other.

As far as they here left or right can look all part of this villa ". ,, Ok, we are waiting for the other our second vehicle. Then we get out of here. Where is there the next opportunity undisturbed fishing ". ,, Since they have the main street and up again PORT Raye`s drive. So they do that please and disappear them quickly." ,, OK when the second vehicle comes we will disappear together here. A famous as long as we throw here before the hinges off ". ,, This is not a good idea, I'll call the police in any case and have them removed by force if necessary here. " ,, OK, they do what they want, we stay here for up our second car comes ".Ronny has overheard everything and of course has the nearest police station which inform, there they should send no vehicle until they have completed their operation here. A little bit later one of the usual big Cadillacs coming with the multimillionaires and billionaires driven into the entrance of the court.

The employee is amazed not bad; he has not yet made the call. ,, What do you look so stupid, I just did not want to wait. What kind of a car up there? "These are anglers who enter there frolic on the beach, I says that I will remove them from the police. " ,, OK, so then to the point, we make the container on " Meanwhile, Gerd has the binding cover behind each rock that up to the villa is lined on the way to the Villa made. He cans unseen reach the yard. With his camera he is filming the yard and the house. Everything will be directly transferred to the FBI car. ,, Gerd, what do not you approach the container? ". ,, One moment please, I need to find first. I make the camera while ". Carefully seeking Gerd around the giant Big House, to found may some problems. He has past the pool which offers him little cover. He knows, because across the US is not safe to move onto foreign soil. Quick one has caught a ball. Then he sees the container and goes behind a giant grill cover. And hold the camera in direction to the container. ,, Good Gerd, very good, now we have at least one image from the buyer, I hope. The property belongs to a company, any private person. But we already know all the shareholders. Of course, is a Wealthy than the other.

What are they doing while on the doors of the container? " . ,, The castle does not seem to get on. " ,, Gerd, I have all so far secured that land is completely sealed off, there comes no more mouse out. When the door container rises, we propose at the same time. " ,, OK Ronny, I switch the power back on. " ,, This Gerd no longer comes when someone hands him a cool iron to the head. ,, Hands, up Sir, what they are doing here?". Ronny hear this call and responded immediately. From all sides storming the police men in to the danger area. The man with the Colt is on Gerd's head is so surprise so scared Gerd can him over helm quickly. All within a few seconds in the action involved handcuffed in the yard. Of course, the FBI is very glad it exults they have here at great expense and effort the multimillionair and buyers catcht. You are satisfied with the action they have it the millionaire Chris Hendricks caught. Just for the second time can he the FBI no longer the scene stealing. Chris Hendricks is grinning in the dust, he's his lawyer convinced him has been cut down quickly. The FBI is convinced that she had buyers can convert soon. ,, Beautiful shit Ronny, I could have stayed at home and can take care of the other containers in Flissen".

,, What's Gerd we have thought us very different but we have the buyer. We believe the buyer to have " . ,, I think Ronny you have not the right, the guy knows what he's doing, he wants to see I do not burn your fingers even as your alleged buyer. E r will try again to get close to the container " ,, your private opinion Gerd, wir seize this container now and store them. I will do so not again loose. When Chris Hendricks as you think is not the right buyer. Has the no idea, since these are not the right container. We are launching some pictures on TV; we will show your good rental items. His people the container opens s have just seen and only the first layer forward. These can be the conclusion to, since s the right containers are. This was once again made great by our experts. " ,, That you have really done well, but I'm flying tomorrow morning back home. " ,, OK Gerd we stay tuned and if we then still have success, I'll get back to you. ,, Everything OK Ronny, then sit e me off at my hotel. The flight I will make a reservation, I hope, because it works. Maybe then I get with what's happening in Flissen ". ,, I d e Electrical appliances are also long since replaced the container. Send me calm again the wrong container wherein ye so now exercise.

We need to lure the guy out of hiding. " ,, It is also planned by my people and Inter pool. I will contact you and inform you. " The next evening the police chief arrives in Amsterdam and moves directly to the train to Flissen. At the hotel he meets his Oberkommissar Schmidtchen and its Commissioner Renate Völcker. The two have been waiting for her boss and then want the next day together again to Koblenz drive. They all have a longing for their beautiful city, family and friends. ,, Tell Gerd, how did it go in the US? ". ,, Everything actually very good, only we the real still do not have buyers. That FBI she believes has left him with Chris Hendricks. But Ronny shares my opinion he seems on his trail to be. They reckon, sinces he the containers now with his people directly for a third time will bring. This art lovers are unpredictable, they have so much money, they want this art simply possess. Most of all! Hang then they sit right in the middle, I think that this house on the beach not far from the terminus of the art is . About the house they do not come to the patrons. " ,, It's a nice crap in this world, there's Milliard poor devil on this earth and then the can easily afford it all back millions of millionaires and billionaires.

Seat here with her fat ass in a golden seat. ". ,, Yes so dear is this world, unfortunately, or thank God, imagine we were all as rich. ". I had to throw up all day if I would realm so that all go past the real life. ,, Yes Renate, since you have also right that would be even worse for the Earth. But we need to ensure ne better redistribution ". ,, Let it better, we this world will never change three, we can only the worst of them render them harmless. The bad, the have the worst so much money, that one of does not reach them. We pack our prison full of chicken thieves and the real gangsters run free and loose around who buy free again. " ,, What's Flissen, you did it again Done container exchange ". ,, Since there we have already a lot of practice, so it worked out great, but only with Renate's help. She had full body use and Bandit has ten distracted. " ,, You Renate did you but not operated as a substitute whore. " ,, Gerd! no ,, that was fun Renate Sorry , but how did you do that? " . A little bit, a little bit true that already with the Hure (woring).A I about got myself of professional for the essential support. But I must confess I've taken everything and it was fun. When I once the police force quit animals shall that would be not a bad JOB for me.

Men, I can only say, a bit tits a bit of leg, d he two hectares b s their job and the container for a few hours completely forgotten. In silence, our people could exchange the container ". ,, Well, kids, I'm glad for us everything went at least here. Are there any news from Koblenz because of the parts inside in the container ". ,, No Gerd which is of course all under the blanket held until we finally all caught ". ,, Is there something new by Gerhard the man from Hachenburg. The poor devil has all his old buddy, within a few lost. The war they have endured together but unfortunately not the shaft in Arenberg here. I've got a bad feeling so I think Gerhard is the whole not yet be over. Even if we could not prove anything against him, but has everything put away as calmly as if he were still special arrows in his quiver "has. So now off to bed, although I am rested, I sleep always great on the plane. I climb in d s flier one and I are already asleep before the box is in the clouds. The wake me for meals and I then slept again one ". ,, Well, we know who is driving tomorrow morning the car. Then we sleep. " ,, OK, driving I will gladly, but only if Renate of her adventures as a prostitute tells "me. The next morning they are after a hearty breakfast back on the road.

In the Beautiful city of two rivers. These two river city also loves her guest Commissioner of Village, Commissioner Schmidtchen. He is in Austria and grew up in a two-river city. In city of Spittal Austria in there the rumbling Lisa from the mountains flows. That's why he gets in Koblenz little homesick for Carinthia. Gerd reconsiders all the action here they had and still have. It was incredible, four dead elderly men and a dead nun a dead Americans 3 Dead Dutchman. You have the container with. The art treasures, the murderers of the nun and have the killers of men. They should be happy with their results, it is actually. Also including the nice songs his Senator and boss of police. But somehow Gerd has the feeling that the thing for him is not yet over. In the US anyway, but here is something in the air. Gerd can feel it."

Chapter 3 Gerhard brings its share to Africa

Gerhard Maifelder brings his money to Africa and ensures, as s his people can see better to live in these countries. Gerhard escape tricky the Belgians and his old Friend Manfred, Gerhard is happy, because he has chosen as his Montabaur current focus. He is convinced, since s Manfred would pass him by without recognizing him.

As much as Gerhard has his personality changed. You are not looking for him everywhere but in Montabaur. With the new identity card and now with the super successful pass he feels already like a totally new person. He is brave and takes the bus from the ICE train station Montabaur. Koblenz, there rises in Koblenz / from Arenberg. The sacred garden and the church have done it to him. Here he finds the reflection. And tranquility to about his plan for the future thinking. The bus stops near the monastery and the sacred garden. He is Gerhard Catholic and Islam at the same time followers. For him belong both go together very well, for him there is only one God. No matter what name you give it. He sits down on the bench standing next to Jesus in his cave The sacred garden consists of many caves and a garden of pain from Mary. But this place this Jesus Grote has become his favourite place. He has no doubts that will anyone recognize it here. ,, Dear Jesus, I ask you Discuss yourself up in your sky with Mohamed, please do something together against the madness of so many currently misguided Muslim s in this world are all a product of their governments are the most artificial of their lives in countries were built by Western states.

Governments in these countries d he never did anything for her citizens had left. Governments all religion used to their own wealth and power to come to get their wealth. These people were oppressed and now make their great liberation. Some cover the land with war, the other seek their safety in flight. Ge r hard as an experienced man and Africa Arabia Kenner have before forty years warned. Africa continues to exploit or so. Aid to Africa has been given over many decades the wrong people in Africa. You just wanted to win the favour of those in power, you never wanted to help the people. Gerhard warns since 1970 constantly before it once because of your own wrong policies of the West comes to an assault on Europe. It line inevitable and daunting will be waves of flights to Europe, a wave of refugees, the so powerful is that of the West, Europe comes to waver. In which the West now forced to speak must help. The receipt for the years of misbehaviour of Europeans and Americans of these people in Africa and Arabia boil with rage and the anger on their leaders to your religious leaders let them do the most ridiculous things. They flee or take up arms, not knowing what they are doing.

As Jesus took you so nicely said, Father, forgive them for they know not what they do. You know Jesus, because your children you following have made similar. You have all killed, who with sword and fire people converted. The Christians had their bad time, they've due nothings in Garbor` thirty years long warred, killed, and murderet. Until Europe lay in ruins, the same is happening now in the Middle East, the religions that misguided religions Sunnis and Shiites. Race towards each other as two trains. Only the two of you Mohammed and Jesus, only you could stop the parties. What in Christianity were the Catholic and Protestant here again there are the Shiites and Sunnis. Ask Jesus help my friends down there. More than thirty years of my life I spent there, please help them. Bring them with God, Allah bring them enlightenment. Please do not help me, but help me my rescued means to this country to bring to my friends so I can give them the promised aid after so many years. I will use this money not bestow greatl will give them to make work. I will make them a chance even to make money. The money I will spread across Africa and Arabia. Only I have to get there before it. My passport I have my money.

Please let everything be fine, do please, as s s I manage to exchange the money here against money there. Otherwise I would not know as I would be to bring my friends. Gerhard then goes through the sacred garden and dares to even go through the monastery herb garden. Still buys tea for his hotel room in Montabaur. In the showrooms of the great Dominican monastery is a brisk business. The tea is so wonderful, Gerhard has it always drunk when he was still living here. This tea helps him very much. And tastes delicious. Gerhard is now sure that he has become so great turns, even the Mother Superior walks past him. Although greets but does not recognize him. Gerhard dares now even the bus to Koblenz to drive. He needed a new phone. He buys two pieces. Because of money it really lacks not him. He wants and needs to be free, must feel safe so that no one can locate on the cell phone him. Of course, both pre payd phones. He can also two different phone numbers alternately use. He strolls through the old town of Koblenz .Get the Moselle and the Rhine along. This city also gives him something again and again. There are many people on the streets but there is no rush in this city.

Except of course in the main shopping area of Koblenz Löhrstraße, the cable car that anyone from the left bank of the fortress on the right bank of the Rhine can bring, is still so small extra kick. He goes again back from the Rhine River, on the German corner at Kaiser by on the banks of the Mosel along back to the old town. There is it on the bench at Görresplatz, directly in front of the beautiful fountain and thinks about the possible settlement of the money transfer to. He telephones the men in Frankfurt and arranges to meet for an interview tomorrow night. They should consider it as they want to assure him the money. He gives then four million in cash to any n place in Germany. E r requires an irrevocable bank document that the money he can pick up in Cairo. This where he has his account already for many years by the HSBC bank there even better, they should consider how they discuss it with his bank and its bank in Cairo. One wonders in Frankfurt that he wants to have the money in Cairo, but that's nobody's business. This is solely his cause. Three days later, Gerhard again in Frankfurt and meets with his Freund Bernhard people to him the money in Cairo redeem want. Gerhard tarry long at Bernhard in the restaurant.

And watched the customers who March through the restaurant and into the upper floors of the scantily clad girls disappear. ,, Will not you once highly Gerhard ". ,, How long must we wait? ". The men wanted to be here, actually. " ,, What are these types. " ,, Do not Bange Gerhard I know the two already over 30 years, I just know for a long time that the Sudanese have a lot of coal in Cairo. Dollars, but this is not over here being come." For him, Gerhard is also a huge opportunity. ,, I'm going through your floors; call me if your types are. Maybe I'll find the right up there ",, Let's go, well Schuss Gerhard, it works still, right?. ". Gerhard going up the stairs, he received directly from some girls who argue almost around him. He does not know about him, which is all about the money. Real good beautiful luxury women body, the one already can take your mind stood before him. Today his interests are of a different nature and a different nature. Enjoying the views and prospects and goes through all three floors and enjoys these sights and insights. He is amazed at the squad that Bernhard has here. For each he has something, black, white, brown, yellow. For some girls, the big boobs from their small holders seem to jump at him.

But today, despite the great offer, he has no bock. His money is difficult for him in the stomach. Bernhard is already reporting on his mobile phone. "Come down, throw that thing away that you have in your hand, the boys are there and are curious about you". "OK, I'll be right down". The men greeted each other briefly and came to the point. ,, you have in cash and want to bring four million euros this past everything to Cairo. Is this money clean? ". "You've already got a few thousand, the bills were OK." "Yes, they were OK". We have already thought about how we can organize this. We remember it transmits you my money into Cairo within the bank and you hand us your 4 million here. " The extra amount of dollars to the euro you get here. "On which bank do you have your money". For a year now completely clean and legal on the HSBC Bank in Cairo / Maadi ". ,, That fits itself very well my account is also at HSBC Bank in Maadi ". Then I will discuss tomorrow phone with my banker in Cairo as we can handle this properly. I think that you give my bank the money ". ,, OK tomorrow make a suggestion, we agree, we will clarify this tomorrow with the bank in Cairo. They can then discuss how to run ". "Then how shall we handle the examination.

Of the money?". ,, We will come up with a machine and the bills have hunted in two hours. Are all these five hundreds? ". "Yes, it's all five Hundreds,``. "OK then we agrees, tell us where we can do everything. We would like to do the exam here at Bernhard ". ,, I call upon you morning if that's clear with the bank then we can see how and where to go. " .. Agree, it's nice to work with you ". Gerhard goes back to Montabaur with a happy smile. He now believes to finally be rid of this money. It's hard on his stomach, he does not think of the lost amber room at all. He now knows that it was a mistake. To salvage this for the 50 million. They should have handed it over to the state. The next day he clears all phone and fax with his bank. He knows his bankers in Cairo in person. The latter will be established immediately with the relevant accountant of the Sudanese. His banker recalls him soon. ,, Everything is OK, the money is ready for us to transfer it to your account, it is available here. " ,, OK, which in turn check my cash here, how can the go the transfer to my account is secured? ". ,, We are making here an irrevocable Letter of domestic credit. If we will have the OK from your friends and freely, and we will forward the money to your account ".

"How do my people confirm that?". ,, signed certified by the Chamber of Commerce or by a notary and by you with a simple fax. Best sent directly from notary fax ". "Ok, I agree, I will now clarify the exam". His partners in Germany also agree to this transaction. They clarify everything with their notary and arrange the examination of the money. Gerhard knows exactly how dangerous this is for him once again. For money everything is possible he calculated with one because you want to put it again on the cross. Even if his bank has confirmed him the money in Cairo and he holds the LC in his hands. For so much money everything is possible. In particular, he has had bad experiences with Sudanese. Even bankers are not angels, who are so vulnerable and keen on money like everyone else. You love in particular because they only work with it and these themselves. Have not but would like to have. He is so suspicious also against his LC from his bank. He comes to the consideration money handover is safest in the small Hotel Trierer Hof in Koblenz. The public prosecutor's office is not far around the corner and the police. Koblenz is manageable and quite secure. In Frankfurt everything would be more uncertain.

Before informing his partners, he already put a check in the Trierer Hof and stored his money there in the largest and best room. He does not feel comfortable in his skin at all. 4 million in cash, some people are killed for 5 € or less. He himself has already lost four of his oldest friends because of the money. One is astonished in Frankfurt about the place Gerhard has chosen to surrender. But it's OK, the men from Frankfurt come right the next day. Gerhard, of course, did not tell them in which hotel he had the money. They meet in the Cafe shepherd near the Forum in the central square. Gerhard insists that these men are unarmed. He does this communicate ells of a metal Detectors and is surprised because neither man some metalic carries. Open the case with the money count and testing machine. Even all the bills are locked the policing, see! these machine. These men, too, are, of course, careful. ,, So men then go, go with a very bad feeling in my stomach Gerhard go with them in the hotel. The Sudanese amazed not bad when he sees but what she has chosen for a basic hotel Gerhard quickly realizes it is a good hotel. The man at the front desk is amazed not bad when he sees Gerhard with foreigners.

These are my business friends from Sudan, we go up to a meeting, they can please the Internet in my room unlock ". "You already have the code to unlock". ,, enough the code all day. Yes they can work with it all day. Tomorrow they will get a new code ". "All right, good luck at the meeting". The men take the elevator to the third floor and enter the very nicely furnished room. They set up their machine and Gerhard freed his money bag from the closet. All men are strained to the utmost. The machine starts to chatter and one glimmering after another flies out of the device during the secondary stroke and is again packed into the empty suitcase. It takes just 65 minutes. Because all licenses are checked and counted again in the case. "So Gerhard, your money is fine, we now give the notary the order to send the fax to the bank in Cairo. The Sudanese the perfect German speaking gives the notary the instruction to send the fax to the bank in Cairo. Gerhard has long Skyp by the bank selected and has the two bankers in the image. "Yes, Gerhard, right now the fax has arrived; we are now posting the funds, in a few minutes it is in your account". Gerhard calls his Internet account and see the incredible $ 4 million in his account. "

,, Everything OK, I'm in a week in Cairo, now gives my cash free,". "OK Mister Gerhard, we look forward to it". This completes everything. ". Without hesitation, the men take the suitcase with their money and say goodbye. They order a car directly in front of the hotel door. They too are as careful as Gerhard was. They also know they are now as likely as Gerhard lived with the stuff. Your money is on Gerhard's account and they lost and they now have the cash here. Bernhard gets the extra money between dollars and euros for his efforts. For that Gerhard has free food and priest all his life in the house of Bernard. Gerhard can breathe deeply finally, it is a ton Heavy Stone fallen from the heart. All this time gone. Well for him, everything is ready for the help of his friends in Africa and Arabia. Friends who need his help urgently. After this liberation stroke. Gerhard remained in Koblenz for two days, retreating to Arenberg in his holy garden, which gave him peace and then went back by bus to Montabaur. Two days later, he goes with the train to Amsterdam and flies from Amsterdam to Cairo. He is his Friend Manfred from Montabaur and Gerry escape the Belgians. They have absolutely lost its truck and hunting looking for Gerhard.

And the million still around. They do not know that for them the millions are no longer attainable. The container from Flissen being equally again in Koblenz In Koblenz harbour of the third containers of home from Flissen come versa. With a lot of prominence, this is opened there. The first thing that falls against them is the corpse of a man. It has been a long time. It stinks terribly after decay. No anything should touch the crime scene is active and the head of Pathology (Coroner) who is present during the opening of the container is activated. Only when the body is carefully removed and all the traces are taken. Catch experts to examine the content front in the container. They are not astonished, these are also old art looted and there are going forward. In the container some part it actually could come from the Amber Room. The container is immediately closed again. Slowly, it gets stuck in the minds of the police, the s it is stumbled upon this saying urgent Amber Room. They realize there fit this effort and now the ninth dead to it. ,, What is doing; they can already say something about the man's death? ". ,, So far I can only say that the man at least four weeks here is in the container. You must have enclosed this man alive in the container? ".

,, Gerd shudders at the thought, we do something. ,, In the next recite more can I say, I need the man on my table. But his hands to show how desperate he tried to open the container from the inside." ,, Four weeks ago, "said the Kommissar Schmidtchen speaks up, ,, four weeks ago there was the container already in Flissen Harbour. He came across Rotterdam. He was supposed to Rotterdam directly to England for the tunnel. Know the devil why this one then after flits has spent. The papers were clearly issued to England. Maybe someone wanted the container for themselves? ". The Doc stands up and hold a piece of paper in his hand. " Mr. Schmidtchen. Here the data of the men seem to be". It is a crumpled customer card you probably overlooked. Dead everything has decreased. ,, Gert van der Mohlen, so probably "is this man. Schmidtchen takes the card and passes this data via his mobile phone directly to Interpol in Rotterdam. The answer is not long in coming. Gert van der Mohlen the dutch people is missing, comes from The Hague and is a sought in Benelux criminals. Interpol has also been announced for the next day. There too is happy because now all original containers are back in Germany. They are very surprised about it.

Because it still becomes any information as what is now in the containers. But they hope to learn a lot when they are back in Koblenz. Gerhard with is in its millions in Africa. Gerhard is very active in Cairo, he has his rest 700.000.- € in cash hidden very well. This hiding place occurred to him while he was talking to Jesus in the sacred garden. It is in the sacred garden very well cared for. Guarded by God and his angels Gerhard has now built up all his old connections in Cairo again. The old companies are brought back to life and several hundred jobs are renewed. The children's home for the poorest children will be reopened.For all this, the necessary money was missing in recent years.

A billionaire from the USA comes to Koblenz

Frank Bruno has gathered his private intelligence in his huge mansion in Sacramento. "All you are here have failed. Cost me already million but the Amber Room you have not yet to h ere ago can bring to me. 8 men and a woman, a nun had to believe it. I can hardly believe it what are you for rivets?. Chris Hendricks is free again and sits well with him gets the most from, I wants this room and I want these s as soon as possible. " Frank ,, o, we have the two new container.

Are already here in the US back under our control. This time, the FBI is no longer in the fingers. This time we are turning the tables ". "OK, I want to be informed at the very latest about how their bungler wanted to do the work. I fly after morning to Germany has a lot to settle with our office in Frankfurt. Then I go to Koblenz for a few days. I have already booked rooms with the nuns. I feel uncomfortable with the Order because you have killed one of the nuns. On the other hand, I will look at the monastery, the church and the holy garden ". "So, tomorrow I want to have a precise plan and nothing goes without consultation with me. His people put him in fact the next day a plan how they want to come to the container, and they confirm him as they also brought the container in Flissen back. Under their absolute control. "But if it goes somehow I do not want to experience any more death. Why did the Dutchman really have to believe that was completely superfluous? ". ,, The dead man's Gert van der Mohlen he was getting caught when he tried to the art from the container No idea how it managed to get into the container. We have it then just in the box are closed. "My God, then the poor fellow has miserably perished, and has already begun to falter.

Hopefully the art works are not thereby harms be. Can you not remove the dead people soon from the container?. " "This has already been done log the worker, he wanted to at least something good to report to his client. He had arranged this but did not know if this was actually done. So men, everything is not here nor do I take fly to Germany I want to see the whole itself. Will see in what strange bay everything was hidden. In addition, a friend recommended a Catholic bishop to visit the monastery there. Unfortunately one of the nuns from the monastery died there. It was suggested to visit the pilgrimage church and the sacred garden. I will do this and I will look at the container in Flissen on the way there. When is he to go on the ship? ". We have organized this; he should go in three days. On the ship. We have a direct ship from Flissen to San Francisco ". "This is good, which means that I must immediately organize my flight". The whole fits then, I would like to have all three containers at the same time in my house ". Do all the containers go to the same place again? ". "No, now they go directly to me. Men do it well I'll be the next 7 days in Holland and Germany. Because the ship of Flissen.

Need certainly 10 days left to San Francisco.

In the monastery of the Dominicans inside one wonders a California bishop from the USA has logged in with 2 guests for 5 days. It is looking forward to these guests from the United States necessarily the Wall propelled church St. Nicholas and the Holy Guest want to see written. The Sister Superior is very excited a bishop from the US has never been in your monastery. You will be delighted also about the monastery and its church are so well known in the foreign continent. Your Order has been this long. The bishop has informed her that he comes with high-ranking and rich industrialists. This does not impress the Sister superior really, she also had already cardinals in your house. The three best rooms in the house are prepared. Frank Bruno has already landed with the bishop in Amsterdam. It is still early morning. In Amsterdam, as the flight to Frankfurt until the next afternoon Frank and drives a taxi to Flissen. He also gets the opportunity to look into the container there. He is glad very glad the body was removed. No matter or other debris can be seen. He does not know, of course, that this is not the container in which the corpse has been. But, of course, he can only inspect the front packs.

He finds it a huge load off my mind, he is sure of view of the first part here is probably genuine parts from the Amber Room. Satisfied can Franko occlusive again the container. All images that Inter pool from the remote monitoring picks of this process are sent directly to the FBI in the United States and to the Soko Koblenz. There you are immediately active and evaluates the recordings. The next day the three men from the USA are in Arenberg. From the airport Frankfurt to the ICE station Montabaur it is just in high speed 20 minutes driving time. Twice as long did the last 25 mails by taxi to Arenberg. There we they friendly welcome and very well catered for. The high visit to Arenberg course was also reported to the diocese bishop in Trier. Arenberg is for the next few days, the centre the Roman Catholic Diocese of Trier. This favours the project by Frank, which is only interested. In the well, be missing is not noticed. Franko Bruno is self made billionaire who does not need any support. He admires this shaft, which he photographs from all sides. The shaft thrilled Frank o much, he now understands why the Amber Room could remain hidden for so long. This e images to decorate the entrance hall of the Amber Room.

It is now the connection to his room. From this splendid bay in Arenberg over the pilgrimage church through the holy garden into its amber room. This is precisely what has been lacking the connection in this stateroom is actually complete nature. Nature has been arranged by man to a work of art. He firmly believes that he is now in possession of this room. Regretted to have very given the Dutch and the men from Arizona done the job to see here after things. He had the old men with whom he has concluded the contract more familiar then probably would have gone all alone and silently across the stage. But here it was because of his involvement around the Amber Room now 8 dead. These eight dead people would not burden him much it will take him about his joy. It does not know and does not suspect there's these dead shall see him still fall very hard on the feet. This he now bring very big problems. Nor is Frank Bruno happy and is eagerly anticipating the most beautiful and most valuable Room This world. He sees himself in thrones and enjoying it. The very thought of owning this makes it unspeakably proud. Then the last two days he spends with the bishop in the Sanctuary in Arenberg and in the sacred garden.

The whole environment suits his Amber Room. In parting, the sister gets a Superior Big donation from Franko Bruno for their order. He sees this as a remedy for the death of the nuns. The Bishop of California without Franko been very active in Arenberg. He still meets his colleague from Trier. Still drives to Limburg to the fabulous new building of his fellow bishops to admire. This has even reached him in California, but he never understood the excitement. For him it was not about the investment but here you just wanted to meet the person. Then, all go together in the two Rivers city of Koblenz which brings the worthy ending for all. Enthusiastic about their experiences here in the beautiful Koblenz / Arenberg they fly all relieved back to the United States.

FBI -Interpol Soko Koblenz- The machine, Computer, Telex, Fax run hard between the Soko Koblenz-Interpol. Rotterdam and FBI San Francisco. One is delighted because we have now identified all venture all Customer of art treasures. All information from the airports about the fly`s of the two to Amsterdam and also the visit of Frank Bruno in Flissen. The opening of the container at the port of Flissen hat them that.

Needs to be this man, the buyer made clear. Interpol has promptly dubbed the videos to the FBI and to Koblenz. So were the men from the United States, the bishop and his billionaire. Also not Arenberg alone, of course, the people of Soko Koblenz also filmed the visit of the billionaire in the shaft. All this could then be later evidence against the purchaser. All the partners in Rotterdam and California are sure that this may be important evidence. They all know the aborted lawyers in the USA, for money they succeed very much. But this is not only in the US so, even here in Europe there are huge gaps in the judiciary if a lot of money is involved. Gerd and actually all the police officers are always angry at these parts of the judiciary. They tear their ass on often risk their lives and so windy lawyers crumble their good work in court. Soko Koblenz sits together once again and discusses the latest events. The first chief commissioner is once more.

Excited. "I'd rather not leave this shit back in the US, but we can, t holds him. We have no choice but to take it very slowly with the dangled containers. His journey in the country of origin of his beloved Amber Room here.

Frank o Bruno very hurt but he has thus helped the investigators. He has shown them who is believed to be the real buyer. Schmidtchen accompanied the Americans yet discreet and unobtrusive for this to the airport. He waits until it directly to San Francisco nonstop a check. He precise information its first chief inspector of the flight and checked even with the German thoroughness of an Austrian that they actually departing. On the booked plant, Gerd is this info immediately on to Rotterdam and San Francisco. There, the billionaire is then monitored with great certainty around the clock. At the day Ronny resumes contact on with Gerd on. "Good morning to Germany, what does it look like with you, has one already gotten out what is in the containers?". "I think so, but you keep everything under the covers. But it is rumored that this is the legendary Bernstein Zimmer the Amber Room, but no one knows this exactly ". ,, That would explain a lot; at least that we have already 8 dead. Let us hope there remains there. But I'll call you on the merits of the container because of Flissen to ship lies in the harbour since yesterday. He is morning here go above are from aboard container. We have led since then are all three containers.

At Maersk together. Then we all three containers together under our control". "Then Frank Bruno came back home in time. I think it will go online in the next few days as the real thing. I assume the Chris Hendricks makes all the dirty work and then protects Franko Bruno. It is then only light and fluffy run everything here." ,, I hope this Ronny, I hope this very ". "Have you considered Gerd "?. ,, I have such a bad feeling, he is out Arkinson submerged and here also two luminaries float around, a Belgian and someone from Montabaur. These are only now in our visor again. By visiting Frank Bruno we found only at second tunnel the air shaft. There was actually a secondary business running. One of the four old men, Gerhard the last survivor, has disappeared. He is the man who has also worked for 19 6 0 until the closure of the shaft here as engineer. We found in the study of small air shaft, as small boxes were also stored s in this small bay. Completely separate from the Great Project Amber Room. The air shaft was then separated from the normal shaft by a wall.

Who has stored things there, the hour at this made aware and now brought these things with the Amber Room out again. For them the Amber Room was lost.

After his old comrades were killed, which it can only have been Gerhard Maifelder. Then we have small amounts of blood from the old man, Gerhard found. We do not know what happened to him. Now that we have but found a hydraulic jack, which was also his blood and his hair glue. Do we have to assume that he was killed it and buried somewhere here in the forest? "In these investigations under the old men then suddenly the name Manfred Kuhlmann is again. His fingerprints are also on the hydraulic lifter. Just as these were found there, has it the old slain by the hydraulic jacks. Then we have also found the fingerprints still one of Interpol sought man, a dangerous Belgian air on manhole covers. The man's name is Gerry Schreinemakers. We are looking for these two men. Have studied Kuhlmann's apartment in Montabaur and found traces of a suitcase in which a lot of money must have been. Some five hundreds lie gen still in the closet. We are now monitoring the house and hope to catch both men. I only wish the surviving old still had something of his money and life ".

"Then you also have some unexplained things". Worse,, Ronny, I even the assumption that the Belgian has contact.

With your husband from Arkinson Has. The whom you left her at the lengths leash.". "That would be dramatic Gerd. Then we must be twice careful. Well that we telephoned, then I can respond immediately ". ,, Ronny, get that beautiful on've got everything in your e-mail, if you are in the office you the description of pictures and fingerprints biography of Kuhlmann and Gerry Schreinemakers ". "Super Gerd, sometimes it's nice to work with you German together". "Why only sometimes?". ,, Well, yes because you also some time a right German guy is mostly an bonierte Korinthenkaker (currant shiter) and farm men are "sometimes. How do you say so nice in Germany, Arschlöcher (Ashools). ,, Well, there where her Amis often are too casual, as we are sometimes a bit too carefully. Only in spying on us Europeans you are world leaders, but there are the machines for you ". ,, Sorry Gerd, but I find this word asshole and Arschloch so beautiful. Unfortunately we have nothing like it. Also I goes, but it does not have as much Character. OK Gerd I register if I mails your e mail have read". Gerd then discusses his SOKO, they have not come any further.In the search for the Belgian and Kuhlmann. Also the monitoring of the apartment has not yet revealed anything.

203

Gerd would have liked to know what the two are doing and what they are doing at all. Lack of money they do not seem to suffer the five hundreds are in the apartment so around. The revenues have to be who they removed the old one. The reward from the sale of items from the airshaft, wen Gerhard was also murdered. Have we now 8 dead but before we have no evidence for this we have to be happy with the seven dead. ",, That is actually a thing Gerd, which is the biggest criminal case with which I do in my career has. What about the alleged amber room? " "Unfortunately, we do not even know exactly whether it is actually the Bernsteinzimmer. But in any case it has to Property Assets of looted art from the war be a V ". ,, this is really strange, we saved all three containers and nobody tells us what really is it? ". "This is indeed strange Renate, but this has to do with the international problems with this art. Think you want only one time to make sure whether this art of German origin before so going out in public. On the other hand, they could only report this when this accursed buyer, as he is still called." "Frank Bruno, only when this is.

Transferred can we announce the content. The rich poor fools, when the desert is in the three fields in Francisco port containers to which it is so keen only scrap ". ,, If we let the joy until he makes his fright in the pants and chains in a barred cell. On stet in the Amber Room is sitting. " ,, You do not think that Frank Bruno the rich man is going to happen in the US or hear anything. His lawyers cut him out of all the allegations. Just as we are now gathering evidence, his people have long since put the counter-evidence together. For all cases, such people are not surprising. Not one of us who again people like us that all traces. They are in court all being pulled apart what we have collected so hard." ,, Yes, sometimes evil. Would sometimes hang my job on the nail. But then I often find there also the smartest minds make mistakes as we do so. Then the equality of arms is again established. Then the courts to decide who gets right closing people; there is something new from the Belgians. " ,, yes, for two minutes, I got a message from Montabaur that the two so dissimilar men in Kuhlmann's apartment are she keep everything they do and speak in sound and solid ". ,, Well you two then we have at least something. Los we go to Montabaur. I throw her.

On the way in Arenberg out of the car. I come back by bus. I will probably then go right from the Arenberg home. Or my Marianne and Sally take me there from. Then we can also our common make walk. My little Eifel goat loves the forest walks and the Border collie Sally anyway. All right, the day is soon anyway around, we then teach you in the morning in the office. " ,, All right then people every success in Montabaur. I also want to again duct go . This is a beautiful walk there down through the Arenberg forest. And the mills home, we will go through the monastery to Spitzweg hut and then only through the woods to the bay. I secretly still hope that my Border anything discovered what us escaped. Often has he dog helped us " . ,, Gerd gets out and his colleagues drive the 1 5 km further to Montabaur. There they enter the vehicle of the sanitation department, is monitored from which the apartment of Kuhlmann. Renate has the feeling that she with the sitting lounge in men. To clear the images of surveillance cameras what they experience as it brings all the wonder. The old Gerhard seems the two of gangsters to have escaped and with the greatest part of the money. They collect all the information and copy the CDS with the recordings.

They are their colleagues Gerd can surprise quite tomorrow. Because something happen in his apartment. The Belgian Gerry Schreinemakers takes his cell phone, according to the ring out of his pocket change it from the left to the right hand but it is too late, and it does not ring. He tries then even this number in the US back. The camera is as low, since Renate even the dial his number on the display of the mobile phone record. Immediately quoted Renate this number as a precaution on his book. If something with the CD happen, ,, what's going yells a voice from the phone so loud that they can communicate without cell phones to America. ,, I'm Chris , I 'm Gerry, "the Belgian roars back. ,, Why you screaming jerk like that? ". ,, Well, you also jerk, I've seen that the call comes from Germany, from so far away. You know Dusseldorf ever meet what time it is here? ". ,, Of course three in the night." ,, what are you now, there is something new from Arenberg?". ,, Yes, but sleep e further I'll call you tomorrow morning about 8:00 am your time on. Then you're safe again receptive. " ,, Do not fuck Gerry, I want everything now do not know until tomorrow morning." . No,, until tomorrow morning, I must also sort some things I have to do tonight. Tomorrow morning.   207

You get the full INFO. It is mostly about your information on your three containers in San Francisco" .The men at the bugging device flinch. What does the Belgians on the container?." Can but have no idea of what really is in the containers. " Everything happens even further what is picked up by colleagues from Montabaur. ,, Was that your buddy from the USA Gerry "asks Manfred. Yes, he was the real customer, but it was so sleep astray I wanted to tell him anything. I must also still in Rotterdam simultaneously hear because there were problems with my old partner Gert van der Mohlen Is suddenly gone. I have met with him in Rotterdam on container. He wanted to serve on the container and bring out some parts of themselves. He gave me said that he feels these are still objects here in the shaft in Arenberg, in windmills. Actually, I'm here because of that. No idea how he knew this. But it should still go to a few million. Gert must have known this from the customer of this picture wants to buy, also a Dutchman. " ,, Yes, Gerry, that was exactly five million, this five million were here in my closet. I got the money with my friend Gerhard from the air shaft. He did not know where to put it so fast and has asked me to help recover the pictures. "

When, recovering the cash money did you also help him? ". ,, I had no choice, for me it was five million, or 500,000, which he had promised. Since I have taken the opportunity and I the hydraulic lift on the head beat and in the shaft locked. Of course, I thought the guy is dead. " ,, That you thought the guy was able to free himself and has taken you your carbon back. You're an adult idiot. The crazy buddy of Gerhard gave you then. For that you killed him wanted 100,000 left behind. "This is again typical German man, you would have to really bite for your stupidity. " Now you run the few million behind her, waiting in the states 50 million. " ",, Why 50 million?. ,, you are a very innocent, we're after the famous Amber Room. Now we have lost all our people. Only my buddy in Arizona's turn, we need you now Manfred, all Dutch are turned off except for Henk. We want to involve anyone anymore with. You can be there, forget your buddy here and forget now 5 million. Let's start with the 50 million we can get in the US ". ,, Pahe, that's a number, of course I'm doing. Let us count the flakes, so we know how much we now have.". We still have five finance weeks USA until we come to the big coal ". ,, we still have fifty thousand, which should be enough. " ,, What is about. 209

A visa, do you have a visa? ". ,, This shit Visa to the United States but I get fast one on the American Embassy in Brussels, I have a friend there. I call the morning of for 7000.- € USD, we have both the visa in three days. " We have to send our passport copies today, I hope, as he can also help you see, because you have a German passport. Gerry picks up the phone and calls directly in Brussels in the American Embassy in. It takes several minutes until everything has been clarified. ,, We are lucky, my pal clarifies that because of you off with the Berlin Embassy, it will work. " ,, What about your buddy in the US ?, Is the trustworthy ?. ,, The leads us to the many millions, then we no longer need it. " ,, Or he no longer us Gerry " ?. The two Europeans are closer in the days looking for Gerhard. Gerry also speaks perfect German. ,, What about your English Manfred." ,, This is quite well my dear I'll be able to move well down in the United States. How exactly is your buddy from Arkinson.? " His name is Willi and is a fine but also harmless guy. He was indeed here in Arenberg and the containers stole. Here, then, the nun and the four old men were killed. The two Dutch and the other crooks from Arkinson are in custody. Willi has left on a long leash with the FBI.

He has then soon made. Thin and is our ticket to the big business. " Willi has the direct line to the buyer with whom I have just phoned did. Willi has made the end and I have the Trust s the buyer won. Bin by you with Chris Hendricks, it's a multi-millionaire. We want the same again after Arenberg. I must once again into the bay, I can, t help feeling that there is to get there a bit for us. The two immediately send their passport copies to Brussels and make their way to Arenberg. The Commissioner Renate Völcker immediately reaches for the phone and warns her boss. Gerd, ,, the two men, the Belgians and the man from Montabaur make up on the way to the shaft. You have to do also something in the Mills, they say." ,, OK Renate Thank you, we'll be careful. We already passed the Spitzweg cottage and are on the direct road to the Mills. I sign on the way. The two run wherever they want if they come here we have them as harmless walkers under control ". Gerd Schöder the first chief inspector has, after his meeting. It the two of them in the convent, dust set off made in the mills. Sally and Marianne are always happy when they can take a walk. They have come by bus from Ehrenbreitstein to Arenberg.

So they are free to choose their way and do not have back to the car. It takes less than 3 minutes than they have accessed through the forest to the bay. Sally rages as always through the forest, but always near her mistress and Boss. Sally closely watched the animals which they always meet here, the hare and the deer are here at home. Sometimes standing up the animals no 5 meters from each other from opposite. All remain very still, until the forest animals in peace comfortably run for it. ,, It's always exciting to watch as Sally behave towards animals. " ,, Sally is a real guard dog she once guarded sheep. Therefore it is absolutely obedient and has no problem with other animals. It is always great with her to go through this forest. It is silence in Koblenz but the smell of the Westerwald is here already felt. In between, the distant view through gaps in the forest in the Westerwald into it. Such a place before Spitzweg cottage they have just happened. A further look into the Westerwald she rewarded. ,, I live in the Vordereifel, which is very nice but here it is a little kick nicer. The width of view makes this out a bit. Then of course the beautiful environment and the city nearby.

It took us from your house in Ehrenbreitstein by bus 15 minutes. If you can manage we can throughout the Mills again to walk to Ehrenbreitstein." ,, Clear my little Marianne, we will do, I know we like e you walk the way are, but I also love long walks. " We'll be right down I have to clarify something here, 'I be sure if these items if they exist at all are not at the bay or in nearby destination ". Then explore the open door to the tunnel, Gerd raises Sally inside. But this can also discover nothing there. They close the door properly again and walk comfortably in the style of careless hikers on. Less than 10 minutes for them the two gangsters have arrived at the door. The three still stroll past just before the turn-off at a house. Although Sally Gerd draws there in the barn they can, t see anything in it. They go beyond the turnoff and then to d he grain Mühle(mill). Where the road branches off to Arzheim. Gerd goes directly to the local barn to see if there is something to discover there. Gerd opens barns door and looks into it, but he can, t see anything suspicious. It orbits with Sally yet the grain mill but discovered there is also nothing. Slowly the sun will come more and more through the clouds and the temperature rises to nearly 28 grad C.

You go further through the mills, a beautiful little valley. Everywhere the left and right of the path and forest a great air and to the constant babble of the brook flowing along. Beside the road, in addition to the pleasant sound of the Mühlenbach (millcreeck) can sally ever again quench their thirst and uses the opportunity to cool down. The two sometimes take a handful of water and cool off. ,, Is not that wonderful here again I am pleased on new if I be the small walk valley. The sound of the water and the cool bris that goes through the valley, it is glorious " ,, Only a little bit lonely to live around here and yet there are here and there individual houses. " You can reach the Sauer mill and go there in the yard. It looks at first glance a little left out, but then they realize that this little place and the little farm still in operation Sally will lead on the foreign land. But she pulls Gerd again at a slightly remote barn. Gerd feel it is because something interests for Sally and he gives in. The door is open and a man is in the works. ,, Good morning, the Lord has fun at work. " ,, I have to hurry up the sun is up and everything is cooking because I have to be ready. I had the shyness for 8 months rented only to German then in Dutch.

They may have very well paid but everything can be ". ,, stop", says Gerd understands immediately. ,, Dutchman you said. " ,, Yes, two nice Dutch who had only occasionally and have supported their walking gear. Here and parked her car here. Only five elderly gentlemen were here, of which the Dutch have taken over. " ,, Please come out here, they're here long at work. " ,, I just started. But I do stop when I want it and think it necessary. " Sorry Mr. Sauer, not sour but I'm from the police. I am Chief Inspector Schöder. It keeps the host its brand back and the amazed not bad. Gerd tells him briefly about the two Dutchmen belonging to a criminal gang and are responsible for five murders. " ,, These cute men should have made here around Arenberg and Koblenz?, "The five murders yes, these nice men of the two are after on the way here. . Please come out, I will examine with Sally the small barn. ,, Come Sally, Sally already has disappeared in the barn. You can still see the traces of the car of the Dutch. They had no time to cover this. Sally Browsed through the hay and found a small package. 50 centimetre by 50 centimetre. Gerd is sure that's an image. Certainly a very valuable painting, Gerd wrapped it immediately into a large piece of paper.

From an old sugar sack one to damage any possible traces. It can browse everything Sally again. You will not find anything, little picture is the only thing that was hidden here. Gerd wonders why. The men have not taken this ?. ,, He calls to the Renate still holds the position in Montabaur. ,, Hello Gerd, everything OK with you ?. ,, Yes everything is OK, I also found what are looking for the two pitcher here. I brought it to safety. " ,, Shall we come and help ",, No remain where you are, I can do it here already. I only want the herein take off again and let the people here in peace. " ,,They're just left, have taken two bags that were abundant heavy. " ,, Certainly full of tools, because the two also do not know exactly what she expected here, I'll call immediately when the two show up here. " ,, Marianne, you go immediately with Sally on, the two gangsters come here. Which are already on the way over here.". ,, Now that it will be exciting send you me and Sally. Without Sally you still had that thing not found. We both stay here; maybe we can still be useful. " Gerd was unable to move the mill Sauer to leave the two. ,, Well then you're going with Mr. Sauer in the house and her closed everything. I stay there and hide myself opposite the small barn.

I have to see what happens. The men also seem not to know exactly what they are looking. " That only thinks Gerd, Gerry knows exactly what he is looking, he looks the picture that Gerd has already taken it. It should also be at least one million values. Gert van der Mohlen stole it from the container when they opened it in the port of Koblenz. Gert van der Mohlen then has given him this type in Flissen as they met in the containers. Since the trace of Gert missing. Of course he did Gerry also tells of his assumption since there still is an air shaft which is bricked up. It is noticed. Who supported on an air shaft. This realization came to him but only in Holland when he all his photos check. As he read the small sign dirty air shaft. With difficulty he could decipher this. He Gert but now had to focus on the 50 million. Gerry is to regulate the other that with the change. But first he wanted to once again into the container, but only after Gerry is gone. For here he wanted to get something on the side. He wanted to be sure he would collect enough of the pie. He then get what he deserves. A gruesome death has given him the Amber Room and d he desire for side income brings. His friend Gerry knows nothing of his death, by the cruel death of Gert.

Gerry would it only right was because he would never part not with Gert and not with Manfred . Not with the stupid Germans with Manfred, who can steal 5.000.000.-. The not being able to kill someone, nor does it requires Manfred. For this hour at the money that he lacks for the action. For the visa, for travel etc. ,, Manfred, we are again looking at the bay, I feel that it is still a mystery in this slot. " ,, There was something on the wall, something I could not see. " ,, You're right Gerry , if I think about it, there was a small closure ". ,, Do you look for what that is? ". ,, clear to me that is lighter than for you, I'm a bit smaller. " ,, That's sweet of you , I will you remember. " You can reach the bay and Manfred climbed into it bluntly, it is not friendship with the Belgians drives him into it. Because first who opens knows what's inside this possible secret compartment. " Manfred comes crawling back disappointed, see with horror Gerry with a gun and with muffler holding in her hand. On only with batting an eyelid shoots. Gerry and Manfred in the head, Manfred bagged so composed as his mate Gerhard he with the tool control head. Only Manfred is really dead and Gerry will rot in this pit. Gerry hate exactly in this small opening has been nothing.

Because he has this opened long ago. Gerry closes the lid carefully and filled it again as originally with sand and sod. There's no entrance to this bay. He makes his way to the Sauer mill. He knows exactly where to look and what to look. Gerd working on the Farm. Based casual on a fork on as the car is Belgian in the court rolls. Jumps Gerry soon out of the car. ,, Good day young man, they are the Boss here from the store. He asks "Gerd. ,, Sure, they still see someone else here " . Gerry suppressed annoying a brisker response. ,, I am a friend of the Dutch who rent their barn. The guys have n here forgot something tool. I was on business nearby and should pick it up. " ,, There is the barn, they are looking for from us, no one has entered the barn. Yet it is still officially rented. When will their friends come back. " While Gerry goes to the barn he answers only grumpy, as if his friend this service too much. ,, I do not know exactly when the two come back, have no idea. They only wanted, as I get the tool. Paid the barn is that, do they still have to get money from them? ". ,, No, no who have paid for the next two months. " ,, OK, then it's all right, I would have designed the lack of rent ". ,, Two months is enough of a lead for him because he wants to already large include coal.

In San Francisco. With no single thought Gerry thinks of just murdered Manfred. Such small minds and Tinker did not deserve to continue living there. In his trunk Gerry has everything that is important to him. Manfred's passport and other papers, but above all, all the money that exists is by Manfred. This money enables him to act now Gerry completely free." He searches the barn and is always angry and restless. He finds nothing; there is no small haystack he has not shifted three times already. There is no area and no bar more he has not been studied. He storms out of the barn and is very angry, crashes on the supposed host. ,, you, they have already stolen the things. " But my lord they calm down as they come to something, I was not in the barn have come to them. " Then they come, they look for you self, I have everything turned over several times here is absolutely nothing but hay. " Yes ,, what they are looking for at all, which should I look for? ". ,, We need search no more; they have here already found everything. Gerry suddenly has a gun in his hand. ,, Los you loudmouth, you've got the picture already found. But I never knew you but their small farmers coal overspending. Do not joke no;, I clutter your whole house in order.

Since no stone is left unturned. I'll find what you've stolen here. In order to give his words emphatically shoots Gerry sharply past Gerd. Marianne and actually host are frightened to m lucky he is now alone at home, so no one but them in danger. But that is enough j a well. Sally growling fiercely, the dog can feel it out there is something wrong. Sally feels, because Gerd at risk. This is not the first shot she heard in her life. She suspects her Friend Gerd out there is in trouble. She growls very danger but quietly to him. Marianne she must calm although she herself is afraid, afraid of losing their Gerd. But Gerd is an experienced police officer he acts cool and dry. He knows it is here very much. You can find out already, there is a dead plays no role here. But he wants to be one of those meaningless dead. ,, Los host, from the house, let's see if you remember the picture when I think of your old pistol under his nose. " This could happen in any case, the criminal would kill for the image without batting an eyelid. Gerd falls only now missing on the buddy from Montabaur. But of course he does not think of his death. Manfred is still in the bay be suspected Gerd, the image will Belgian safety alone get for them.

Gerd has no idea that the guy already murdered is and buried in the duct is located. Marianne has not noticed, there's has escaped Sally. S ally found its way through the basement to the outside. She sneaks cautiously to the barn. She feels that her boyfriend Gerd is in danger. Gerd observed the Belgians in all his movements; he is waiting for his chance to attack the man. Then it goes quickly when they leave the barn. Sally jumps to Gerry from the state, without having first given a sound. Gerd uses the surprise and lunges at Gerry. The balance loses and shoots into the air. He comes back to his feet and runs directly off must leave his gun. Gerd sees this not immediately because it has slipped under the hay. Gerry reached his car and Sally Missed him by only a few Centimetre, for attend examined Gerry the key. Sally Gerry would like to eat through the glass. Gerry gets the key control and drives off. He races out of the gate and driving at excessive speed by the so beautiful windmills. Gone are the hardly anyone believed at some winemakers and beautiful vineyards in this valley. In the house you are happy about the good outcome of this action. The landlord and Marianne come out and are obviously glad, because everything went so well.

,, Yes, Marianne our Sally was once again great. " ,, Yes, it's our Sally, but if you should take a couple of days it's my Sally ". ,, Gerd does not answer calls and Renate its Commissioner. To the already with Schmidtchen on the way to Koblenz. You are amazed about the history has to tell Gerd. ,, Then Sally up has once again prevented you a hole in your wash. Shall we have a F a h invention initiate after the Belgians and after the guy from Montabaur ". ,, No, we both have the touch, we know that they need to Brussels. We fit in there from, you are both expected at the border and are then shaded ". ,, OK, if you say so, but who have babbled something of the three containers here. They supposedly know something about this container. I hope that not only waste in the containers in San Francisco is. Then our project with the FBI and Interpol is in danger. " ,, After the experience today, we will not know this for now. But if both but then fly to the US this is a sign that it must be something else." ,, I just get the message from the highway patrol, the car of Gerry Schreinemakers is near Niederzissen been spotted on the Autostrada A61".,,, Do you see my dear Marianne, we and our police, we are on the ball. I am absolutely sure that.

We can no blind spots, followed into the American embassy him now. We can turn to the FBI and Interpol the mole at the US embassy then simultaneously". ,, OK, it's late enough. We want to go home now. Commissioner Schmidtchen has adopted as early as the closing time, he was already asleep next to me. " ,, As long as you drive he can sleep peacefully. I'll see you tomorrow; I still have to buy a tasty meal my Both Sally and Marianne ",, Oh you has again the Eifel goat with you ? ". ,, Then they can think of to-morrow even remove my little Monika. Who looks forward always to Sally. " ,, Ok, both of which are still with me in Ehrenbreitstein. I discuss this with Marianne and Sally. You then bring your little tomorrow to the office. Marianne and Sally they pick you up there. So then you two until tomorrow morning. " ,, Marianne, you stay still here in Ehrenbreitstein? ". ,, Do you want to get rid of me?". But ,, No Renate will get rid of their small, she has noticed that you're with Sally in Koblenz. Can you or do you Monika pick up tomorrow morning in the Bureau. " ,, Yes, of course, we are looking forward to the small, great weather tomorrow is again fashionable. Since we can drive together to Braubach.

I always wanted to return again in the Marksburg by Braubach.".,, Well, that's at least clear. " ,, The landlord is still very pale experienced by the. ,, Commissioner which would only have been if they had not been here. Never again I rent the barn to strangers, which is a lesson to me, but the men were so nice." ,, Yes, we wonder every day about how many nice men or women then suddenly criminals. But their range of beef cattle from your own I suppose. If they again battles they call me. I do so appreciate a powerful piece of beef " . ,, Mr. Commissioner, where the straight I say still have wonderful cattle bones frozen for our four-legged heroine " ,, Since Sally hearken, on the word bone reacts immediately. " Gerd's cell phone rings again, Renate's turn. Gerd, I forgot, what about the lost man from Montabaur ". ,, He will be on the mountains, and will not return to Montabaur. The now knows that we are or were on their trail. " The two others will meet again in Brussels. Sure Kuhlmann is already on the way from Arenberg and Montabaur with the ICE train on the way to Brussels. Which may be before his buddy from Belgium there." I just called, not you will be surprised on your hike from the guy. " ,, Thank you for the care.

Otherwise you can bring Monika tomorrow morning. Marianne wants up to Markburg . " ,, Prima is pleased Monika, but only if Sally is ". ,, You know without Sally goes to Marianne also nothing. " Ok ,, then a good walk back to Ehrenbreitstein ".All right, until tomorrow morning," ,, so you two, the delicious bone we have now we can go pull ". The landlord goodbye and less the draw, he looks the three who saved his life after a long time. He thinks about what he might have happened if the Commissioner had not been there. Secondly, he has won a new customer for its beef. The Commissioner, Marianne and Sally walking now through the narrow valley so beautiful, have a little bit time for the beautiful vineyards and the nice houses of winemakers at the front of the Mill Valley. "Here, Gerd, when we go up the path there stand the cattle of our landlord." ,, This is the walk from the Mills of Arenberg, it's funny at once all roads lead to Arenberg. Me is never so extreme noticed before. When they have behind a vineyard from which you have no idea when traveling only on the main roads the great vineyard. They enjoy the valley and quickly forget how dramatic it was an hour ago.

Gerd takes his girlfriend and Sally in the mouth of the mill valley. "It is beautiful here in my Koblenz and it is even more beautiful to have both of you". An hour later, they sit on the terrace behind his house. The sun lowers fire red behind the mountains of the Eifel. It is always a great sight of all ever recorded and enthusiastic. ,, I know such great visions only from Africa but here at the height of Ehrenbreitstein I have the most beautiful sunrises and the most beautiful sunsets in the world. " ,, The Gerd really was, you see where the sun sets over these mountains I live with Sally. " Sally is unimpressed by this sunset crack them around the Giant bovine bone with the greatest joy. Enjoy bones with the best view over Koblenz and the fortress Ehrenbreitstein. Also in the distance the elevations of the very nice hills of the Eifel. There Gerd can always see the hill chains at their foot the home from Marianne and Sally. From the terrace you can also look at the German Corner and on parts of the Mosel. Koblenz is already the dream city on the Rhine and Mosel. The most beautiful city in the world, on the cultural heritage of middle Rhin Vallay. To the east of Arenberg and Immendorf with an altitude of almost 340 meters.

Behind by Immendorf the Westerwald start immediately. Then you can already see the first Westerwald place Simmern which can be seen already well from Immendorf. Behind Koblenz, on the left side is the Hunsrück and Eifel mountains spreads out. Right s you can see from the terrace just in one corner of the well-preserved fortress Ehrenbreitstein. Left the castle Lahneck, the castle Marksburg and The beginning of the small hills Taunus. Of course on the other side of the Rhine, the brewery Königsbacher and Koblenz with the nearby castle Stolzenfels. They let the evening pass by. Gerd throws the barbecue and makes for herself and Marianne. A nice salad to the grilled meat, but most of all like a vile Gerd good bratwurst prefer much better than a steak. The next day is a big meeting at the Bureau. Marianne and Sally bring then Gerd to the Presidium and take there the radiant joy Monika in her car with them. Marianne is accustomed, as Monika until Sally greeted before her turns. Monika's mother Renate looks at her daughter, she is not good at talking to the Eifel goat as she always calls it. Then this woman makes it impossible for her to Gerd approach. She does not know what Gerd has eaten at this laying goat.

But she also recognizes how much the Eifel goat cares for her daughter. She is called to the meeting and has to leave the window. M to speak in the Bureau about how do you want to bring the whole thing to the end. From Brussels has been informed that Gerry is at the US embassy. But Manfred has not been seen and heard. But you know that he got his visa through the US Embassy. In Brussels, Both will get their visa, but they can go not a single spot in the US without being monitored. This calms the Koblenz CID much they want to see the killers behind bars. It gives them the opportunity to act together with Inter Pool in the United States from Koblenz. You will be at the forefront. That this is possible will be a rejection of the actions of the NSA. This wild action is unfortunately noticeable. One does not understand the anger. Even Gerd never understood. What has been spilled out has grown in a time of blocks. Everyone wants to know what the other is doing. Know as much as possible from his neighbours, even if they are friends. This is not the same in the family, there are always people who try to learn everything. When it comes out it also bangs in the families. But it is just so, everyone uses his possibilities to learn everything.

But now they are benefiting from this action for the first time as a detective.

The prosecutor who has bundled these investigations stands up. "I am going to have a look at what happened, please, please, please, Mr. Chief Commissioner, if I leave something out. You are more deeply involved in the matter. " Gerd immediately speaks. ,, Mr. Prosecutor Mr President, I would like to anticipate even know what is actually in these containers for its contents there have been so many deaths. " "Everybody clapping, everyone wants to know that". The police president who is also present is standing up. "Yes, people, that's something I'd like to know. The BKA has taken as they know all investigations, but leaves us because of the previous work free hand. The BKA has spent in consultation with Bonn the valuable container in a secure location. The containers are then emptied first in Berlin and the individual pieces are checked by experts. We have no information about it. We are puzzling just like them, but in the rumour it is about the amber room. When it comes to, then I understand how to fight for it. But even I do not know where the containers are located.

I thank them the Soko Koblenz, which they have so managed Spectacular then the Container from Flissen and bring back from San Francisco. The ladies and gentlemen, was a feat of which we are all proud. A tour de force for Germany, but just as it is pleasant to see how the police in Europe and with the United States functions are grown in this matter. It will have a role model for the future. 7 dead, there have been, including a completely innocent nun. But according to our findings, this was simply too curious, even the head nurse soon caught it. But now peace has been restored in the monastery. This action has even led to the visit of the Dominican monastery from the USA. But we have stepped up the cameras in the monastery something is until this case is closed. The whole thing in the US will go on when our two men are in the US. The FBI thanked you for the telephone number you sent over. You have this number on the screen. As soon as the mobile phone is switched on, they are included. If the two men are still in USA. Gerry Schreinemakers and Kuhlmann from Montabaur. Fly over again and back with Interpol and the FBI. More can`t at the moment say only that we may have a trace of the old man, Gerhard Maifelder.

In more but when you're back, I think we have done here what we could. Power continues as before. I have all led the visas you are already in the Bureau. I hr are allowed also take your guns and use. When and how will the people of the FBI explain you. " What will happen there, I have no idea. I wish you a good flight and success in the USA. Catch me from the artistic peasant; I do not care where he. Is in the prison here or in the USA ". Two days later, they learned that Kuhlmann has entered in Dallas on American soil. Gerry Schreinemakers is nowhere booked and nowhere landed. He still has to be in Holland. Inter pool is a connected and seeks Gerry Schreinemakers in Holland and Belgium. It remains for the time being missing and is not found despite intensive search. Gerd and his crew end up in San Francisco and immediately contact Ronny by the FBI in connection. You stay a few days in the hotel and enjoy the environment of the most beautiful city in the world, says Renate. "Most beautiful city in the world, my love can only be Koblenz?". "No Gerd this city is the only one that Koblenz can reach. is certainly a bit better. Yesterday the Indian forest, these are trees we have never seen in the Westerwald or the Eifel.

Mammoth trees which have a circumference of 20 meters and more. Forests whose stems protrude into the sky. Everywhere the sea to the middle of the city extends. The sea even divides the city. The huge bridge that is so old and so beautiful. The steep and narrow streets and out there Alcatraz. Unfortunately, only museum," we has. ,, Renate, water enough in Koblenz and we see a sequoia oar ". ,, The Gerd you do not believe myself. " ,, But we have a large sequoia in Arenberg in the sacred garden when you push on its bark. If you how soft it is. Of course, the mammoth has no circumference of 20 meters. But a considerable 3 meters are also that ". ,, Los comes, it will be our last day we have time in the port something is happening. Get off on my boat in the heat it will be beautiful on the sea. We go out to the deep sea fishing, from morning we are then in full use for the containers. The network is designed; we just have to knuckle down and want to see wriggle the buyer is. " A little later, they are all on the high seas and fishing like the world champions but not such tiny ones as from the Rhine and Moselle. There are real fish and Renate has the most luck. Ronny has helped along there; they got the best bait and bring a giant fish.

After another out of the water. While the others were just flouting. "Conclude now, Renate has completely thrown us out with fish, I can no longer accommodate". Tonight enjoys her again the old city of San Francisco from tomorrow begins another life. " ,, What do you do with all the Fish Ronny , "The lives of all the injured I throw all back into the water". "Well, I thought we had to eat five days of fish now." ,, Ronny laughs, no, that does not need it, tomorrow morning I'll get even into your hotel right after breakfast at exactly 9:00 I stand at your hotel. Now you have to do I have me even to the rest of fish and take care of the boat taxi back to the hotel. So get off the boat into the shower and dive into the nightlife of San Francisco, you see me until Morning early again."

Chapter 4 Back in US

Of course, already waiting for a taxi at the contact point on SOKO from Germany. In such matters can rely absolutely on Ronny. The next morning the Germans are picked up on time. There is a meeting at the FBI headquarters. Since all German commissioners speak English this is easy. They are led to a screen, here ladies and gentlemen, they see the three important containers.

With such valuable content. One had compiled the three containers so that these are so easy to monitor by three cameras. We have only one local police station. A guard is always ready in the vicinity with always three people. We ourselves are from here in 10 minutes. Let us stay here or go on the spot asks Gerd. He does not trust the cameras can be easily manipulated. You only need a short message from the control centre and all cameras show an old picture in a few minutes. Gerd is sure that this station is not always occupied. He says nothing because he does not want to deal with the FBI. There is something so does on the screen one time close up image. Since a forklift truck is approached although there are container bridges. They become attentive and look to what is to happen there. Gerd does not look bad when he is looking at the forklift truck up close and is lifting a container. Gerd has long since discovered, as this truck is too weak on the chest. He does not make it and drives away again. That was all that happened that day. Either the forklift driver was wrong in the container or he has no idea how hard such a loaded container is. Gerd shakes his head. ,, The container weighs at least 20 tons NEN.

Coming as one with an 8 to NEN stacker. The forklift driver must have one at the clapper he has ever tried it. But why do they want to load the containers with the forklift? "They will not want to be loaded with forklifts". ,, Or have said Gerd because they want Saturday loaded on a Ship, will act exactly as in Koblenz. The day or at night n on Saturday or Sunday when a bridge crane runs falls on that. But a forklift is independent ",, That would mean that we have to wait until Saturday or Sunday. Now they must probably provide for a suitably large forklift ". They also determined 20 tones here at the port, which should not be a problem. " So wait again, probably another four days until Sunday? ". "It looks quite like my dear Gerd our nerves are being examined". Again a 4-day break, Gerd is quite sure that you can only get the containers. With forklifts without attracting attention immediately. OK we go back to the office and take a break. Gerd immediately gives the delay to his president. He gets permission to stay. For four days back and forth that would be nonsense. The FBI also has no choice but to accept this delay. Meanwhile, the phone also has Arkinson moves. But too short to get it to places. One is sure.

That this participants knows what is going on. He only briefly contacted Gerry Schreinemakers and given his News No. Of course, he also knows the FBI is looking frantically for him. A few days later, on next Saturday can be said the two Kuhlmann and Schreinemakers the US have left behind. They have flown to Italy, incomprehensibly, to Rome. This is the FBI only out when everything is over here in San Francisco. While they are waiting here are the two in Europe. They have nothing to do with the removal of the containers here in Francisco. They seem to have a new job somewhere in Europe. Probably in Italy. On Sunday it is really going on in the port of San Francisco. Already all on his place, they are sure to get going today. In fact, a huge forklift truck arrives with 3 low-loaders in tow. "that fits says Gerd, these are the right devices". It does not take an hour since everything is lured and loaded. The trip goes down, they expect all so that it goes back to the villa after Bea r Vallay because bends of the first low-loader to the south. The second loader according No gestures and the third loader leads in the direction of the Golden Gate Bridge. Ronny is totally confused, so they were not expecting. He immediately splits the other cars over radio.

Now every truck has only one tracker. He immediately provides support at his headquarters. These are also very confused are seemingly overwhelmed by these events. There is a lack of vehicles, on neutral vehicles. Ronny maintains contact with all vehicles alone now follow the individual truck. Ronny remained only the last of the low-loader of the route across the Golden Gate Bridge has chosen. One of the pursuing FBI vehicles announces, a truck has taken the right of way. He has lost the contact to the low-loader right now. Ronny beats furiously on his steering wheel, he can`t believe this info. Their secret action has been recognized, and they are all shaken off. "Watch out for the road traffic, you try to separate us from the trucks, s". Is a Helicopter went up and searches for the first L KW. They were so sure there's has waived this time at a station at the Container An unimaginable failure, so Gerd assesses this action. That would not have happened to him in Germany ". They pass the Golden Gate Bridge and are all so confused that they can, t even look at it properly. They are all shaken. But they still remain at your low loader. But the colleague on the other low-loader also reported traffic lights.

Someone with a huge jeep wants to push him off the road. Meanwhile, a second helicopter on the way to this colleague to support him. But for the time being, this low loader is also lost. They drive off the bridge as there is a huge bang. Your vehicle is raised, turns in the air, and overlaps. With much effort they can free themselves from the vehicle, all of which are only slightly injured but fully finished. This is something that everyone has not yet experienced. Since someone has learned a lot or has been warned. Gerd remembers. The words of Gerry Schreinemaker had said to his mate in Arkinson. He knows something about these three containers. Gerry knew about the security of the container over his dead Freund Gert van der Mohlen. Meanwhile, three helicopters are looking for the truck, at least 100 cars are looking for the trucks. She must have disappeared somewhere in big halls. On the streets is not one of the three low-loader to see. "We are combing all the halls and large garages that come into question. These heavy vehicles could not have come so far. But, unfortunately, are all in a different direction thereof and the space for the search is so insanely large over the city distributed ". "Gerd sits with his people in the office of the FBI.

The ambulance examines them and connects the smaller wounds they have. "Gerd, sorry this is once again a huge blame, no idea how that happened. There must be a leak in us. Unfortunately, ours, some of our people are also corruptible. Such a shit I might burst ". Gerd sends a mail from the FBI office to Koblenz and informs the police president of the bankruptcy here. We will respond immediately. I think the truck could not so easily disappear. " I see a danger not but in which one makes the container and looks into it.

Then the whole deception manoeuvre has burst ". We stay two more days, when nothing has happened, we come back to our whole success. " ,, OK i'm agreeing the police respond President, two days are good. But we are not successful, you saved us the containers. The murderers of the nun and the four old ones are also fixed. There you can again see what makes money from people. From those who have too little and also those who have too much. " ,, Is not this day our daily bread, all depends in the end the money together. " "What about the two men with the Belgian and the man from Montabaur?" "So far only the man from Montabaur has arrived". One is on the track of this but has hopefully under control ".

OK Mr. Chief Commissioner makes the best of it and good flight. I think our job in the US is over. Two days, we book the flight for you and send the data by e. mail". "Ok, Mr. President, then I expects the tickets. This is so depressing her; the men of Interpol fly home at night already. " The monitoring of Frank Bruno has also revealed nothing. He did not move a meter out of his house. He certainly laughed. Wonderful he once again led the FBI around the nose. Calmly, he allows himself a whiskey and grinning in the mirror were at his bar. But the Amber Room he has not, e r has yet to get all hopes so. So fast does not put him an FBI. His agent, Chris, has become a full idiot. The Koblenz fly back to Germany, we have not found the truck. But the containers are opened for sure. Thus, everything is clear and the buyer fully informed. It is the trick went off Gerd trick backwards? , No, not for the Soko Koblenz. Gerd has a stomach problem something is wrong with this matter. What about the two men, he asks Ronny to whether there are now results there. ,, Yes Gerd, both a week ago left the country from the United States. " ,, They are both left the country. " As both, we have the departure of Gerry Schreinemaker and Manfred Kuhlmann ".

,, How so, if only Gerry Schreinemakers has entered Ronny. How can they both have gone? ". We are already working on it and check all entry possibilities to the USA. Somehow, Kuhlmann must have come to the USA. " Well Ronny, I wait until morning when the whole thing is a little over or lazy". "I know Gerd, but I do not know what. If I got something out then I'll report immediately ". Gerd is thinking about the whole situation and wants to know where the containers are. After all many requests it turns out, as these containers are still in Koblenz. The all, the two are in a military restricted area until they are recalled by the Federal Office. They believe here at the moment the safest. " Ok ,, I think so, but from tomorrow double insurance. I have a suspicion bad suspicion. On the other morning everyone in the presidium thinks Gerd has a titmouse. He sends the trace back to Arenberg. He sends them into the shaft and back into the air shaft. His suspicion is confirmed in the air shaft, the body of Manfred Kuhlmann. He's been lying in it for a long time. I t is now clear Gerd that someone is traveling with the passport of Kuhlmann or Gerry Schreinemakers from the US. Someone did not hold tight.

It is only possible that internal information has been used. Guarding the container is substantially increased. Not only with video Camera but with more local police in the barracks in the old barracks in Arenberg / Urbar in is partly the police school. Gerry and the substitute, presumably from Arkinson have arrived with Kuhlmann pass a week ago in Italy. You will have travelled by train to Germany and may have been here for a long time. Back to Arenberg at the starting point of the action. As one says so beautiful everything is back home in the realm. Gerd can, t understand why nobody has taken the container under the microscope. Here the problems are safe again delayed the responsible ness everything. The Department of Art has banned any tach and the police are the transport only free if the action in the US has ended. This is what she is, Gerd wants to be vigilant, and has asked for a free hand from his police president. He got it, but his influence is very small. In Koblenz, some people have been working on these containers, which have already caused so much confusion. The plan is firmly established and the men of the security team are believed to be fooled. Just as they have already been fooled.

They have got the money for they have technicians and the technical possibilities for many things. You have a plan that makes this possible. You have already prepared this plan. They too have gained informants against good, very good money. Because money plays no role for the men. Gerry and Henk men from Belgium and Arizona a descended this time in Bad Salty, course again under a false name. Who come back from Holland and Denmark their partners are also considered tourists in Koblenz hotels housed with their real papers here. These men are completely unknown here and. Also not noticed by the police. The plan is difficult but grand, they are all sure they will get the containers from the barracks. Many police or soldiers or not, they will get the million 50 zig from. You have received the money. They have already set a lot in motion and have invested a lot in this campaign without anyone having noticed anything in Koblenz. The police are also of the opinion that nothing will happen here. The corpse of the man from Montabaur in the air shaft in the valley of the mills valley has left a few days to go. But now everything sinks back into oblivion and the gangsters can go on in peace. But they also do this inconspicuously.

Gerd the constantly follows only gets the answer everything OK. It's nothing. They want to transport the containers to Berlin next week ". Hopefully ,, says Gerd, I'm glad when things finally are gone at the Federal Chancellery in Berlin. " Gerry is very active, he sits every day at the company and nail he wants to organize a transport to Africa. 3 pieces 20 feet container with car parts and old cars. These should not run over Holland but necessarily about Hamburg. The Manager of Kühne and Nagel work to find in Hamburg a ship owner for West Africa line. Gerry organise one 400 tons crane. The needs to raise at least 30 to at a range of 50 meters. ,, Because I would rather suggest them a 500 to crane at the reach they need reserves. How is the underground? ". "Yes this is a problem, this is simple field, now just mown and also once worked with a milling cutter". "Can I look at the ground not that our crane later sacks or falls". Yes ,, this is good we will interpret the highway into the field with concrete slabs. The is starting tomorrow possible, where we set up a site. We plan as state Concrete plat to move "for the crane for the access road and the stand by. ,, That's Ok, where is it.? This is at the border of Arenberg when they rise from Urbar directly opposite.

The barracks ". I know, I'll be there tomorrow morning at 11.00, are they ready? " "Yes, is OK". "Gerry is now the company Kann Beton in Bendorf where concrete slabs are loaded and support walls. Gerry counts the plates and supporting walls. There are some used walls like an L formed walls which are simply placed on the ground and the wall stands. Just like the Berlin Wall or the huge barrier walls of Israel. 4 full low loaders are transported to the construction site to Arenberg / Urbar. Wheel loaders and a small crane await delivery. A company is already to erect a large information sign. You can already read. A construction site is being built here for three months. As a reason for this construction site a water and soil investigation. Is given, by the Land Rheinland Pfalz. On the construction site, everything is running smoothly the organized construction company from Arenberg is diligent and moves well. From the opposite, the police officers of the police are watching. You have only wondered but now where the information plate is everything is clear to them. Soon this wheel source will have disappeared again. A small crane, installed in the record time, place the floor panels that form from the entrance to the field.

Forth the heavy-duty line for the crane and other heavy equipment. In the evening this road is already passable and the next morning they begin to put the walls. Just like the Berlin Wall has looked out. More than thirty meters can now be seen in the construction site. 2 peace,s. 20 feet containers with the label "Rheinland Pfalz Wasserschutz" (Water guard) complete the picture of the construction site. It is now Friday 11.00 clock and the crane company comes to the building road to take off. "Well, that's great, our crane can work safely. He takes his phone and marches the giant crane. In three hours. The crane will be here. " "Where does it go the invoice.?" To the Land Rheinland Pfalz or to the City of Koblenz.". ,, No, we are making them the bill ready to land a special construction department, we need the crane only until Tuesday. Have mainly on Sundays and on Monday something to load. Then again to dismantle the facility in some weeks. We pay for the use in advance ". "This is something again some new advance payment from the country we had never. Otherwise, we always wait for many months with 100 reminders." "As we said we have a special status and we then generally reckon with the country.

With a slightly higher margin just because of the advance bank ". "If it is for them is the OK. A few minutes later the invoice is e. mail there. ,, 2 5.000 € lays Gerry on the table and is the lucky crane Manager quickly release. The construction company is deducted attending the machines again. You will also be required again only to break down in a few weeks. Gerry also paid a flat rate and paid in advance. What Can the second crane in the harbour at Bendorf at the company, we need there to lift the large parts of the ship. The parts we need here for the construction site ". ,, This has also just paid and this crane is now built at the harbour. At the company Kann concrete factory ". "Great, I drive down; the ship has to come every moment. We also need the crane driver on Sunday and Monday. The construction manager of the construction company appears. ,, It's all we could move away for the time being or is there to do something. " "It would be good if two men and a wheel loader remain here until the crane is set up. Maybe we still need support ". "Well I leave two men here with the wheel loader what do they think of how late it can be for the men. Just because it is weekend and we are working Friday normal only until noon. "

,, At the latest at 18.00 everything will be done sooner rather ". ,, OK then the men will like to stay. "Exactly 3 hours later, the crane rolls on, in less than 1 hour it is constructed for operation. The driver makes a small test run. Gerry asks him nor extend the arm only halfway. This has security reasons because of the police helicopter. We need to the can approve more than 25 meters high. " Gerry had to cheat no one can see the actual range of the crane, ,, no problem, how about on Sunday day off. " Sunday we have free from, 7:00 to 9:00. " ,, This is getting a nice job, working 2 hours because this is worth it does not come. " ,, Unfortunately my good is no different. " Gerry pulls 2 x 500 € from his pocket and gives it to the crane operator, ,, for you and your husband tension, so that you get the timely do not forget. For us, this time frame is very important. " ,, All right, "for this coal, we are already at 6.00 am there." Well then all the best until Sunday morning at 6:00 am. " Here's all for the three men completed their construction they have under control. ,, I must say that I never thought that I will site manager of such construction site once, the construction site is very glad ". The giant crane takes up the half effect a concrete wall.

From the street or the windows of the barracks, he now looks out like a recovery tank. He is not as enormous as this really is. Gerd Schöder has this Friday is also used to after Arenberg / Urbar to drive. He had to laboriously check with its top line the first. They did not understand what he wants barracks near the containers in the police. ,, I want only one thing, gentlemen, I have seen puke front of the pharmacy have horses. I have, since s experienced s Dill Emmer with the FBI in the United States. I would not go so here. I have a hell of a bad feeling, to be honest, I have a stomach ache. " ,, Schöder now they do not overdo it, where should the containers be safer than in our own barracks. We have this with a steel frame surrounded and the container to the point foundations attached. No truck can move these things. On Wednesday we are the containers going anyway. The pioneers of the Bundeswehr (German Army) will bring the boxes to Berlin. "I wish these things would already be in Berlin when the inside is actually what we suspect it's a billion-dollar value, or even more. " ,, Have the picture what I found in the barn, they have already passed on this? ". ,, Schöder, they think I hang me such a crap in my office or at my house on.

The image is a real Picasso and is estimated at 1.7 million. The picture has picked up right. " Then they go for God's sake Urbar, or is that already Arenberg? ". ,, I do not know the limit Urbar Arenberg runs very strange. Once you are in Arenberg after a few meters again in Urbar ". ,, Come Schmidtchen we drive off and look at the thing on. Up in the barracks everything goes without problems you are facing the two containers; ,, they are actually packed as if here Fort Knox. The containers are six-point foundations. They have a rotating steel frame which is each again bolted to the foundations. Gerd that is absolutely certain, the container rises no away and gets no unauthorized to be closed. Most with the welding torch. ",, You're right, our concerns are unwarranted, the cracks nobody and nobody gets here from the premises. We go home and we get a nice weekend. " While out driving he sees the new construction by the Office for Water Protection. ,, Yes the boys are looking now ubiquitous for new water and b ears and drill. Schmidtchen, chauffeur you to the huge rig that looks from here like a crouching leopard tank out. The Saturday runs extremely quiet for all, Gerd moves to the Vordereifel.

His Eifel goat and Sally. He enjoy some t there with her the walk through the quarries and climbing walls. While it straight back to hike leave a call reached him on his cell phone. He will be called immediately to Koblenz. There the hell is going on since 6:00. In Koblenz, it looks as if AL Kheida or IS of the city are attacke. ,, Everywhere Cops it anywhere is fire, in Ehrenbreitstein. ,, What a bummer, Marianne, we must immediately cancel I need to Koblenz, where the devil is going on. Bombs and fire stops in several places simultaneously. Until Gerd is in Koblenz, is it all back over. He gets a huge shock, that's all over but can only mean one thing, our containers are gone. " ,, You're crazy Gerd "says Renate standing right next to him. ,, This is "excluded. ,, Nothing is excluded, let's immediately call in the barracks, I drive already high. Renate come on, plug one your weapon and read you give guns out of the chamber. " ,, blind, without knowing what's going solves Gerd Schöder a red alert au s , it leaves low loader. Search on the go on the holy Sunday. He has experienced as the containers were stolen from the port " . He is considered crazy, but when the top of Urbar in the barracks no one answers seems to be something in the matter.

All available police car racing to the police barracks. Gerd immediately sees when he is in the court that enters the container disappeared. But nothing is damaged even still closed the door. The containers have been simply lifted from the earth and disappeared along with their foundations. Because of course the steel frame has been of no use. " The men stormed into the office, sitting there, the three officials bound and gagged at their tables, ,, you are still dazed and barely able to answer, they were almost suffocating. You gasp for air. The ambulance and doctors are on their way. Gerd ,, can be by Renate describe what was going on in Koblenz. But he could also have guessed they were all alarms the ineffective are a lot of smoke. Much wheel track from low bed saddle. They wanted to prevent the police for some time. For the time you the containers from the site needed to lift. The camera of the police court could n pursue it this incredible bold That . The giant crane has a gripper packed containers in the steel frame should they protect. The powerful crane has container within 20 minutes as toys from the area hands raised. According to records of the camera time was at 6.45. Gerd shocked at his watch.

Now it's already 8:30. Since the low-loader have been around for at least 15/07 on the. Go this way which may be now maybe in Frankfurt Bonn and Cologne or more down in south or North of Germany. Gerd claps her hands over her face; he no longer needs to enter the construction site of the water office. He knows that behind this wall of protection a Giant crane must stand. He can imagine how this crane the container like toys; he has lifted from the ground, with the foundations. . What a disgrace, the Amber Room in the hands and now it is once again disappeared. But he is sure that they still catch it. No mouse comes more through the border. No more low-loader on the highway until Monday evening. Gerd is sure they will catch the container. The officers of the guard are questioning Capable again. They tell of many explosions in the city and explosions nearby. All colleagues are going on and raced with the all aviable squad cars. Then come two men stormed in and kept us their weapons in front of the face. We really thought the IS or Al Kheida are there. Meanwhile, in Bendorfer Rhine port at the company can again quiet again. The two containers were loaded within a few minutes in the big ship.

With closed hatches it is already back in the middle of the Rhine as if nothing had happened. The large crane is already dismantled and Transport Ready for Monday. I m a corner not visible parked. The loader is possible at a nearby hall and the tractors in the next hall. The halls and the vehicles and the crane are hired for the next 10 days and already paid in advance. No one looks for any missed her. This was a military precision action taken to those who have done it a fortune will bring. No matter how long it will be in the US until the container. The man of money is now time, lots of time. In the ship a team is completely the containers to be working n. V freed on the foundations and the steel frame and provides it with new cargo documents. Will anybody notice that this ship has with the three containers from Holland. Here comes from the direction of Koblenz created on Monday morning. In a few minutes, these containers are stacked in the containers that go to Hong Kong. In three days the next ship comes to Rotterdam. And the containers are transferred to Hong Kong. In Germany now runs a massive manhunt by Gerry Schreinemaker , the Ami from Arkinson and the two Dutch helpers. All participating German companies.

Are long Ratio pulled ore and really tortured; the police are sour, really angry. But now the world knows the Amber Room is back. Only nobody knows where it is, it has not changed in the 70 years of searching, everything is back to normal. Very few people are privy. Now the hunt begins for these men, only that can explain and clarify where the containers are. The four men, two new Hollander Gerry and Henk American Guy enjoy life in the Hotel in Bad Salzig. For now, they absolutely avoid publicity. They have long since new passports and other names. They have been previously well supplied with money. Wait a few days and disappear individually by train to Switzerland. There they get from a small portion of their promised great wealth. The major remaining a famous they get only when the Amber Room at the buyer's where always. Will be his place. But the United States is large and also not excluded. The Amber Room is surfaced and disappeared from the scene. No one knows to this day whether secured in these containers is ever the Amber Room. Nevertheless Arenberg gained fame as a deposit them as important and valuable room in the world. The old mine is destination for many people.

The FBI observed for years to the merchant and billionaire Frank Bruno. But who has set up many opportunities in the world about this room, it need not be in the US. In Koblenz, the head of the Homicide goes within. He can no longer hear the name Amber Room. Gerd, go long, he knows he could have prevented it. He has it suspected but actually he can`t believe it. They were all experts, the containers so sure no one can steal. They are gone, probably forever. All actions were in vain. Only one, the old Gerhard has wind get about the matter, despite its distance in Cairo of course he noticed what happened there in Koblenz / Arenberg . Gerhard has buried even some reserves in Arenberg. He thought long whether he should contact again in Koblenz with Gerd. He is great and so easy submerged in Cairo. Here he controlled everything. His little old factory running again, the auxiliary organization. For the poor and destitute children is again twice as large built up as before. His friends and girlfriends are all back to work and bread. In Addis Ababa and South Africa, he has all his little company brought back to life again. With 4 million that was not a big problem. Now he wanted to collect his things back to Germany and there.

Above all, he wants d as Amber Room reloaded for Germany. His friends shall not have died in vain. The killers are now indeed convicted in the US with A lifelong imprisonment. Life imprisonment is also life sentence in the US. The men will never come out again. But Gerhard he is already 78 years old, his life stay on earth also coming to an end in next time?. He but is still full of energy and bursting with health and vigour. His head is still in order and is working at full speed. But the only way he can keep everything at bay. It can be no room, no time to rest. Rest is also to be sluggish for him. Be lazy is deadly for the mind and body. Gerhard still trained bay it. Head training, physical T raining it would have served a 50-year credit. He has now really all he had wanted in his life done. Children, grandchildren, ex wife, girlfriend. Forty years after the closure of the shaft have brought him in Africa and Arabia as much. He confers with all his friends and business partners and employees in Africa and Arabia. You do it all now without him. He will always go back and check. This control is necessary for some time. He, Gerhard is the only of the buyer knows personally. Gerhard was personally by the purchaser in Sacramento.

If someone then takes the container this is to be his last major action in his last part of life. These containers have brought him out of Berlin way and have cost his friends late life. The need to return to Germany, Gerhard sits down at his computer and writes from Cairo an e.mail to the Hauptkommissar Gerd Schöder. They are almost became friends in time in Koblenz. Gerd Schöder to this mail go, his cell phone reached amazed not bad when he sees the mail from Cairo. It skins him almost from the stool, he can`t not believe the old Gerhard still lives there. There is only am I in a few days in your office in Koblenz. We get the container back and we get the criminals and the chief criminals". ,,What's Gerd "asks his Commissioner, ,, you do so as a radiant face." ,, I have a great e-mail received from a friend in Africa I thought was long dead. " Gerd leans into his seat next to Renate back. This can be a new beginning; with Gerhard they have once a thread in his hand. This he does not want to relinquish. He trusts the old, young and believes in it, there is this embarrassment could be re-created from the world with the containers s. A few days later are Gerhard office by Gerd in Koblenz. They greet each other like old friends and take in the arm.

They have great sympathy for each other. ,, Mr. Inspector, I'm back, I think we have the same goal. " ,, Let the with the police chief, we are from now when you. Though you'd have this so I do not really offer, because you're older by a lot. But fortunately no less fit than me ". Ok ,, Gerd that I like very well, from the Mordverdächtigem (murder grounds of suspicion) also round not bad?. ". I missed everything about the newspapers and news in Cairo. Now completely new people are in the game. The Miser sack the billionaire has sold us and my friends on my conscience. For this he must pay even if the actual killers are convicted. But the guy has betrayed us and the killer has rushed on us. I swear Gerd we will grab him. " ,, We have to grab him who has disgraced us all the FBI, Interpol and our department together, ". ,, I did not understand how it was possible that these devils could steal the containers from the police barracks ". ,, Very clever Gerhard. The guys have faked a construction site really have almost hiding a giant crane and lifted the containers together with their foundations from the barracks in a few minutes on Sunday. Previously they have in Koblenz a giant organized spell so than the IS or Al would Kheida occurred in Koblenz.

Then they tied up the few remaining officers and gagged. Since the containers are gone. There is no longer any trace of them. We can only assume; , since s they are on a ship already in Holland. It will let the dust settle on the thing and then the things sealed and resealed with new papers on Send. " ,, But this way you know yes Gerhard, you've done it like ". ,, Since runs incidentally a case against you, I have already talked to the prosecutor. It will stop this process, if we can get with your help the container ".

We're ready to go; I have arranged everything in Africa and Arabia and brought here in Hachenburg everything in recent days in order. My papers and the residence is OK again. " ,, You were already a plan Gerhard what you intend to do?., the first thing we need money, we need to be independent of your authority. You have to leave you take, do you have holiday Gerd?." ,, Sure, I almost another 8 weeks of vacation. To take a piece from this when I talk to the supervisor authority, where I need to sign anyway my active involvement. Otherwise, I might get big problems. " ,, Then do it my dear, because we have to start in the US. We have to pick up the thread again with the buyer.

Let heaven's name the FBI and Interpol time being out of the game. We do not need it before we pull the strings firmly in the hands ". ,, Even with the Finance Gerd I accept completely. Also, your authority may not know what we do; at the end you must inform your supervisor. For no police force is quite clean. Anything for money is also there possible. Unfortunately, we're all human and everyone needs money. " ,, Where did the money come from Gerhard? ". ,, From Cairo, from my local company , they supported us from there. But I have only once cash enough for our action. " ,, Gerhard I need two days to discuss everything with my superiors. They will not want to know what I'll do, then you can go on the cart them later none. The bear had enough spot than you stole them the container from the police barracks has ". ,, I believe you my dear Gerd, here is my passport copy, even the latest with fingerprints. But you can get faster visa for both of us.

Also the same that we may need to make the visas for two of your people for a few days, for safety reasons". ,, I have a good friend at the FB;, we will not turn on with? ".,, No Gerd, only later when we know where to go " .

Three days later, the two holidaymakers in Sacramento sit on the edge of the small town in a beautiful but small hotel. Enjoy the first night after the long flight in a sports bar. ,, That's the only thing I love in the US, these sports bars in every corner of the pub another sport on the screen. You can choose yourself what you want to look. Only in these pubs, there are sometimes to eat a snacks and always a good beer. Tomorrow we take a car and Tune once as if we were to look at the area. "
,, Have you taken all the stuff we need "for listening etc.. ,, Clear, Gerhard, but my assessment of the purchaser is up to every trick. Since we do not come with plain into play, because you're right, which has a luxury house, because you can only be amazed." ,, Even milliardair in America, which is still something special today. " The two are in bed early, and the next morning, the first at the hotel breakfast table. Gerd turns the stomach when he sees what his table mates to cram in itself. A layer of bread, a green salad, a layer of egg, a layer of bread, cheese. Jam out to another location bread salad and ham. At dinner the men and women get a problem to closed her Mouse. Then the whole portion is brought with two hands in the form and pressed together.

Left and right of ketchup and mayo are running out and drips on the chin. Gerd must turn away so it is not bad his eyes. But he is tired Nevertheless the operator knows the breakfast habits of their German guests and served sausage cheese butter and eggs. Meanwhile, the car rental company has also brought the vehicle. ,, How long do they want to rent the car? ". ,, We remain about 6 days here in Sacramento but if it is possible we would like a different car every day. " No problem, ,, gentlemen, but replace the course will cost something every day. " ,, That's OK, we will pay that. " ,, Have a down payment? ". We have, we pay in to art, and for the rest they take the credit card. " ,, That's OK, please 200.- US dollars and give me the card. " He inserts the card into their device checked and says OK, then by tomorrow morning. " ,, Why every day another car Gerhard ". ,, Commissioner, I wonder why, because we circle every day through the same area, we do not want to attract attention. " ,, OK, that illuminates me, let's go. " Drive about five mails out of the city.

On a hill stands a huge villa. ,, The Gerd, Villa Franko Bruno, he has a few. But all other names, I know, I was already in a near San Francisco right on the beach.

But this villa is up some here to Enlarge. Especially looks of who's coming up there as early as Monday on Friday to visit. At the villa we never come trickling down, no chance Gerhard. As far and as many walls as there is no listening device works here. " They circle round the estate at some distance. Come nowhere a way unseen approach to the villa. ,, I was for three days in one piece at the villa when you need there, do you live no longer get out. This villa has everything you need to live. ",, We will orbit in a distance and watch everything with the telescope, we have to get in there, anyway. " They see no way that day. They speak in the evening through all the possibilities. Cable eavesdropper erection, but al l this requires a technical tour de force and which can be seen from the villa. They will not investigate long. In the evening they get a phone call for help. Two gardeners sit at the bar and talk loudly about their work. You soon notice, since s it comes to work at the Villa at Villa Franco Bruno. Both complain because of the many work to them by manager and how little money. They get for it from the comparison. Again and again, everything in life for money, here too, the two Germans also seems back the money to help.

Gerd addresses the two. ,, We both come from Germany, like we would look at the gardens at Villa but we do not get approval. What's guys, if you take me as your mate, not a bad idea German what you pay, figures yet for this I you helping?.",, Clear without paying you come there never pure. " ,, OK friends, Tomorrow I'll pay each of you 300.- USD ". A, ,, be made German, which is a weekly pay for the miser. It sucks with the rich; the rich people are all the more covetous they are to their employees. " OK, we're at 8.00 am here ready for collection. Frizzle with the workers a few beers then pass this. ,, I am tomorrow at 8:00 am at the door and pick you up. But I need it only in the Villa regulate I have an employee from need to get. " Gerhard and Gerd, hit you self on the back, this turn of events they did not expect. Now they can use their devices to install the villa. The next day it goes as discussed the matter with the gardeners. No problem Gerd comes to the villa, at least once in the hotel grounds. The two gardeners get their money thing in the morning. Gerd makes them aware that maybe he needed three days.

The boys are looking forward to the mighty are for each 900.- dollars more.

Gerd study his work itself out, he himself has a large garden in Koblenz and knows of course. He goes to the car the gardener and gets a rose scissors and a small rake. ,, I will occupy myself at the house with the roses, I myself roses and am very interested in. " Ok ,, German do what you want but do not break anything. The host will see occasionally after us. He also loves flowers over everything. " Gerd the rose border goes along, magnificent roses stand here in a length of at least 200 meters. Gerd starts very gently so as to cut them something free. He can look through the window into the mansion, he sees that he is here at the height of the study. He goes back to his knees and cuts very cautiously. He looks around and sits down at the Rose strain is a unit and covered it very carefully with sand. ,, Can you hear me Gerhard ". ,, Yes, and how, where are you ". I'm just under the window at the office. " ,, Since ringing even in this room the phone. Gerd must immediately turn his listeners it rang so loudly in his instrument as if it were directly in the study. ,, It's just a short conversation of the landlord. " Gerhard logs immediately with Gerd . ,, That's great Gerd, such a technique only have the Americans ".

,, Morning I check how to get to the Internet cable, let's see if I can still find it today. "Gerd diligently is working through the Rose Pray, his gardener colleagues amazed how quickly and diligently the German's. At the corner of the house Gerd discovered a box. He undermines this short and discovered the bottom of a channel the cables running in the box. The reputation after work bothers him, but he has discovered what he seeks. The installation it must for the next day pick up. The right equipment for it provides with Gerhard Tonight together. They have everything they need to buy at a store in San Francisco. They knew what they wanted so, could not know what they had luck with the gardeners. All the equipment you can buy freely available in the US without seeing its personnel must provide data. The next day they assembled everything and brought the villa under their control. The gardeners have each their dollar 900.- and are also super happy. They already think that he German is strange birds who work and pay more for it. The next difficulty for the two now is to go unnoticed in the vicinity of the villa to the reception of the device extends only over 1000 meters without interference, then it is less clear.

,, Now it pays off every day use another car and a new dress every day it. Gerd has even taken off his three-day beard and sometimes used a blonde and sometimes black women wig. So they always keep the residents of the house for the curious. They are used, the starting and keep curious motorists here. The villa of Franko Bruno is already an imposing building. To remind you on a fortress in Europe, Gerhard has no 600 meters away from the villa in the car for built a hiding place for the technique of his car. A new car battery keeps the wonders of technology going. So they can go unnoticed record everything what happens so via the fixed network and the internet. Unfortunately, they have no way listened to the mobile phone. That would have been possible only with the FBI and the NSA. But Franko Bruno here has certainly over defences. His group will already ensure. He is told the boss of the group and stemmed Italians for good relations in the underworld. Gerhard and Gerd are convinced that they have no other options to get the contacts of the man. Gerd is always surprised by how secure Gerhard is. How well this physically everything is gone. He does not show any fatigue with his now 8 0 years at a very tight performance.

In the next three days, they will come to this place only three times a day, look at the surroundings, and exchange the tapes of the recordings. Access the e-mails and disappear again. It is weekend and the Sunday is inaugurated in Sacramento, for the Tuesday they booked their return flight. Today they want to explore the nearby area of Sacramento and just before dark tap will go to you. Sacramento and its surroundings is a wonderful country landscape. The place where alternate green pastures and desert Similar dry areas, the City itself is a big city with some skyscrapers. But not nearly as many as in Los Angeles or San Francisco. Nevertheless, this city is the capital of California. There is also a wonderful two river city like Koblenz. The American River flows into the Sacramento River. Gerd has here by two rivers again to connect to his Koblenz. Only Sacramento is much bigger. Measured nearly five times the size of population, you will always find fast to her billionaire who has built just outside of Roseville his villa like a fortress on the hill. Gerhard and Gerd drive in Sacramento always the case that they depart far from the Autostrada no. 80th also use the opportunity in the railroad Museum to go to the magnificent old locomotives.

To see who then conquered the West. Also, the beautiful History park they visit. But they have no time for more. You must be back in Roseville of the dark. They manage about to get dark they are almost back in place where they have installed the equipment arrived. But right there already parked a car and forbid them to go there. You gasp, they discovered their technique their devices. Stop their vehicle at a distance and keep behind some trees and bushes for cover. ,, So a shit, have discovered that our activities? ". ,, We must get closer, you stay here with the car Gerhard I will crawl me ran with the telescope. " Gerd proposes a wide arc and then comes the small hill in the tall grass crept down gently. Exactly on the vehicle parked there on their technology. Carefully as he learned it from Win n Eton in many films and books, he comes down inch by inch. Behind a stone, twenty meters from the car and the pair, he dared to lift his head out of the grass for the first time. About the stone away he can now see without glass, that it is patently Lich just about two young lovers is that has chosen this very place for their love exercises. The two act as if they have already done these actions together more often. Also from the villa one seems interested.

To observe them. Gerd has this n viewer now with his telescope in his sights. The man also seems to observe this act. Gerd, the flashing of the two telescope lenses in the setting sun seen. The figure stands behind a window in secure cover. Whoever it is seems to have fun with the love life of the two. But just as Gerd considers that this could be an idea for them, could be one simple case. It is getting dark and the young people gather their clothes and the picnic basket and drive away. Gerd can see how the man at the window follows the car with the telescope and then disappears from the window. Gerd waits 15 minutes before he crawls down to their technical hiding place. With the participation of the young people have raged from none 10 meters from the spot. Safe he crawls from the cover of the stone out there. At any moment, he is prepared for someone to jump forward and attack him. But he is certainly up to the hiding place he has scrupulously to each that the chief grasses have moved as little as necessary. Quite he could he applies here despite his Indian art not be avoided. He reached hiding with a very deep breath, the well-camouflaged technology. His is completely untouched, which means that everything is OK.

He carefully removes the band and the CD containing the e-mails. He can, t exchange either of them unfortunately, he has to go back to the car. Later he has to do the same tour again. But now he is no longer so cautious. Then they experience a huge surprise when evaluating the news. You can hardly believe it. Gerry Schreinemaker has phoned Franko Bruno from Italy. He even stated his address there in complete safety. They also learn from this conversation that the containers are still located in Europe. Unfortunately, he does not say where. Gerry, s Call is only because of the money, the part payment he has picked up in Switzerland was too low. Its cost in Arenberg for the theft of the containers were very high. Again, the money is again the trigger. The instalment has just covered these costs. Franko Bruno still promises him some money to make free, 2 million USD. ,, OK they heard Gerry just say, then it clicked and the connection is terminated. Then a discussion followed with Franko`s friends the bishop who will again to Rome and then from there to Arenberg. After that, they evaluated the many e-mails from these was on the fast nothing out. Read at least not yet.

273

The two then the next day to evaluate their technique. Again and finally expand everything. The facilities at the house to which they no longer come is very nice. In the evening give a few beers that they have drunk with much pleasure. The next morning going it then early to the airport to San Francisco. Gerd is when it comes to flights or always to travel very punctual. Here is already 3 hours before departure at the airport. Check-in, handing over the luggage and then retiring, he loves traveling. Then quite comfortably a round by the Giant airport, check where the departure gate is and then the second breakfast in peace.". Gerd is just cutting the second round, which looks as similar as in Koblenz the rolls as someone taps him from behind on the shoulder. He thinks it is Gerhard who wanted to the toilet. "That was fast Gerhard you did not find the rest room." "I am glad my dear Commissioner, that I have found you. Just come to my realm, do not register with me and do not unsubscribe. That my dear is not at all." ,, You Ronny, where are you from?.". ,, I have guessed that you come back here for the problem in Koblenz and you want to hear something from me. The state of this is where you are foreign. Unfortunately.

I got it yesterday out that you're in Sacramento, or better were. Whole 7 days. I can imagine what you wanted there. But believe me you can, t learn more and find out more when we have the FBI. You know now how good our NSA is. Frank Bruno can, t do anything without us. We have also fanalized here. But the thing which deducted in Koblenz has all respect. The theft of three containers from a police barracks that my dear Gerd Hammer hart was a no. Stronger. " ,, Come sit down, beautiful still meet Ronny you. But you can imagine that we were not keen on it ". "I can think of that, but that's how it is in life. Time seems "the sun and sometimes there is also rain. "This was not a rain with us in Koblenz that was a hurricane and I had to act in order not to be reared with this theft for a lifetime." ,, The dear Gerd I've also thought and as a police officer I would Of course, precisely the resumed F threads here n ". "What do you have for a pensioner with you, is not a bit too old for this job with the police". "Gerhard, who is old but very fit, is the only survivor of the five young soldiers who brought the containers from Berlin across the Westerwald to Arenberg".

"Not to be grasped, for so old I would not have appreciated him". Gerhard comes just around the corner, he already suspects who is so lively with Gerd entertained. But they have also been in Sacramento always looking out for n observers maintained by the FBI. But they had no DISCOVER then, but they would have stayed an extra day if they had been on the hook. Spy on the Americans in this perfidious way they have done this is not allowed in the US and only reserved for the FBI or the NSA. "Well, men," says Gerhard as he approaches the breakfast table. Everything already clarified Gerhard and Ronny introduce themselves they knew through the stories quite a bit from each other. "I do not need to investigate your suitcases, he certainly has disposed of everything that has helped you with your work." ,, Then you can rely Ronny. But I promise you you'll get a full report. Where leave out when I certainly how we got our information. " "If they are good your information then I do not want to know that, but what can you have learned more than our experts and the NSA?". ,, Dear Ronny, wait for my report from ". "Ok men, it was nice to have found you, also see the FBI does not sleep, we also do our work.

I wish you both a good flight, report when you're back in Koblenz ". Gerhard travels with Gerd to Koblenz and remains a day at Gerd the Bureau. They deal with Commissioner Renate Völcker.

And Commissioner Schmidtchen with all the information. Your police president is enthusiastic about the success. In the meantime, the traces of Gerry Schreinemakers and Henk have been recorded in Rome. The new Dutchman must also be near her and will soon appear on her screen. The many e-mails that have sucked they bring. Fitter long screening of more light into the dark. But these information would all have been unusable had they not noticed this one call. They were at the right moment in the right place, with the right tool. The FBI could not listen to this line; this is an absolute secure line e ne of unknown subsidiary of Franco Bruno's empire. Dear Koblenz, I have to go home, please keep me up to date when there is something new. I have to relax a few days and then have to go back to Cairo." "We have to thank you very much Gerhard, which was great from you. I have also collected all the documents and you will be very likely to replace all the documents if we see the first success ". OK, then for the time being by, by,

I must now take a break once. In Koblenz and in Rome, where there are already two officers on the trail of the three gangsters and the Bureau in Koblenz everything runs smoothly.

Gerd makes a report to Ronny, he can, t conceal where the containers are now Ronny course. They have the e. mails decrypted. You now only know that the containers have not left Germany yet. But they do not know where they are located exactly. You suspect all in de m container port in Cologne. The container Harbour in Koblenz has already turned several times upside down. Every container that goes abroad is examined, no matter in which country, therefore also the men to Garry who this course will learn the containers that declares to Hong Kong were switched back of performance is in a domestic limited hours. That seemed to them the best and to be secure and to be the most unobtrusive. The container port in Koblenz. From which it knew because it was times searched unsuccessfully already three s, the best policemen will not believe that close to her nose. Stolen in Koblenz and secured in Koblenz. The three men involved and also their client considered this solution to a brilliant prank.

When the initial excitement is over in a few days, then the containers are transported by truck. This seems the gangsters currently safest. The ports and ships are all heavily monitored. The criminal investigation department Koblenz would never have come up with this idea to go again into the harbour. They are looking for solutions in the USA and the containers are in Koblenz. Especially since the actors are in Italy. The wait there, but only on their new passports, they are all together and Italians can from today free. In the EU without visas moved. Gerry of the Belgians, needed a new name because he was being searched for killing, and because of heavy robbery and attempted murder. Henk the American is on the international search list and Mike the Dutch also. They can no longer move with their old names in Europe. They radiate as they hold their new passports in their hands. That could create their clients only, he has always supplied with everything. His money and his relationships make almost everything possible. Even they can now travel comfortably with the new passports back to Germany. But they must first collect their well-earned money in Switzerland. You are satisfied with it and rejoice in it as they could propose such a trick.

Of the German Police, and still can. Unfortunately this did not work with the transport of the containers to Hong Kong. Your client, his people here in its German company have Franko Bruno informed that there are huge problems in container transport in Germany. All containers with foreign destination are opened. That will delay their shipments to all the worlds. That was important information for Franko Bruno has implemented this info thanks immediately and the ship the data of the containers at the port immediately Bonn has made some changing. The containers could not be moved abroad. Koblenz was a good and clever way for Franko. Franko Bruno was known in the business he always has a nose the other is ahead. The employees of his office in Cologne were SLOS idea about the contents of the containers. They did not which well it is in the containers. Franko Bruno has reluctantly taken his people from Cologne by this. But unfortunately he had not seen any other possibilities. His competent men are still in Switzerland and Italy. Now they are back with new papers on the way to Koblenz about the settlement to take over. There are already three good men.

They have proved with their last grandiose action. It all worked so well, and then the German police stop the possibility of the fast transport to Hongkong. The containers were already on the safe hydrofluoric been ready to ship to Hong Kong. Without the trip of the first chief commissioner to the USA, this would never have been discovered. Now that you know the police in Koblenz with great certainty that these have not left Germany three containers. They were able to find out about the many encrypted e-mails. But, of course, they had also discussed the location of the three helpers of Franko Bruno, through the telephone conversation about the secret management. Of course you had no idea that these three men had changed their identity again. Now travel in three different flights to Gert. One goes to Cologne, one to Stuttgart and one to Hannover. Two days later they all meet in Cologne. Since all speak three good German and English drops to no. The none of the three Italians speaking also German, She deposits the new passport in Cologne at the Hotel. They are equipped with full powers, the containers now to transfer by truck. To sent each of the containers in a different direction. The new Holland and even.

Newer Italians takes the matter in Koblenz harbour. They quickly found the containers and planed the trucks for pick-up. Gerd gets a call from Ronny from San Francisco.

"You will not believe Gerd. But our friend Franko and his friend the bishop have booked a flight to Cologne. The bishop has an appointment with the cardinal in Cologne and the Herr Franko certainly wants to go to Arenberg in the monastery. In any case are so my information from our common friends from the NSA. " Ronny that fits together with the things that we have now found out. Please come over as well, if it is possible. I think the whole story is coming to an end here, it seems to be pointing. It is now safe that these accursed containers are still in Germany. Koblenz and Cologne, we have already three times on the head Place. The place they are not, we are looking. " We've also tracked his three men in Italy, we're shadowing them round the clock. " Gerd course do not know yet because s s act these three again with new papers in front of him. "Gerd sent me a short report and asked me officially. I am preparing my flight to Cologne tomorrow. " ,, OK Ronny, the Bureau is sending you in the next hour the invitation and the request.

I must urgently go to the port of Koblenz, send me a mail when you arrive. Cologne or Frankfurt that is almost no matter, Seat down on the train to Koblenz, the moment. We are hopelessly hopeless, I can, t shut down anyone ". Gerd then shuts. It self once more with its Commissioner Renate Völcker to Koblenz container port. He then sits together with Renate and the experienced harbour master at a table. "We do not know where to look, the containers are still in Germany, but all our searches have been futile." "You have been to me three time; so far nothing has changed here. Every container that comes in and everyone who goes out are thoroughly investigated. We even open some, just those that are not sealed, but they are opened at their destination. " "There can be no container escape a control". ,, That's good to hear, we hope that can escape us none of the three containers ". ,, We want to hope for the best, "Renate adds that the guys are departed who have set us up a few times." These three crooks are now again turning the wheel. If the first Commissioner had left the port with his commissioner a quarter of an hour later, the three would have crossed the three of them. These three greet the harbourmaster.

And place the papers for two containers before they have to pick them up since their company has relocated the dispatch. Ok men that's are no problem, bring me the papers and the change of shipping and the collection certificate. Then I invite you the things directly. Times look where the things stand. You are lucky children or we too. These two containers are high on the huge pile, nor are they there, so hurry. " Ok ,, Master, we do it with the papers and come back. As long as the boxes remain ". The men go back and are glad to have taken the first step. ,, Why Gerry, why only two containers, let's all get at one time, then we have done this thing. " , I think Henk if we get three container in which all lights on. Three containers are widely sought in Germany. We pick only two, and the third, we get a few days later. " You can be right, let's do it. " Two days later, the two containers are picked up; they leave peacefully on flatbed trucks Koblenz. Two containers of the three so sought are for the time being disappeared again. If the Koblenz these lead still a hols. One will discover this in time. " Ronny has now come to Koblenz Interpol practice control everything behind the borders of Germany. Especially in Holland and Belgium.

Nowhere is there new knowledge. Ronny amazed to know about this because has earned the Cid Koblenz. It passes two days nothing happens; only Frank Bruno has arrived with his bishop in Cologne. These two are also totally supervised. After the conversation with the Cardinal, the two of them continue to Arenberg. The two low-loaders with the containers have already unloaded these at the new location. One is in Flensburg and the other in Rosenheim. Ready for further transport to Austria and Denmark. Then it is again a very deliberate move of the three. "Men" says Gerry to his two partners; these two are only once safe. No one will find these containers. Now we are on the way and win the third container from the port of Koblenz ". Gerry's phone rings and his big boss are off. "Hi Gerry, everything went well". "Yes Boss, two are in absolute security". ,, Gerry avoids talk of containers, which is also much better for such since. His boss understands immediately. "But why only two". "We have to handle this carefully; we are now getting one by one". "Ok as fast as you can and come to Koblenz. I am back with the bishop in Arenberg in the Klosterhotel. The bishop has been eating a fool at the hotel. In particular the sacred garden and the church. "

,, Franko, we live for security reasons in Cologne. "
We should meet in Bonn not in Koblenz "."But
Gerry I want to meet you in Koblenz, but down at
the container port. I come there with the taxi
quietly and inconspicuously ". ,, OK but then only
morning I'm off to Cologne. " ,, I then come
tomorrow. At what time to Koblenz? ". "We meet
there at 2 pm, you can go to sleep, read the others
in Cologne. But watch out on the there is no
organize, you know woe when they sniff alcohol
and women". "OK, I'll be there tomorrow at 2 pm. I
drive a Ford KUGA, black with Cologne number ".
Ok ,, see you tomorrow Gerry ". At the door of the
bishop Franko goes up and down already excited,
he wants to with Gerry still in the sacred garden
and into the church. The Sister Superior, of course,
is once again thrilled by her American guests. She
also immediately reported to the first chief
commissioner. The courses already know that the
two Americans are back at the hotel. But he thanks
very kindly for the support of the upper-
swimmers. Everything seems to run at the
moment of their Place, according to the plans of
the police from Koblenz. But no one suspects the
two containers are gone again for the CID. Art
chief are one step ahead of the Koblenz again.

But the se the information will also have to get late to respond. On day Gerd brings the FBI man early on the hotel. Somehow he has already a very bad idea. He has often been right with his hunches, slow knows Gerd the extremely naughty behaviours of its thieves. He now dares them the most impossible and naughty. "What is Gerd, you are so restless, actually I wanted to take with you a good German breakfast". "We can do that later. Later my dear I have set myself on pork Haxe and sauerkraut ". "How do you get on pork Knuckle with pickled cabbage (Sauerkraut)". ,, When I went through the old town of Koblenz I saw there a place a Bavarian restaurant ". Ok ,, my dear as we go along there, I'll take my team with, I was already long gone. " "OK, where do you want to go now, I have to go to the port, I have such a funny feeling that the brothers us again really want to make mistaken.". "Yes, you have to let the guys have the right thing." The container port is already in front of them and the harbour master happens to be at the gate. This does not make it any easier but faster. "What is great master, what are you so thoughtful". ,, I wanted to call you, I have yesterday two containers ben out actually yesterday.

This is actually nothing but I had such a strange feeling. Then I checked the car registration mark this morning. Those were wrong, why someone gets containers with falsified marks. Had they been three I would have reacted immediately but I wanted right now Please with you A ". Give me the copies of the papers, but when the character is sign was wrong. So will agree nothing a shit. But it can also have other reasons that the containers have been picked up in this way". ,, Yes, I immediately thought of contraband or smuggling, we had already been here in the harbour. " "Port master from now goes here no container from the farm we have not controlled.

Today come another feed marks les X-ray machine and examined the container ". ,, Commissioner, the two are three containers of which now gone, who have come together in Cologne. " Where is the third container?, perhaps we need only examine the container. " He's right there on the top I have in a few minutes down here ". Gerd gets very restless and calls his experts, who have to open this container. An hour later, it is clear; this is one of the three containers from the shaft. A success on this day. "Put the container back where you picked it up.

Gerd possessed now an invisible from it total surveillance. Immediately give him also out the search for the two single containers. All freeway cameras have been tested on all motorways in Germany. They had the wrong numbers of trucks, and they were hopeful that they had not been replaced. You're back in business with Gerd is happy and his whole troop is full of joy when he says this with the invitation. To hock them they are also really excited. The shank and the success of the delicious beer to go are simply exquisite. Even the Commissioner Renate brushing away almost the whole leg. Ronny, of course, he always complains about it just does not exist such a thing in America. "You have now been at every corner cut houses since Schwarzenegger was your Senator?". "Yes, but schnitzels are not a big leg from pork with cabbage. On the next day, they are fully occupied with the search to expand and evaluate the current results. 1 to. 3.00 clock they get the message from the hotel in the Arenberg Franko with a taxi on the way. The taxi we course pursued by them. "Stay friends, we need to know where the guy wants to go. But I already have a clue. I guess he wants to go to the port. Gerd is absolutely right.

A little later he gets the message Franko Bruno is the container port. A Cologne Ford Kuga takes on the man. The two men look out of the car windows to the container. After a few minutes, the two go back to Arenberg, stopping only briefly at the police barracks in considering the place where the three containers were. The driver then launches the Ford Kuga Franko into the hotel and runs again to Cologne. GERD has long been a vehicle of the ordered Kuga. Invisible success. So the most clever gangster also make mistakes. Still in the night the Koblenz police who know these three men are in Cologne Hotel, the alleged Italians. Mistakes are always to be made on both sides. If you feel too secure and if you consider yourself to be good, that is often the beginning of the end. Gerd is now sure that he has returned to the winding with the perpetrators and the container. Everything is back under his, control under the control of Soko Koblenz. The guard the container port is now monitored reinforced around the clock. The three men are under their control, every step of these men is immediately reported to the Soko. The Bureau and the LKA and BKA involved with people in it. But the SOKO Koblenz has been given the lead.

This has all the details and only her achievements in the USA have made the re-entry possible. The BKA also bears the responsibility for the theft of containers from the police barracks. The Soko and the LKA, this storage was not right, not safe enough. They wanted to get rid of the containers and go to Berlin. Now they have to, unfortunately, the containers hunt again afterwards. Two of these containers have disappeared, because they were only too late a day. But on this one day.The containers can be where else. But only the direct thieves know this, whose criminal list is getting longer. But now they are at the safe hook. Franko Bruno telephoned on the remaining secret phone line with Gerry. "How does it look like my dear Gerry, two containers are safely housed, we still have to get the third". "My dear Frank is not so easy, be glad the two are safe. Getting the third is not a children's game. When the men of the LKA, s who now guard the container port, then they are to us now also on the track. Unfortunately, we were so stupid and had to drive to the container port together. Surely, the people have been watching you too! ". "Yes, that was stupid, but we could not have reckoned with this total surveillance."

"OK Franko, I already have an idea. I know how we can leave the hotel undetected through the underground car park. There is a small most unknown transition to the Urban Underground. Only a small tight tunnel for cables and pipe, I will now have two other vehicles with Wiesbaden number and secretly go with my people the hotel. We go straight into the lion's den, we go directly to Koblenz. There we check again with our old papers, which we still carry with us. " ,, I have new US passports for you. If it becomes necessary can get her this immediately. " ,, You've probably quite a passport factory in your trunk, OK, we get it . " ,, No, but I have an excellent printing and the necessary blanks, this we will need many of our international operations, Register if you are in Koblenz, again on this phone that no one can locate because no one has the data. " ,, OK Boss, here runs about all the new cars are already in the city garage of Bonn . We do not take with case; we only take that with what we wear on the body. I have paid in advance for the next 7 days. You will hardly miss us here. Only our guards will soon realize that we no longer appear at the hotel. But I think the earliest morning. Then we are again immersed in the middle in the lion's den. "

The police men guarding the hotel and sit down in the lobby and also the garage exit in the eye may not notice how these three men leave the hotel and drive through the city garage to Koblenz. They have in greatest Hotel booked into the Mercure right on the Rhine. Go shopping only once and buy the necessary clothes and what son still missing. They have everything personal left behind in the Cologne hotel. So the three as late as possible disappear it will be noticed. Their weapons they have in an unremarkable. Special case that looks more like the case for laptop and accessories. ,, Gerry logs on to Franco who is happy it worked out the move to Koblenz. ,, What did you now before Gerry ". ,, You'll hear it when the time comes Boss, I will now first of all clarify the situation at the container port. Then I know already what we will do. " A little later, Gerry is with Henk as hikers along the Rhine at the container port. There they are looking for with their telescopes from everything where they naturally suspect police officers in plain clothes. In the area of the port they believe are the e not. You could find out too quickly. That's why they focus on the close environment. Luckily there Friday and there is little to be loaded in the container port.

The whole surrounding industrial area is quiet. This naturally for art thief`s advantage, since they can make all the changes taking place shift change of the police station easier now. About two whole days and evenings they have the harbour and its surroundings Monitors and notes made about where the individual officials who now in turn monitor the container terminal, where they are exactly. They have made a careful plan it. Them, it is clear that since so easy on a Saturday or Sunday is nothing. Just this Friday afternoon.

They consider the right moment. The police have actually scheduled the Saturday or Sunday for the trial of theft. But Gerry is an above-crook, not for nothing that he is mandated by Franko get the Gerry's skills has often claimed. Gerry's men retreat to the common meeting men. ,, I have prepared everything, the truck; with particularly low he loading area for container transport is less than 500 meters from here, no low loader. I drive these. I have prepared already the camp for this truck. Up in Arenberg in a landscape gardener. In Arenberg the place where it all beginning the container you will be there not suspect.

,, Back in Arenberg, which will never suspect the cops, we turn the three policemen guarding the Terminal. " ,, Just Henk, I switch the harbour master of, and operate the container crane. The moment it reappears on the court. Your then take, you can also with the crane deal Henk " ,, Clear, an easy thing for me. " ,, Well then I'll get the truck, in the time you have the container on the hook. " ,, so we do not need 30 minutes and are then gone. Every 40 minutes to query the guards by radio. This time allows us, it is just but then I'm on my way to Arenberg. I'll take the way across the highway and then go back to the 42 directly from Urbar to Arenberg. You Henk come with me and the Ami follows with your cars." ,, All right, Gerry, here we go directly, we numb the individual police officer with the gas which we derive in the cars . I take two and Ami the one over there. " We need almost the same time, men on the last use. " Gerd makes his way to the terminal and hit the harbour master who just wants to conclude his office door. He looks for a moment in amazement Gerry, Gerry, he recognized immediately. But before he can even do nothing she has the spray gas inhaled. In se moment he bagged already in it together. Gerry the office opens the door.

And pulls the heavy harbour master back to his office. Balanced this in his chair and pulls him a hood over the head. Captivates the man firmly in his chair so , because she sits there motionless Gerry gets the key of the crane, he knows exactly where it is and sets the giant crane in motion. There already is Henk and takes over the control pendant. The American is already climbing up the container stack and is ready to hang. Gerry is already on the way to the truck and comes straight in the bin as the container already approached floats. In less than 4 minutes the container is discontinued and the container with its container corners on the bed locked. The Ami is already running past them and goes to the meeting point in Arenberg. He will report if something suspicious is doing on this route. They have practiced yesterday the transport, so nothing can go wrong today. The wireless connection is working and the truck roars from the terminal. Gerry knows that she has not yet managed to see, even if it looks like. You have the container in less than one managed minutes. 10 minutes less than they planned had. What they did not know that for the police she has shortened weekend with the start of Friday noon, the query time to 20 minutes.

The moment the truck from the terminal of the responsible official races tried already to contact the three officials at the terminal. When he does not reach all three, it reports this immediately. When the message, the Soko a civil vehicle has been reached on its way to the port. Gerd Schöder passes immediately a large search for a truck, with the container an unfortunately, these are at the moment some in Koblenz go. It does not take another five minutes until the first stops. But of course, it turns out quickly, as This is uninvolved. Gerd picks up the phone, he has already a hunch. He picks up the phone and ordered a patrol on the road from the 42-hour. About Urbar to Arenberg. He knows this guy the Belgians now who will try it again with his usual insolence. Gerry is already close to Arenberg when he sees the police barrier. He is the last roundabout in Urbar and just before the next round about in Arenberg he sees a further police barrier. He turns right a b in the industrial area Urbar / Arenberg. He is caught in a trap. No longer comes out of this industrial area. He must go back to the main road, but there you have now sealed off. He must turn and comes with its heavy Truck the fence on the horse pasture. The double wheels sinking into the wet grass.

And before he realizes what's going on is the truck comes to spin and is one stroke diagonally stalled and stopped in the meadow .Both men jump out. Henk reaches for his submachine gun and shoot at the approaching SEK. Henk is made immediately fatal and Gerry recognizes quickly that he has no chance here. He is unhurt led away in handcuffs. All police officers are awesome around the container. You know what are closed for values in it. Fortunately, the truck is not overturned. The Ami in the car of had noticed the happiness he came too late and can escape. But on the motorway to Cologne she can, t bring him from the street. Unfortunately. Franko Bruno and the bishop is already on the plane and high above the ocean to the United States. Franko Bruno is no longer available for the German police. The entire police top of Koblenz and Mainz gathered on the property in Urbar / Arenberg. A heavy crane moves and saves only the container is set to a police trailer. Unfortunately, he may once again been unable to open. This is with an escort directly only in Berlin at his destination place without great speeches of Arenberg went to Berlin. They want to get rid of him urgently transferred other responsibilities.

Gerd and his team including the prosecutor and of course Ronny go even eat pork knuckle. This time they drink themselves too completely with the tasty Koblenz beer that tastes better to Bavarian dishes as the fade Bavarian beer.

In any case, the commissioners feel this taste of the beer that. The SOKO Koblenz has managed the last part but not the other two containers found that are still in Germany. Gerd takes before this matter with Gerhard discuss and maybe even solve with the help of the statements of their captives. But the highway patrol could give important information. You are still looking for the other container, it will take. The opening of a container is clear that this part of the former Amber Room are. Here are some other valuable pictures and objects in the container. The search for the complete Amber Room continues. This is no longer in the hands of Soko Koblenz. The Koblenz shaft has been thoroughly investigated and it was not found in this bay than in the containers. The SOKO Koblenz has done excellent and is only quiet B BSERVERS in another matter Amber Room. So far, no one knows this is here, these parts are they have and hunt. These parts already cost so many lives ha ben.

Are the parts doe`s fabled complete and genuine Amber Room?. The hunt on is not yet finished, there remains the uncertainty, this is now the Amber Room or these are only parts of the Amber Room . Share the replica items are?.You need to find the two containers, they must not be lost. If it should not be the Amber Room, it is definitely important art objects in these containers. Ronny the man the FBI says goodbye the next morning, his flight left the next morning back to the US. ,, So dear Koblenz SOKO, we are all good friends to me. Unfortunately, we had only a partial success, I wish you the place it the other two containers ". It is a nice departure of sealed been friendship between the police in Koblenz and San Francisco. ,, You can really on love Koblenz friends. We will also with us to try more from the art thieves, heller and bandits, what they are all together to get out. We keep in touch and hope we find something. " Ronny disappears behind the panes of the departure hall and once again waving the Koblenz commissioners to his friends. The glad that ultimately the first negative experience with the FBI have been transformed. They are very good workers, although they were all very well glued by the special commission.

But this just happened only in the interest of German Art. ,, What now dear friends, as we go further in front, what do you think we will find the other two containers and we will ever know what was hidden in our bay in the mills mine? ,, Gerd, we can no longer do we have to wait and see what the federal police are. " ,, Yes, you're right, I'll do a few days` vacation, I must travel to the Eifel ", ,, you just want to your Eifel goat and to your dog's adopted. " Yes ,, Renate, the two missing me a lot . We want to wander through the beautiful little valley of Nitz, well into the high Eifel (600 metres). But that does not mean I'm going to the service completely forgotten. A friend and dealer of art, a dealer from Frankfurt who sometimes does, not take it so exactly with stolen goods, which will be active throughout Germany. For me and look out for the goods. We both suspect that these goods were already transferred is provided in another container and was re-sealed by customs with new seals. We suspect that product already abroad again, but know everything is not known. Just as well that stuff can be somewhere in Germany in an abandoned hall. While the boss of SOKO with his girlfriend Marianne to roam the beautiful valley Nitz creek.

This is in a deep valley and is bordered on both sides by a beautiful forest, a dream trail for everyone without any major problems. For Sally, it has the advantage, since s they come in this heat without any problems of water, which it is getting pretty close to the Nitz creek, e along. Pick out just before they reach the chapel a place to make their snack. Said the Commissioner would call from Carinthia this break. Sally rest down to the water and quenches the hundredth time their thirst, it is more a game with the delicious water, the small river. Shortly before Mayen at the beautiful castle Bürresheim flows into the Nette stream and disappears with nice stream in the Rhine River. Above the chapel it then goes to a picnic area and from there to an old mine. Gerd, ,, what do you think. We want this mine, I've never been there? ". ,, OK if you two still do it, I have no problem with it. " Gerd's cell phone rings, oh his friend from Frankfurt's turn.

,, Gerd, I have a hunch of where your containers are ". ,, Just a hunch Walter? ". Yes ,, it is no more than an idea, I've heard that these containers should be in the Eifel and the charge is prepared for transport to Belgium.

And then to the United States. " ,, Walter that would be the hammer back to the US, the money aristocracy does not let up apparently. They seem to want these containers. " ,, What do your informant, in which area of the Eifel, already far west direction Belgian border or here on my side. " ,, What do you call your site? ". ,, I am close to the Nürburgring in Mayen ". ,, If my information then vote should the containers are on a Farm. In the vicinity of the Nürburgring. " ,, You will not believe Walter, I'm on a hike near the Nürburgring. " ,, Then look at you ask for, but be careful. ". The containers seem to be in the hands of very hard men ". ,, That these containers since her rescue from the well in the Mills, it's about very many millions of them already some have flowed. As will likely prove a strength. Did you name the backers in the US? ". ,, No I do here comes from Frankfurt only one of the middlemen, someone from the lowest region of the underworld, so be careful. " Thus the call ends. ,, What's going Gerd, what are you doing for a long face? ". .. This shit Amber Room did not leave us alone; it haunts me well into the holidays. It should be located in the area of the Nürburgring on a farm is very remote now. " ,, That is the end of the walk and go home? ".

,, No Marianne our hike, we can`t take us, we will make only one change of direction. We are now going in the direction of Kürrenberg and from there directly through the forest to the ring. Maybe we discover in this way a bit. There are many remote farms. " ,, Well, my Commissioner then we do a professional hike through the Eifel forests and fields. Then I go once by car to the old mine,". ,, only if you take me. " ,, You have yet again chasing criminals. " Gerd takes his cell phone and informs Gerd and Renate of the special commission on the latest information. Please send Ronny a message that is to keep your eyes open and ears in the US, who is this new buyer. But I suspect it is the old buyer who has now found a new undercover partner. If the whole will now be handled by Belgium. A new organization is busy. I just wonder how the containers have arrived in the vicinity of the Nürburgring; I do not think it possible we all have Motorways and main roads blocked off. " ,, This Amber Room (Bernsteinzimmer) its vortex is just, but it's unspeakably valuable. That was long lost makes it even more valuable. " ,, It prefers Gerd we still do not know if there is ever the Amber Room. ,, You're right but that makes.

The art dealer probably batty for these containers. They have this again at their mercy as it seems." ,, It's mind boggling, I have you can leave the stress holiday. I am now back at work, how so, you walk now official with the Eifel goat? ". ,, Renate under let these comments about my friend, yes to now I am exploring after the farm and the containers. So my holiday ends tonight officially today. I think, since us a wandering couple with a dog walking stand out as a horde of policemen roam the forests. Please give any information to the police after Adenau out. Streaking around police officers and cars could warn these people. " ,, OK, ok that with the Eifel goat I take that back but be careful. I also make myself with Gerd on the Nürburgring and two other civilian couples are also on the way to the ring, we walk on the other side. Of the ring and browse carefully the environment. " ,, This is a great idea that is our fresh air fanatical Bernd fallen ". ,, The is already up and running in his hiking boots in front of me , burning to run on it." ,, Good colleagues, we remain in constant contact with each other, who is the second group? ". ,, Commissioner Uresla and Franz Rudolf ". ,, Ok, both greetings from me, my phone no., The two already. Have you informed Ronny."

,, Yes, we have Mr. Police Chief, who was very surprised that it continues in this matter as quickly. " ,, Yes, we were also, but where so much money is involved it goes on and on. We only marvel at how quickly your contact has been found in Frankfurt this, hopefully it is also true with this information?.". ,, This, unfortunately, we know only when we really found the container. It's been crazy these containers circulate through the whole world, but we have at least one guaranteed ". ,, Then good luck at all, let's get started." Gerd, Marianne and Sally of this transition are like most already halfway to Kürrenberg . It's uphill pretty hard and its business. Only Sally seems to make this increase fun. Upper arrived they go back and forth through the forest always the winding forest roads are no easy oh by feel.

But Gerd has an unlikely good sense, always amazed Marianne that they migrate toward the right. They come through Herresbach and pay attention, there are many farms that are remote could be where the hiding place of the container. But they do not believe that these containers are somewhere in the yard, which must be in one of the great barns.

Space would have them in all barns that can see them. ,, Gerd, you would not want in any of the barns? ". ,, unfortunately I have no choice my dear, how can I find the containers otherwise, I have to dare. " ,, Well, we are looking for all barns on, Sally is looking forward it safe, just as we do this discreetly, you can probably see us when we move from one barn to another. " ,, This forces us, unfortunately. To make this at any detours barn and if we do not manage it today then we'll do tomorrow. Possibly some other luck. In fact, it gets dark after the fourth large bills and another is looking futile. ,, Now what Gerd, where is the nearest hotel. ,, Over there under the trees is our next hotel, we do what and we've always wanted, we stay under the trees and the open sky. Sally is awake already for us and above us. The wild animals are Sally beautiful scent knell and a detour to make us ". The wild animals that do not bother me but this little unpleasant crawling stuff that crawls on the ground that will bother me more. " ,, Unfortunately it caught us so, and we have neither tents nor air mattresses but the ceiling will be enough for you to make long on you can easily and cover with one half ". ,, And you know where you sleep.

I'm on duty and only need my jacket and Sally will keep me warm " . ,, So I have not imagined our first night in the open air, which will warm you my dog. " Gerd puts the blanket carefully and sweeps every wrinkle smooth, anticipating he has prepared the ground and all the branches and stones cleared away and the square lined with grass he plucked diligently. Marianne amazed not bad how nice he did it. This is getting more beautiful than my bed at home.",, You shall also feel comfortable in the woods, so feel at home, but we have quite a few nights on the balcony and in the garden, which was up lovely! ". ,, Yes, that was wonderful but here in the woods! ". ,, show the nice weather there are nearly 25 degrees, the sky is clear as rare. We can experience the beautiful sunset behind the sight of Nürburg. The sky is colored red as if the Angels actually bake cakes for us. The first stars are visible and just the spotlight goes to the Nürburg. Beautifully illuminated. What is more beautiful than the wait when it gets dark, then if all the stars appear and the moon will illuminate us?. " ,, You're right, Gerd, it's beautiful, come lay with me I need you now. You cuddle up together and enjoy the encroaching night.

The rising moon, which unfortunately hovers just like a sickle over everything. It will be a wonderful night and Sally keeps her body heat that nobody has to freeze. It is on this night not cooler than 17 degrees. Gerd is the first wax; Marianne is still a bit tired from the wonderful love playing in the great outdoors. Gerd prepares a breakfast and on a small fire of coffee boiled in a tin Gerd in nearby brook has washed out. Of course, he has the peaches have been in the can before eaten. Sally helps him. There are fortunately a little what is not plastered Sally. She has long smelled good sausage that already exudes its good smell out of the box. After everything is well prepared wakes Gerd his great love that has nothing of an Eifel goat. Marianne is surprised, because she has slept so tight. ,, You've already done everything Gerd, the smell of coffee makes me alone wax. How did you manage to make coffee here in the wilderness?. "
,, A good Indians succeeds something playing. I feel like a rascal as a scout, it gives me a lot of fun to live like that. Down there by the creek you can make yourself fresh, I cut the meat and the bread and pour before the coffee into the cup. The rising sun begins to dip everything in its light; the beauty of the night will be replaced.

By the beauty of the morning by the rising sun. After breakfast, everything will be re-wrapped and stowed in a backpack. The walk continues and the search for the Amber Room. Three barns in the area Herschbach must be checked. From up here you can see all three barns. All are located on the small stream and the old dirt road to the little is busy. There are barns are not located directly at the courts, only agricultural implements be accommodated with great certainty. There are no large pastures nearby. ,, Look Marianne, in which barn you'd container hiding, if you had to hide them? ". Marianne looks at the position of all three attentively ". ,, Gerd, I would take the first barn from our point of view, which is somewhat hidden among the trees. It is also the largest barn, it must once have stood there horses. Behind the barn are still a Paddock and a small pasture to see. That would be enough for two or three horses. But like everything practice is there are no horses more.",, That's what I was thinking, we observe this barn up close before we approach this. " Come on we set off and put us there at the edge of the forest, from where we have a good overview of this barn. I have such a good feeling in my stomach that we have found the container ".

Hopefully. ,, Gerd, this amber room drama is ended. " They reach the edge of the forest and hide their sent, and Sally has understood, since s it may make no alarm here and must lie quietly behind the bushes. Gerd phoned all his colleagues who are also in use, they all have discovered nothing suspicious. Gerd are his suspicions here on his barn not award he wants is to wait for what happen. But it happened a few hours nothing, so Gerd itself decides the barn on the fur to move. Marianne now takes but Sally on a leash to prevent them running behind Gerd ago. ,, pass to Gerd, be careful, there is no one seems to be, but you do not know. ,, Would not it be better if we go together as a lonely wanderer there and Sally any men startle there?. " ,, I have also been considered, but I want to know first what is there in the barn, I have the best out alone. If something is you can send me Sally, and if any vehicle is to come then you send me a text message. " ,, OK, Gerd, but be careful.`` ,, Gerd has already made his way and sent used to cover the many bushes that are on the road to awe raise ne. Just high enough that they offer him the crawl coverage. Even Marianne can, t discover it from its location. At the corner of the barn Gerd discovered.

A peep hole or air which probably serves the circulation of air in the barn. This vent is almost completely obscured by the bushes that have taken over many years there wide. Carefully, he bends apart the thin branches of small birch and looks into the barn. What he sees there leaves him breath, there are two fully loaded trucks, he can`t know what it is. It could be big boxes on the plane he can see the inscription of a circus. Can`t read the name of the circus but because of the darkness. It buzzes in his pocket; Anna sends him a text that a vehicle is approaching the barn. Gerd writes back, thanks, I'm in good coverage and continue watching what was in the barn is going on. OK, it just comes back. The vehicle stops directly in front of the barn and four men get out and open the large heavy wooden gate. Flash light flows in the barn and immersed the barn inside in a flash light. Gerd can read the inscription on the plane now, circus Sarasani stands there in large letters. So there is a failure, unfortunately. Thinks Gerd here has only made some things a circus. But why so far from every street. Gerd decides to wait even further and this waiting will be rewarded. A second vehicle rolls up, a small truck. Loaded with large prefabricated parts.

For powerful wooden boxes. This makes Gerd very curious. Lot of men Please hurry, the crates will be transported further tomorrow. We need to reload the containers unloaded when they are empty and recharge the boxes. Tomorrow at 14.00 clocks everything must roll over the border to Belgium. Gerd is awake, what lays the tarpaulin of the circus Sarasani?. The crates are carried in and assembled. Four huge boxes appear. Now, Gerd, who wants the containers, when these are under the tarp are reloading into these crates and reseal and reship. When the tarpaulin is withdrawn, the containers are searched for. There is someone with a giant front-mounted truck and the containers are unloaded and the crates are loaded onto the truck, each truck two boxes. "What men are when parts are in the crates that are longer than our creates. Then my dear Boris comes our special tool and our expert used, we have no choice but then professionally disassemble this part to fit in the box. Under no circumstances. Shall we transport these goods again in containers. We had such luck in the ring-hunting around Koblenz. We already prepared these tarpaulins as a precautionary measure and were able to drain them over the containers during the journey.

This had escaped us the police because of the speed in which we did this and we have come so through their so tight meshes. Now let's tackle the rest careful. I hr does know how many lives already cost this action. The heavy front loader disappears again. "Where does it want to go with the device boss". "He has to get away again, we could only get him for an hour, every further hour would only make us suspect." "That' Boris, we have to reload everything with the hand". "Yes my dear we must, for the many money my dear, you will probably be able to work once, or". "OK, ok, then read us". With these words, the containers are opened and the first parts are removed from the container. Gerd pulls his mobile phone and films the unloading of the first container then his battery is all and he has to go back to Marianne there he still has a rechargeable battery to recharge his mobile phone. Cautiously, he now makes his way back, unhappily in the feeling of having these rags back on the lap which have been fooling him and the FBI. Over so many months. He manages to get back to Marianne and Sally and load his cell phone. "What is Gerd, did you find the containers?". "Yes, I did when the thing is loaded I must inform all of it.

The bandits have completely littered us. They were cleverer than we thought, but they just made the bill again without the landlord, without the SOKO Koblenz. " After the phone is recharged informed Gerd his colleagues that they should collect them all in the village Herschbach, there will they go. Then we will see how we proceed further. First we have to secure the door to this barn inconspicuously, which come there nowhere than back. Over this agricultural way. I will try to avoid this long distance and then wait for you at the entrance to this path. Please let me know about the exact location via mobile phone and parts. The three do not to be discovered a long detour to yes and then reach the point where the dirt road at two courtyards passes to the barns, where it ends in a dead end. A little out of this junction at the entrance to the town, the commissioners meet and discuss the situation. Bernd brings Marianne home to Kottenheim, for her, this adventure is at an end. Gerd had therefore fight because she's left him back Sally's. Then he certainly.

Can still use the clever bitch well for further use. But Gerd can, t dare to involve Marianne in this matter.

He is leading a police officer, two men at his school-house in the wall of the barn. The barn is surrounded by the police, and no one is to escape them. Meanwhile to a possible arrest of the criminals they want to document everything that happens in the barn. The two camera officials have a very good cover and film everything that happens in the barn, every piece that is unloaded and reloaded, is filmed and saved for eternity. The recordings will be broadcast directly to Koblenz via the Internet. There you can hardly believe it, either, because s this action they are now more concerned s. They were terribly upset about how stupid way they escaped vehicles these containers. Now they can adjust the international elaborate search, they have their containers again in their hand and equal to the entire bandits. But just not the main builders who have caused this whole thing. The police president consults with all involved and also with the FBI in San Francisco which are also surprised by this twist. After the written guarantees of the FBI with the USA customs all return to Germany allowed the competent Germans make these crates can now be transported further. This message hits the head of the Soko as a hammer.

He must immediately stop all activities and have the boxes pulled. Over the border to Belgium and to the ship. They want the true contractors. Gerd leaves the cautious ring around the barn until further observation is prepared. It only takes a few hours for specialist departments to take over everything, but Soko Koblenz will transfer the additional line. The two well-camouflaged camera men can continue to film in all peace and secure very important evidence for the later arrests.

In the USA and here on site, the Presidium in Koblenz is working hard to find out the data of the men involved in the barn. It turns out that there are German and Belgian. One of the previously involved is back again in the new action. One can only guess, since, s these two driver are no longer just the leader. One of the men, the apparent leader gets a call on his cell phone from a landline number. The Kripo (crime police) surprises with this how surely the art robbers and killer feel. It comes to meet them very much, they listen to the voice of the man that is the Dutch or Belgians, it might Gerry Schreinemaker be. But the call, they can quickly get out of the area of Nürburg, from a small hotel at the Nurburgring.

Bernd Marianne has brought home is just for him the call reaches in transit at the Nürburgring by his boss him. "Hello Bernd, where are you?." "I'm just at the Nürburgring". "This is great. Please go to the hotel name Rennbahn, from there the Boss in the barn was called. Please find out who has telephoned a few minutes ago from which telephone.". "Everything clear Gerd, the hotel, the hotel' Rennbahn, I just see.

Still 500 meters, then I'm there. I'll get in touch if I get new from there ". ,, Be careful of the latest state of play is from the very top, we have to pull the truck. When it "must also be up to the United States. "So a shit boss, then everything starts again". "Unfortunately Gerd, but we will at least know what is in the containers and then in the boxes. The guys filmed everything from their super location.". ,, Na least bit, I am now outside the hotel, sign up if I have some experience. " ,, OK, boy, do I wait for your info, you have delivered Marianne? ". "Yes, of course, it took me all the way to vomit her Sally". "Yes, she and the dog, now do it well Bernd". Bernd drives his BMW into the parking lot of the hotel, it begins this week falls immediately a car with a Belgian number plate on. He parks right next.

To the car and looks completely inconspicuously into this car. When the call came from this hotel and the goods are to be brought to Belgium which he now wants to check the hotel looks Bernd immediately establish a link. But he already sees in the back seat objects which suggest a customs officer. A Belgian with German customs documents, Bernd sees under the blanket some inches of seals. Since the flags of the Germans and Belgians. Are almost the same, he can only done so at the identification who is on black, red, Gold. It is difficult to see whether these colours are long or cross-striped only at the eagle on the colours Bernd can recognize this. But he wants to have such a seal sent by the Customs to know exactly. He entered the hotel with this new insight and only looked for a man he could think of a Belgian. But he does not succeed, the phone is directly at the bar is constantly used. He sees that there is little chance to find the man so over the phone out to learn who telephoned so everything in the last hour. But he wants to get the connection data. Thus he concentrated on the car with the Belgian license plate. He goes to the reception and checks in, because he feels he has to stay here because of this strange.

Belgian with German customs seals in the car. Bernd has checked this in the meantime on the Internet, which is there in the back seat of the Audis are original German Customs seals. He lets the car call out at the reception. Please the driver of the car with the Belgian label. This driver should immediately register, and to come to his car, it was damaged. Bernd wants to see the man first and then address him on a better occasion. It takes only 5 minutes there stands the Belgians in front of his car and can, t see any damage to his car. But Bernd has photographed him with and without his car long ago from a safe distance. No more than 20 minutes later, he got the name of the man and his address via Koblenz. It is a Belgian customs official who knows how to deal with the export right in the EU. But as he comes to German seals he has to explain later. Bernd telephones with Gerd and clarifies this about this man. "Bernd will stay with the man who will show up here tomorrow and put the seals on the crates and provide them with the right papers." "How is it with you from Gerd?". ,, Here everything is normal, I just have to replace the camera crew. Give us around some problems. " "OK, be more careful I stay here at the ball and announce me immediately when tomorrow.

The man from the to you inch starts". ,, Ok, I'm going to change teams before making a nonsense of weakness or simply fall over."

Gerd, sneaks with the new team in place to connect with which he did with Marianne and Sally break." I'll get the two cameramen here, then I'll bring you to this place the right is well covered. You only have to pay attention to the utmost calmness ". Gerd first brings the two back, who soon fall asleep and the fingers are clammy. It was the highest time when they were relieved. Gerd then takes the two new and introduces them to the inspection hole. They are building their camera and recording equipment. Since the impossible, is one of the two men, a cell phone happens going on and everything is stiff and silent, the three men in front of the barn and the men in the barn. They also forbade absolute mobile phones and they all look excitedly in their pockets. Soon they discovered that this mobile phone comes from the outside. Gerd immediately responded and whistled Sally. The immediately released rushed comes and jumps at him. His comrades are apologizing because they may have spoiled everything. Gerd has to go on the offensive.

He Has a quick ride with Sally to the nearby dirt road and goes by the barn without looking into it. He does not come far he is put out of the barn from the front and from behind. Fortunately, he is without a weapon and without badges. The men come towards him from the front and from behind with a drawn weapon. Sally recognizes the situation and bangs her teeth; Gerd can only calm her down. He knows that these men will not hesitate for a moment Sally and shoot him. He knows what it is about, and must now keep the peace. "What do you want with your mutt here at the barn?". "Sorry guys, but I'm on a big walk with my dog, we want to go to Herrschbach and then back to the Nürburgring in our hotel. ,, Two men beside Gerd in the middle and Sally noticed the this threat. play crazy again but Gerd can calm her down. ,, Sally who want to harm me who just want to ask us. " But Gerd knows exactly in what danger he and Sally hover. They are led into the barn, and in Koblenz on the presidium and on the camera one is astonished as Gerd her chief commissioner of the head of the Soko suddenly appears with his hands over his head in the barn. On his side of the Border Collie of his friend Marianne. They do not know what to think of it.

You'll see how a net is thrown over Sally and the chief commissioner is knocked down to the ground and both are pulled behind a projection the camera can, t reach. The commissioner and the dog that has caught himself in the net have disappeared from the picture and are no longer visible to the spectators. They are all very dismayed at this unhappy circumstance and the development of the observation. They believe there now everything has been in vain and they are now forced to strike. One of the cameramen understands the situation and withdraws very cautiously. He informs the Presidium that they have caused this incident and that the Chief Commissioner has saved the situation in which he met the people who have no idea who they are. These think there they have captured a harmless walkers with dogs. Everyone breathe out but is concerned about their commissioner. Luckily, they have some time to discuss the progress. Bernd of this new situation undergoes turns immediately and wants to rid the police chief to be a man saddled straight his car and makes his way to the barn. The Carinthian Commissioner follows the man in a respectful distance but the ride goes directly to the said barn.

Stops at a much earlier stage and makes walking.

On the way to the barn, he needs to speak with the men at the camera se have now installed their cameras fixed and locked the monitoring system. They have pulled themselves back a bit and are now trying to turn around the barn to find the place where the main commissioner and Sally have been drawn. They know what they are doing and are doing it with the utmost care. Bernd has discovered the two and speaks to them. They are frightened and believe themselves to have been caught. "No banged colleagues I belong to Soko, to the chief commissioner. Where is the commissioner? ". "In our opinion, this must be here, right where that is another of the air holes". Meanwhile the man from the Belgian customs office with the German customs seals and the corresponding papers arrived in the barn. Everything is packed in crates and a few things had to be separated actually. To fit into the smaller boxes, one is astonished in Koblenz Bureau front of the screen is not bad. As you this art objects all sees and directs the images directly to the experts. ,, You did great Henk made, "the men of the apparent leader says in the barn,

,, Your money you get as always in bar in Brussels, with you in your Restaurant. "No problem Boris, I trust you, so as always. I'm done here now, and I'm pushing. You just have to view this as soon as possible you're in port, loading onto the ship in a few days. The ships wait not one hour and those who are going to the US especially on time." ,,We evaporate immediately, and we have a full tank all vehicles and arrive without further refuelling in a trip to the port of Antwerp. " Good, then a good ride, I tell the captain that you come in any case, these boxes get a special place. As I have seen you have already attached the big signs. Fragile goods / utmost caution. The master of both cargo assumptions is based on this. " "Well, friends, I'll go and wait for my coal in Brussels." ,, Do not worry about your money; you can rely on us up as always. " "The astonished officials could see how much they can rely on these gangsters. You already know that these gangsters can, t leave alive this man, more than 50 million depend on it. They can, t use any confidants. About all not someone who knows where the crates go. The men in Koblenz advise what to do. "We have to try to protect this man we do not believe he will ever see his money".

Mr. police advice, we give its data to the Brussels police, they should definitely take the guy in protective custody. When she arrived in to Brussels." "Well, how do we deal with our Commissioner, we wait for our Commissioner from Carinthia to report, he tries to get an overview of the situation of the chief commissioner. Gerd the chief commissioner, is awake in his corner, the lead behind which one has drawn him. Beside him lies Sally without a muck of itself to give. But he, too, has a great deal of effort to stay awake, his eyes are always falling. It is clear to him that you have injected him something and also his Sally. He tried to keep his eyes open, something that always succeeds only piecewise by force. He knows now that it is important, he hears the conversations next door and hears the trucks depart. He tries to free his hands from his shackles, despite his constant impotence. Then he hears a voice as spoken by a trumpet. Hollow and very weak. He can hardly believe it, he has never heard of his Carinthian colleagues. Gerd, it does not sound very understandable, please do not move, imagine yourself fainting, they leave and want to leave you. We release you when all have disappeared and there is no longer any danger.

That someone will come back. Behave calmly that my need, since you're still conscious. Bernd hopes that Gerd has heard him if not, it is also not a problem because he must now hold absolute calm. They all listened to that one holds both Gerd and the dog probably harmless, as simple pedestrian, I will bring them back. It is assumed that they are there for a few hours, until they are long in Belgium. They have both KO. drop and will not remember anything. The barn teaches slowly and no one cares more about the inspector and his dog. Gerd would have liked to Commissioner and Sally but it is still too dangerous when one of the men would return it would be noticed. But you already have a rescue vehicle nearby and a paramedic is already at Gerd and notes that both are stunned. Gerd just fell asleep after hearing the voice of his friend and colleague. It was as if he had already arrived in heaven. Since there is no acute danger one has decided to wait another hour. After that man took both from the barn. A team moved up and secured all the tracks in the barn and in Koblenz the recordings were evaluated. All involved were identification and now consuming monitored. Even the FBI has come back from the US to monitor the loading.

It is Interpol of the Soko and the Brussels police officers difficult to arrest any suspicious. But none of these men could go a step further. Besides the customs officers is on the way to pick up his money. In his local pub was held all on a long leash. It monitored the place and is sure as put the host with the customs officials under a blanket and holds the money. They want both to be arrested and no longer give them the opportunity to give something further. One does not believe that one will need these two further. The interest in them has been lost and the money has not been paid to the landlord any more. The customs officer has come out of his apartment and is glad to be his homeowner and will no longer appear there. The man noticed is uneasy and suspects the danger for him, noted that followed him someone he is careful. He has a hunch after he has left the barn and has done its job. He did not get rid of the feeling that something in these crates is stuck. He walks through the historic heart of Brussels tries to get away with it shake off its shadow. He does not see anyone, and he already believes that he sees ghosts and makes his way back to his pub. He takes his cell phone and chooses his mate at the former customs office in Germany.

"Hello Harry, everything is OK with you". ,, Yes, it's all OK, but the promised money has not arrived yet. " "Are you alone in your pub". "Yes, here are only two tourists, think from Germany.

You can get rid of them". "I'm trying, where can I go, what's going on?" "I am on the bridge to the port at most 1000 meters away from you, but you have to clarify whether I am pursued. I have such a funny feeling that. I want to get rid of myself as a witness ". Then the conversation breaks off already. But the police have already identified the location and had listened to everything. Also, the host is immediately and makes his way to the bridge. There is already great excitement and a crowd start in the channel there. There are some men already jumped into the canal to pull a man out of the water. The channel is fortunately not more than 1 meter and it does not take much effort. A little later, you get the man in Koblenz and Interpol certainty. Was shot this fraudulent customs officials on this bridge and the criminals have again disposed of a confidant. Unfortunately, they could not protect him anymore, so the murders around the amber room have grown to and one is unsure how to treat this further.

Meanwhile the crates are on the way to Antwerp, the trucks are not 50 mails before Antwerp. Since these crates can, t escape them and there is no danger for further persons. At least is not for men in Europe. The next one will be relocated to the US again. There has never been such an excitement and such a sweep through Europe. But an art treasure was never as valuable as these from the mountain bay in Koblenz. Even if it should not be the Amber Room but only some parts of it. But doing other important works are guess that the experts have already found out. The value is estimated to total more than 550 million € from the experts who still carefully studying the pictures. The commissioners have the boxes once again be drawn and sad look the ship with the cargo behind her, but they have the guarantees of the US government, as s all get back to see these pieces. Gerd looks sad after transport and he does not think so right to return. Americans can still insert his opinion some vetoes and a year-long struggle then begins to these treasures. Ronny knocks him on the shoulder. "I know Gerd what you think, you believe we do not keep our word?. But we guarantee you the return." "This is the only thing that calms me, what have we done.

To save this treasure for us?. But I think now, the experts are the first; we have been able to document everything in the boxes. " "You see Gerd I take the copies with to get hold of what they will get. We have everything. In picture and sound, I am also curious about what the experts are finding. The ship is sailing back to San Francisco and I have made sure you are there again for our support. The FBI has already clarified this with your Bureau and although you have time smeared us so, but we have had and this great understanding. We need your support and show our appreciation for your performance. " ,, it would be disturbing if I bring my girlfriend, she makes a few days of vacation in San Francisco. I told her so much about the most wonderful city in the world, this city is the only one still standing in front of my hometown ". "OK, Gerd I check with my director, I could imagine that this works". It has worked and Gerd flies 10 days later with his girlfriend Marianne to San Francisco. It is a new adventure trip for both. Marianne comes under the home of Ronny and Ronny woman cares about Marianne. While Gerd cares with Ronny and his colleagues at the Amber Room the FBI still suspects the super-rich people.

From Sacramento as final purchaser, one suspects that these crates goes again over several middle men. Once they messed everything up because they beat too early. Gerd has been looking for a room with Ronny and some other FBI men near the port. The ship enters. In a few hours and they are ready to wake the ship. Of course, they have noticed that the captain of these four cases is particularly loaded and has hidden among containers. This time, the FBI has become wiser through the old experiences. Today there is a surveillance team waiting for each crate, not like on the first transport, when suddenly all the containers have disappeared and they have only been able to follow one and because of the confusion they have also lost them. Today everything is ready and the men are waiting. The customs authorities shall also ensure that all data relating to the master of the vessel are given to them. But they will only sue him if anything completed. It does not take long because they are loaded four boxes and natural as suspected shipped separately and individually hiding between the containers. They had expected because s these boxes are repacked into containers s.

But no they are hidden in between. This time, they are all well prepared and not a box escapes the FBI. The Transport of boxes going this time to the city of San Francisco, in an old shop house. All the boxes are unloaded and taken up. To the astonishment of all the policemen, these crates remain there for three days. They stand there and are no longer touched. Filed as worthless stuff stand her like junk. The FBI suspects that these boxes are empty and have been loaded on the ship. Only Gerd knows better, he has a man on the ship. Who has not left these boxes out of his sight. The FBI always swallows hard as happy to know this, these Germans them one step ahead. So they do not run into the danger but still have to look, because then they would have betrayed themselves. The entire hall is completely supervised, of course you also from old experience whether someone followed the crates. The Fed's caution has paid off, but now she almost saved Gerd from a mistake. These days Marianne has travelled with Miriam Ronny's wife throughout San Francisco. You may find there was not exaggerating Gerd, for them this is the most beautiful city in the world. Just in addition to Kottenheim and Gerds Koblenz.

In which she also partial lives. Today she booked an offshore trip that made her pretty busy. She does not go normally on any ship, even if she is on the Rhine or the Moselle she will be dizzy. But today she has survived a high sea tour on a small boat. She has really popped up and now feels really empty. She missed the beautiful San Francisco, but tomorrow she wants to go. To the old Indian forest on the outskirts of San Francisco so she goes to bed early today. This forest wants and has to experience. Not far from her no three houses next to the house of the FBI man Ronny both she is a guest, is likewise a meeting announced. It is about the four wooden boxes from Germany. The boxes Ronny and Gerd supervise with the help of the FBI. Marianne is awake at night because there is so much going on in the memory of the waves in her head and stomach. She takes the dog of the family on the leash and gets some air. The night is wonderful and you hear the sound of the Atlantic as a backdrop, her feeling of nausea is not just good for you. She wanders a bit and feels, as it gets better with every minute and every GONE meter. Wufi little crazy dog she pulls something in the doorway of the neighbours of the three houses away lives.

She hears loud voices to the probably Wufi has responded and it has taken in the way. You suddenly clearly hear the voices and a loud argument, she wants to polish off the affairs of others do not care. It is not quite speak the English language. But since is also someone here who speaks German and then another. She listens as it is about an art delivery from Germany. more often they hear the words Amber Room. Because it blocks electrified on the ears. Amber Room, that's the case where Gerd worked for so long. This is the case which is why he's here in San Francisco. " Now slips away completely into the hedge and hear things they should never have heard. Wufi begins to bark and the men fall silent Instantly. Marianne hastened to come to the street and goes with Wufi they still yapping leads on a leash on, as if nothing had happened. Two of the men her look and shakes their heads. These women will run whatever stupid in the night with their jumping dogs which through on the area. ,, Can women have heard something, where did she go? ". ,, The disappeared in the neighbourhood, was probably drunk the old ". Only now Marianne is really drunk were from that she has suddenly become afraid of these men.

It is sometimes amazing what can so happen. She lies in bed and thinks about the part, it has to do something but not until tomorrow morning. Could would here today, the cars of the FBI or taxis pull up these men react suspiciously. You can feel it again and again to Gerd if this hunts a fever. These men are the hunted, the need to be more cautious than their hunters. She Marianne by chance by seasickness, more learn about these four cases than the entire FBI in the days in which the boxes are stored here. It will inform Parliament of it tomorrow morning Ronny and Gerd. To sleep is hard to think. Wufi the little dog feel the tension that goes into Marianne, she has to endure this tension until the next morning. Rosie the woman of the house felt the next morning immediately that something is wrong with Marianne. ,, What's going on Marianne, do you have a bad dream. " ,, No, not a bad dream, please call immediately your husband and Gerd over here, but they need to come up with inconspicuous cars ". Rosi picks up the phone and doing as I said; the men come immediately and stand for 30 minutes later in front of the door. The men can, t believes the story, but everything fits the story of the four boxes.

It is inconceivable that sit the ringleaders of the whole art smuggling on any three houses. All the wheels of the overbearing FBI immediately start. Gerd would wish that they would have this technology available in Germany. In a police patrol car and more technology is installed as in some German police station. In thirty minutes, they have all of there so unimpressive draws his threads over these neighbours. It's not even an unidentified police he was involved already in many art thefts, but he could never be transferred. That was part of Annette is explosive and giving them new opportunities. Now that you know the end customer is a man of no good reputation and the combination of very closely with the first customers in Sacramento. It looks as if the two want to share the delivery. 2 boxes here in the Neighbourhood and two boxes of Sacramento said Marianne heard the men talking. You can hardly believe it, which had a lucky Marianne. Fortunately she has got away scot; These men have no mercy at every reason to suspect the suspects die immediately. The walk through the native Forest falls for the day of for Marianne. But Rosie is aware of the danger hovering aware of Marianne.

,, Dear Marianne, you are here not in your Koblenz is so sure you're in the US in the middle of a bad thrillers " . ,, Yes, that is when you love a man of this life and loves adventure. I have to live with him and his world. Marianne to the sometime we want to live in Germany but then again we know how beautiful and free our country as large and free the US is. We are a melting pot of residents from around the world, but we are all Americans at the end and we want to stay there. So sure, it is now in Europe not more. Ronny and Gerd have since analysed the documents sent by the FBI. They have also found who had. To be the two Germans Marianne has heard, these are but submerged and not seen since the evening. These two were involved from the beginning in this deal and are distributors and brothel owners from Frankfurt. One soon discovers that these have booked flights from LA to Amsterdam; they are trying to cover their tracks. After two more days, the boxes are loaded again, and as already actually two boxes out to Sacramento brought to the local multi-millionaire who was involved already in the first experiments in the matter. The other two boxes go. I n another warehouse nears the airport. One quickly realizes.

That this building belongs to the art dealer and neighbours by Ronny. They seem to both is all to be quite safe now to this delivery around fine. The art dealer in Sacramento, this crate, each at least 60 million values are even in his court. But his property is also tremendously saved but he has no idea that you have already guessed this location at the FBI and all safety systems are already under the control of the FBI. The Hall of other art dealer is currently being prepared. Gerd Koblenz. Commissioner amazed not bad as swiftly and silently goes. If we had anywhere near such facilities, we lack in Europe also as a powerful and so super-equipped troops. We could prevent much in advance and explain much faster. It has quickly discovered the flights of the two men from Frankfurt and pulled them equal in Amsterdam from circulation. Directly after this message to the FBI it starts in San Francisco and Sacramento. All involved more than 30 men are arrested. Even the multimillionaire Franko Bruno is not comes all his many money and many lawyers from this number out. The works of art ever reach the West again is also open. Gerd and Marianne still enjoy three days of special leave and then go with a rental car the whole west coast of the United States.

Down to the Mexican border. Do not stop in San Diego and then fly crammed with beautiful and terrible experiences from LA back home. Back in their homeland and their great great city on it again waits after they've been longing again. Longing for the mighty United States of America in the small peaceful Germany. But there is in the home and immediately new disappointments, the two art dealers and criminals you fancied on the way to Europe, who have booked their flights. Long before the Soko have escaped the arrest, or not flying. They were seen not in Frankfurt and not in Amsterdam. Interpol rotates in Amsterdam at the wheel. The two criminals have once again the police in the US and in Europe can be deceiving. Gerry Schreinemaker and Wolfgang Nussbaum are all flight lists and passenger lists did not arrive in the EU. This is the first wound point in this whole action for the Soko Koblenz. Just these two are responsible for some of the killings here in Koblenz disappeared. The Soko sits down immediately with the FBI in San Francisco in conjunction there you are also very surprised. They promise to act immediately. Mr. Schreinemaker and Mr. Nussbaum sitting in Italy, they have guessed, there is shadowed them.

You have to pre-flight in LA and made it to Mexico and from Mexico to Spain and went from there to Switzerland. Here they learned once with fresh money supply the Franko Bruno had referred them to Switzerland. For the 20 million for each of you, there are good new papers. They both go on together from Bern via Zurich to Germany. They both have not yet earned enough to just know they believe that some very important paintings are hidden in the forest of Arenberg. They could not do enough loaded and have with the other men. The now almost all are dead or behind bars, 10 images with oversize in the forest well wrapped had to be buried. According to expert opinion, these were at least another 10 million revenue. The buyer for these images they found in France. Well equipped with their new identity are both courageous, they know have been arrested almost all their previous customers in this business with the parts of the Amber Room. Franko Bruno is of course against a large deposit on the loose. Again, this is not purified; he knows these images and is also interested in spite of all its problems. His already delivered to him art was confiscated. He could not stop the payment to Gerry and Wolfgang.

They are the two escaped crooks back at the place where it all began, in Arenberg. We know there is not, and with their new Swiss passports and some changes to their faces. Beard and hair they are confident that no one will recognize any of the special commission Koblenz. But as it was so often in this art theft and. Commissioner Random helps SOKO back on. This two men check in at the hotel with the nuns. Dare you, as never before, they were here at this hotel and their murders in Arenberg were covered. They were just the instigators of the actions. The perpetrators themselves have long since been fixed. They make their walks unobtrusively through the Arenberg forest. Almost opposite of sour mill they have buried the 10 images. There have already been several months and to look the images under difficult conditions. It takes a few days, they fall forward to. But they can be explained, can explain why they have in the monastery always so dirty shoes and pants. They see no choice but to rent a car and to put appropriate clothing in the car and then getting to replace them. Wolfgang ,, I can`t believe it, I'm sure the pictures are exactly buried opposite the guest house of the mill Sauer me. But we are looking for the third day.

And have not the slightest trace. I could almost believe that someone watching us here and has already recovered the treasure. " ,, No Gerry, we were so careful, I think we were further up the hill because of an old pit was already there that we could use, now many months have passed and everything is completely overgrown. It will not be easy to find this place. Because we must be careful not to damage ". Both sit down once back and think about how to proceed. It was a pity we did not get everything into the container ". ,, Clear was the shit, but now we have here is the wonderful bread to 10 million It's been really something that we have nothing to lose, we are wanted by Inter pool and the FBI. You heard it strikes us the murder of some of the many deaths to have come to this Ominous Amber Room to death. We need to be clear about when you caught us we are here for many years, possibly decades disappeared ". ,, time we've actually got the devil is not against the wall, we had expected this is the reward for the big money. For Franko Bruno that's just been small change that has 50 million earned on that deal. He was just unlucky that was the FBI faster and better. We have the art treasures warned him not to bring directly to Sacramento. "

,, No matter what happened, we want to do better than the others did it. " ,, How do you like to your new name? ". ,, The dear I really like is from Wolfgang so Schreinemaker become Belgians, the Swiss Robert Koppel ". ,, Yes, that sounds really good, for me it is so similar from Wolfgang Nussbaum Hans Rosenbaum has become. We will be able to live further with the other 10 million as these two men GOOD and no worries. But first we need to find the pictures and discreetly get rid of here, and then we can start with the fine life. Up to Robert, read us the images found in this wonderful valley that has made us so rich. " ,, We wait it off Hans, damn I have to get used to Hans. " ,, I'm doing no better, we must be careful that we do not betray us, as practice always practice our new name. " Come ,, Robert, on with you, we need to find the images. Other there is nothing to the wealth, although our 20 million that we have are very good. " We must be careful, we have wrapped the images lack of time only in plastic. " ,, What wrapped images worth 10 million only in plastic buried ". ,, Yes, we were in Stress the containers were picked up and we had to take. We have tried everything to get even the images in the container, but had no chance. "

,, All right, I have understood, " the Bureau in Koblenz all SOKO sitting in front of the computers they sift through everything to go all the documents by. ,, children, we must have missed something in this whole story. If the two upper crooks and alleged art dealers are submerged, then that means there. Franco Bruno's paid them and they want to disappear now and need. I am once again gone through all the images we have of the artworks. Verifies that please even if you have some air. We missing much at all over the verification images. These missing images I have not found in the crates for Franco Bruno, nor where to Hendricks. I have now looked at the recordings for the third time. These images appear anywhere. I am now of the opinion here nor anywhere in the Mills could still parts of the treasures be hidden. some of the images have to be here in Koblenz. Here in Koblenz exactly said in Arenberg be. The experts also examine all the lists have now been found. Lists that have not yet set up the lost when they shipped the first containers ". Gerd ,, if you've checked that and has the Americans which also confirm we need but no longer deal with it, but then we do the job properly. "

Also good,, Bernd because I go strongly believe that we still have these images here with us. Because if I everything they had to bring not have time these treasures somewhere far away in ". ,, Just love Commissioners, because I have already thought, I'm going to check the two art dealers and bandits. Could determine, there is in the EU has arrived neither of the two " . Where commissioners is actually Gerhard Maifelder, he is the only one who had nothing to do with the death of a nun. The wanted to return to Cairo, please try to get the guy. The still can get a lot of money. Who has yet secured a number of other art treasures that were in the secret passage. Perhaps, the help us, please make me the guy approach ". ,, Good Boss, I think you men, you and Gerd you should carefully leave the forest around the manhole, maybe you can find something to her and we can wait quietly to the two. I stay in the office and call on all hotels in the area whether two men are staying there somewhere. We could now have the two in Switzerland they already have new identities and the new papers to. " ,, Very good Commissioner, it is a very good idea, so the two could already be in Germany, run completely unknown here already around. "

Therefore ,, chief should ye try searching the forest ". ,, The Renate my dear, I have already taken my companions are waiting at my home to start ". ,, Oh my goodness, you want to climb through the forest with Sally and the Eifel goat ". ,, Commissioner, "ok I'll take the Eifel goat back but I find the name of that great". ,, Pull yourself together Renate , I do not want to hear this term for Marianne or I'll have you terminate the friendship. " ,, All right Gerd I have to get used to it but cancelled is not pushed well ". ,, No shock you that at last from the head. If we want to remain friends, between us can never be more than a friendship. " ,, Well then cut it off into the woods with the Eifel, oh sorry with Marianne and Sally ". Bernd the Commissioner of Carinthia turns on and what should I do with the story? ". ,, You my dear are our backing because it has Renate right could the two are already looking for the treasures themselves. They will at least know about where they are located, because cry Maker was when loading the art treasures with it, even if only with a telescope. The guy is even resurfaced, is a small miracle. Come Gerd we meet like random walkers at the Sauer mill. No but rather up in Arenberg, we go separately to walk down.

And catch at bay with a search on ".,, No Gerd that you can. t do to me, although I love nature and but the Run Arenberg down that's too far. The piece you run with Sally and Marianne alone. I think anyway that you assume three right streets and I the left. We are mobile and I will Parke in Sauer mill and start there. " ,, Good Bernd, that's a good suggestion, we do it like you said it. " Ok ,, boss I nozzle going on, we've got that look great weather for such a forest walk. " For you ,, Corinthian but the mills should be a pleasure, something like native air.`` A little later, Gerd, Marianne and Sally start from the car park at the edge of Arenberg in the direction of the Mills. For them, this is like a little vacation and Sally the greatest pleasure, they are already browsing in the undergrowth but never runs a game to see if bunnies or deer, she looks the dehiscent game only and enjoy it as they chase it. Gerd and Marianne have the bitch never when they walk on a leash. ,, Gerd, tells me, this is yet again not a normal walk, we going here through the bushes and undergrowth. Miss do you need me and Sally again for your service inserts?. " ,, Well, yes sweetheart something like that, we are looking here possibly some art treasures. We have found that the men who did not get everything.

In the container five older men and had to hide some treasures here somewhere. The gangsters must have noticed that and this I most certainly have reburied. " ,, reburied that sounds like a funeral. All is very about Amber Room around pieces of the Amber Room which has led us to the United State. " ,, Yes, we could find on the basis of lists and the footage missing some parts and can only be here or should be. ",, Then you have it once advance the Sally and I are set as auxiliary Commissioners, we are more for the Koblenz police traveling as a private." The three have now arrived at the height of the old mine and make the first catch. They sit on the floor in some small bushes and enjoy a piece of sausage and bread. Sally does not miss such a delicious break. Of course she gets a tasty meat bones. ,, That's right Gerd, we push ourselves the fat sausage in and the dog gets lean meat bones ". ,, He can also afterwards drink any liquor to digest as we do the same. " ,, OK, we let ourselves enjoy the official vacation day and do not argue. The mobile phone interrupts the conversation and the breakfast in the woods, Renate's turn. Gerd ,, I have something figured out what you could be interesting. You know t Yes I have good relations.

With the monastery, after the death of my friend, after the murder of my friend who was indeed there nun is the contact become closer. " ,, Now tell already, I do not want your life story but I want to know what you learned important? ". ,, Ok, could not you well again at the, end up with Marianne; do you have a bad mood? ". ,, No my dear Commissioner I did not I get the same if you do not accosted. " ,, Good boss, as two Swiss have arrived since yesterday evening whose description could fit the two on walnut and Schreinemaker ". ,, Well, that's something useful, Bernd knows humble? ". No ,, I inform and equal'll get back to you. What you chew because there already?". ,, I enjoy my second breakfast in the middle of bushes and trees". ,, I can think of with Sally and if she with Marianne." Yes ,, my Commissioner as it is. " ,, Then it might even be good that the two already roam about in the forest and looking for their treasures. " ,, That may be, you drive best equal to your monastery and see you around there, maybe you get so little out over the two Swiss? ". ,, Ok, then sit equal with Gerd even in conjunction who has just arrived in the parking lot at the Sauer mill ". ,, Ok I'll do". Two seconds later, Gerd has tuned the just brings his hiking boots from the trunk.

Of his chief commissioner. ,, Hello Gerd, I put off the same, just put on my walking shoes. " ,, Well fine, be careful Bernd, I must warn you, there are in the monastery two suspicious Swiss surfaced that could be our men when it our two Schreinemaker are walnut and then we will meet them determined?. No 30 minutes later Gerd's cell phone goes off again; Renate is tuned and informed their Commissioners. ,, Hello Gerd, I am here in the hotel and the two Swiss sitting not 10 feet from me and cut a mighty breakfast pure. Belatedly, I think, for me it is almost lunchtime.

I have photographed them and sent everything to the recognition service. The way I see it have only changed her hair and the beard, our boys will soon have their true identity out ". ,, When it comes to the two concerns walnut or Schreinemaker ". ,, OK and thank Renate, I also inform the same Bernd, but knows we had on the two bumping could. " ,, As I see it, the two need at least 1 hour long can search her in peace if the exit I sign. They concern a car here. " So the conversation is over, leaving behind a thoughtful chief inspector. ,, What is going Gerd, there is some News ". ,, Yes, my dear, if we're lucky then the two are already here and have breakfast.

Up in the monastery. Schreinemaker now called Robert Koppel and Mr. Hans Rosenbaum. " ,, They have now picked a great name if it is the two? ". ,, We will know hopefully soon, now want to start again; I once again pack everything into the backpack. Gerd calls still Bernd has already begun at his search just on the other side of the road. Bernd amazed not bad when he hears the news. ,, Because we would have once again the incredible luck of the able, I doubt after all the problems mind that are the two men or not, that this Schreinemaker are and Nussbaum. But I thought that are far behind Swedish curtains. But you see how hard you can make mistakes, in particular when so many agencies and countries such a thing involved. Where do you put it? ". ,, We are almost opposite of the mine and have just finished our second breakfast ". ,, Ok then let's get going then we can focus on the observation of the German / Belgian Swiss. You always amazed how quickly you can get a reasonable new identity with money. "Then read look for us, you have to find with your Sally yes better chance of something here. I understand just how the two so money can, t be while gone to this great danger and go back to our region.

Have 20 million each, and could in the lap of B out of life. " ,, This is our lucky people have the money, never get sick of it. This applies to the good people and the bad people. Anyone who has tasted the many money usually goes in this greed as ". The two men in the monastery hotel have eaten their breakfast, their late breakfast with great relish. You now have the rest away. With 20 million in the back and good new papers you can feel in this great Klosterhotel very well. They set off on their only yesterday morning of rented vehicle. So they can better hide their search, because it is still not so long ago when they played here just crazy, that there was a dead. Nun and five other deaths here and in the surrounding area. The nuns had already become a little suspicious. Why her to dirty walking gear. So they are also faster in the Mills, and are clean and well maintained as hikers back. These five old here disguised as hikers the way. Now they feel more comfortable as a car driver and they have noticed that the nuns who serve them filed their distrust in the hotel. The believe the two but only, they do not feel and do not know, there the Koblenz detectives sitting them again in the neck. The two do not make a single step more without being observed.

The discovery service has undoubtedly notice from the images which Renate has sent them from the Monastery Hotel from the two that these two men with Swiss passports and the beautiful new name paddock and Rosenbaum with 99% security Schreinemaker are and Nussbaum. This alone by the face detection but also of the two. Is already being tested to make it even safer. Renate has brought out of the hotel rooms fine hairs with roots from the hair brushes and transported to the laboratory. Just two hours later, the result is 100%, these two Swiss is the Belgian and German walnut. Renate informs Gerd as they drive with their jeep from the farm. This too is a quirk of Schreinemaker the Belgians. He loves to drive it Jeep, one he has not broken already on his last adventure. The commissioners have swept through the area without discovering anything without finding the slightest trace of the art treasures. Sally also had nothing where she could have taken a track. Before the two get out of the jeep they park something in front of the saddle, they call in the USA, at Franco Bruno. "Hello Franco, we've heard you're bailout outside". "You idiot, you dare to call me here, but at least you called on my secret number.

What do you want from me?". "We want to know; what you are paying for the art treasures you already know, you have them on your film". "Do you have the art treasures?". ,, Yes, we have, we are almost out!. What are these pictures and parts worth?." "You know I'll give you 10 million for that." "For 10 million we can sell this to an Italian, put something on it". ,, Call me if their actually did these things, I want a photo of each piece. Then I tell you, for each of you 10 million. Just do not sell to the Italian, it would be easier if I could still trust you ". "Come, but just over then you can see the parts themselves, we certainly do not come to the USA". "Your spinner, I'm on bail outside I can, t leave the US". ,, Well, well, we have registered 10 million for each of the pictures. " "This is clear if I lose the other it would be a small disaster but I would have these things. But I also work to get parts from these boxes. " "OK Frank we announce ourselves as promised with the money, you can. t transfer it to Switzerland we have these accounts dissolved". The discussion ends up and the two Swiss have to go on searching for and need to find if they now want to get back every 10 million. They have doubled their amount just because the one art dealer does not want the other art dealer.

To get it. There are sums that are normally unthinkable and there are people in this world for, these amounts are only pinats. The many millions on this earth have too little and too dying just too much, and a few can buy the whole earth. And not a single wish remains unfulfilled. The three commissioners, the SOKO Koblenz, who are dealing with such rich people a lot lately, are fully in agreement that they would never exchange with such people. They live sensibly have friends can go out to make what they want without being bothered. But these rich and super rich lead a life of fear around their wealth and in constant fear for their lives. They are captured of their money and their lust for more and more. They can do everything they want, but they are never free. The commissioners know that they have to work and constantly fight when they want something special. But it is not that real life. Bernd and Gerd meet at the Kornsmühle (Grain mill) for another of the many mills in the Mühlental, which has to offer besides old mills also great vineyards and also some wine grapes and wine cellar has. A valley full of experiences, only her Soko has no eye for these beautiful things. They are in use for the good things of the super-rich and the action against.

The criminals. The produce these things on the criminal way. At this presumptuous Amber Room (Bernsteinzimmer) from the shaft mill Mühlental already are 7 dead. They want to make sure there are no more dead. But of course nothing is certain, they can only do it. You all do not suspect, since it will be even more complicated. Because Franco Bruno was so stupid as he calls the other art dealer and this explains that he has now already purchased the remaining artefacts. He looked like a child over the stupid face of his opponent, which he can see on Skyp. He is acting immediately; Gino knows where the two are artisans and bandits. He reacts promptly, turns off Skyp and immediately calls his office in Frankfurt. Two hours later, three men from his Frankfurt office are on their way to Arenberg. With all the data from Rosenbaum and Koppel in the bag, also with the address of the hotel of the Dominicanians in the two booked. These two men Rosenbaum and Koppel are coming back to the hotel before the dark. They had no idea at all of how the rope around their necks was so slow. A knit at the two ends the Italian Maffia pulls and likewise the Soko has already laid hand. Robert Koppel and Hans Rosenbaum are still in a good mood.

They believe they have found the deposit of art treasures. With the hunt of the objects they want to start tomorrow morning for today it is too late. Hilarious and Enterprising showering the two. As you can see the 10 million each in their Tashkent. So that they are really outark of all, do you know what we're doing today?" "Yes, we eat well and then give us the sketch, the pictures and what is still buried there can no one take us anymore. Now it does not matter any longer. We are completely strangers here and now enjoy our millions. " "OK, Hans, my suggestion, we go first to the Pizzeria Roter Hahn (red rooster) and then to the Klönsack, to us really a nice old stile place". "Balling up the idea was not bad, they kept right, it was a ball. But a ball as the Italian Mafia desires. This balling was not in the sense of the two art dealers. But they had their fun in advance. Robert has eaten his hot-beloved super delicious pizza and Hans his gypsy schnitzel. "I did not promise you too much my friend, did you?". "Yes, my dear, this has done really well again, it was super delicious". ,, The two now make their way pastors Kraus road down to the pub in the Klönsack. There is much movement on the pastor Kraus Str., More than normal moves in the evening on this road.

The participants do not know this of course. In addition to the Italian Mafia, two employees of Soko Koblenz are also on the street. They all march as inconspicuously as possible along the road. The men of the Soko would have been very astonished. If they had known that the three men, before the spectacle shop Mafia men are also watching the art dealers. Only the artisans have a different goal than the SOKO Koblenz. The three men from Frankfurt go unobtrusively into the small Arenberg cult pub. The landlord, mania, which today is even behind the counter is amazed not bad. As only the two stranger men see now three quite dangerous-looking men follow them. These three seem to be among the two who thinks at least the host. Until he can see from his position that the two men under the table are directed two large revolvers. The third throws a contract on the table. Here gentlemen, here is the contract you have with my boss. If you do not fulfill these then you have several holes in the belly of here immediately." If only you are moved, it's over with you. " We have excellent silencers you only hear a low noise and you sleep peacefully in this beautiful pub. " "Then Gino ordered once that he should be more out, then it is not a question that he gets the items.

So we agreed with Franco. Payment against the images we send from the treasures or with you it could be a personal acceptance ". One of the men goes to the door to talk to Gino in Naples. His answer is crystal clear, one ant word of a Mafioso s for a contract. He has with the two is a contract. Mani the landlord of the pub has long been on the phone with the commissioner Gerd the head of Soko and clarifies, previous function on the situation in his pub. "Gerd, something is brewing, I can see how these two men are threatened with the gun. Just the second of the men comes in again and his mine is dark. I have already sent my guests who were sitting at the front of the bar. My service is already on the way to their car.

What should I do Gerd I am now with the 5 men alone, if the mutually I am as a possible witness with turn? ". "Mani, you go on like this so far, but are careful. At your door are already 2 of my best people, put them so that they sit inconspicuously to the men. Reinforcement is already on the way to you, you dare to the you these men continue to serve ". "Sure my dear, send the men pure I will greet them and sit at the table in front of the TV as if they wanted to look football".

"This is good Mani do so, so fast does the Mafia not shoot in a public pub". The door flies up and the two from the SOKO Koblenz come through the door. But, ,, Prima you two, unfortunately, are my guests counters disappeared I do immediately to the TV. Dortmund is playing today." "Are there even more TV guests?.". "Yes, there are still some of the sports club, registered by your club". "This is good, and then it makes watching more fun". Bernd then writes a text message to his boss. We are at mania and have everything under control but against five we are powerless." "The answer comes promptly, there are still three men for the pub in the march and a SEK is on the way. Keep everything quiet until the three of you are at the same time, the SEK has sorted out.

And is ready to intervene immediately. "Mani is on the way to the new table, what shall I bring you men?" Today I have a special beer if you like. Bavarian white beer with and without alcohol ". "Then please bring us three white beer without alcohol". ,, OK will be done. would the five gentlemen drink something? ". "Yes, I have just heard you have alcohol-free white beer, we would like five too".

The weapons, the three Mafia people already plugged in again, this did not make a great impression on the two mellow art dealers. "What is your Boss just now, you just talked with this?". "He wants the fulfillment of his contract, we know long ago where the goods could lie, which there is no other possibility. We could make you aside and seek for ourselves. For we know you have not yet found these parts. We would have organized 100 men tomorrow and would not need you at all. Do you think we and our boss Gino is stupid, he can save 10 million and more ".For the two bandits and artisans, the air is thinning; they feel this and try to get their weapons as inconspicuously as possible. They put their guns in the socks and one under the armpit. It looks like a thunderstorm in this place, after a violent thunderstorm. The next three spectators of the football match come in. And sit down with the other three men. It looks like a lot of deaths when it bangs here. " "Bernd goes to Mani, these two know themselves also because he is so many times also with Gerd up here. He also has a savings here, even if it is not too often since.   ,, Mani that looks very threatening at this small pub, do that you get it. " "Bernd When I'm Off Smell The Guys Lunte".

I have a better idea, I'm Dortmund fan, if the first goal falls then I give a round half litter off for all. Then I already know what I am doing at the table of the gangster with it. They all slide off the tray and you can access this mess ". "Mani is too risky for you but a great suggestion, it could work". In fact, the first goal will be in the first five minutes.

All cheer and jump off the chairs. Mani is in front of joy, beer, free beer for all, he calls loudly into the pub and taps into hell out of doors for all. His whole collection of beer jugs must believe it. He juggles 11 jugs full while the Dortmund team shoot their second goal. because the SEK (special police) ensures that no other guests can get into the Klönsack. Mani puts the first 6 years on the table of the disguised policemen and protests them ". The loud sound loudly against each other and drunk and Dortmund is cheered. It has long been agreed with the six men and Mani. As s This will provide beer mugs for the next table for turmoil. They have discovered that now the two artisans have their weapons in their hands. They could see how they carefully pulled them out of the sock holders. Mani goes to the counter and knows that it is not safe to do what he is planning. He puts the five jugs on a tray.

And goes over the small staircase to the table on the raised floor. "Hello men, here please your swimming pool". He raises the tray with his right arm and it crashes with a bang on the table and pours all five men with the delicious beer. There is a shot is fired from a weapon and another one that hits a ball one of the Mafioso's in the leg and a bullet whistles hair's breadth. Manis ear over and drills into the beautiful bar. With a jump, the six Soko officials are over the crooks and have overwhelmed them in seconds. There is not much to do for the SEK. All you have to clean up the criminal, first aid car come to the slightly wounded Mafioso and pick up. The KTU picks up the one ball from the counter and quickly the shack around mania is empty. Only Bernd and Gerd are still longer in the Klönsack and still drink some jugs of beer. Help Mani collect the jugs and wipe the beer. Only 2 beers are broken but 6 litters of beer bring the upper part. Of the bar for swimming, you need some time to the beer from the floor and the tables to be transported in a bucket. Four brushes are used to clean the floor. The Chief Commissioner and the Chief Commissioner are satisfied with this successful day. These five men were fixed without much effort.

Five trigger-men has served them very nice host of Klönsack. There will be a long night for the commissaries, which are on the way back on foot. 5 mails for Gerd and 7 mails before Bernd, they renounce a taxi and they arrive almost sober in Ehrenbreitstein and Koblenz. It is a splendid air and the two have very good mood, now the project Amber Room in Koblenz is almost complete. Now they just have to find the last art treasures and save for now German museums, where these works of art have no other owner. It is now also firmly that only parts of the Bernsteinzimmer here in Koblenz were stored. The next day the office application starts a little later in the Bureau for all. The Soko and the police department from the LKA are again with the boat about Amber Room. At about 10:00, all rested and not intended to be art treasures worth 20 million already on their way to the wonderful Mills in the. The entire Mühlental is full of police cars. A millennium is to be combed on both sides of the mill valley. Three police dogs are on duty, but these dogs do not know exactly what are looking for. They suspect their noses in the forest floor and in the meadows. It takes exactly 4 hours until a whistle indicates that something has been found.

The dogs were there and then metal detectors which indicate the presence of metal parts. A group of men and women Advances on the experience of excavation has ben. Everything has to be excavated carefully by hand. It turns out there's this art treasure grave has completely covered s a landslide and has changed the situation of the slope. The Hundreds successfully pulls out of the Mühlental. The mills and vineyards are free again for the tourists and the inhabitants of the mill valley. Only the Kripo (Crime investigation) and a strip wagon watch the excavations of the Mühlental treasure. Gino the art dealer from Naples would not be a worthy member of the Mafia in Italy and in Europe if he did not have his people there. Even though his three killers have failed and are broken at the Cleverness Koblenz Soko and are now in the custody of the Koblenz police. But he Gino has long since unremarked observers on the spot in the Mühlental. But he can`t do more than watch.

He must watch over the cameras of his people, how to be pulled out of the pit bit by bit. There are parts of which he still wants it, since is they have to be in his possession. He Gino had also paid 20 million for what he sees now is four times.

The value. He thinks about what a huge treasure was recovered by the four young soldiers from Berlin. They brought the treasure into the shaft in difficult manual work, and kept it there for decades. They have remained little. Only the one Gerhard Maifelder was able to save a lot for himself and his people in Africa. Something from the money of Frank Bruno who would soon have is completely destroyed. It is by the use of Hendricks who sent his killer to the Mühlental and thus set a series of murders in motion. But the death of the nun from the monastery Arenberg have to be held by three of the five now-old Nazi anti-aircraft officers from Berlin. Gino now has the chance to see these great remnants of the pit. You can see how these bronze busts take pictures, panels and more from the pit to be unpacked from the film, cleaned and repacked and placed in large closed box vans. His men who filmed everything and direct transfer do not suspect her boss can pack his stuff and set out for Koblenz. Gino knows that his against the part in San Francisco. And Sacramento have poorer cards here to get those treasures. Franco and Hendricks have so much exaggerated the use of violence that could spoil everything. But he Gino had almost the same way.

He is glad that the employment of his people in the Klönsack Bar so well expired. He wants to thank the host personally for his action has prevented the death of some men. By the evening Gino Fabritze has arrived at the monastery Hotel Arenberg. The next day he takes care of his people that the local gruesome Koblenz prison is in the city part Kathause in custody. You can only wear them on account of their unauthorized possession of weapons, and in a few days they will be released for a bail. Gino sits for a long time in his hotel room and always looks at the video of his people, who have turned it from the site. These are all things if he had seen them so clearly before, for which he would have paid much more than these 10 million or the high-rocked 20 million Franco Bruno wanted to pay. He would have paid them 20 million and regretted very much now because he did not come earlier to Koblenz. Gino is one of the few people who, besides his addiction to money and art, can be a normal person. He is the type of man and the rich does not believe companions and protection by others. He is now in Koblenz and wants to enjoy this city and he begins to admire this city. This great city on the two rivers, and the great restauration.

At the old mighty emperor on the still image and his horse. Show above all the huge and well-preserved fortress on the rock of Ehrenbreitstein. He also visited two of his Pizza shop belonging to the sphere of influence of his Mafia, maybe he still needed help. Of the pizza restaurant owner he finds the necessary for his feeling. He would not Italians, Sicilians if he did not need a woman in Koblenz. But he finds course quickly in a small bar in the near the train station, its pizzas owners have already given him recommendations. He quickly finds the suitable lady at the bar, the lady whom his men have recommended to him. It will be a huge German-Italian night. Only such nights bring Gino the clear head for clear decisions. He spends time and again to watch the videos in his hotel room the next day. He pursued also transporting the treasures and the temporary storing in a well-guarded barracks of the army up here near Arenberg. It has also been learned in Koblenz that a police barracks can, t be the right safe place. From there, the complete container has been stolen. Gino goes through. All the stops of this gadget again. It is already a madness that was only triggered by the insane acting of Frank Bruno and Hendricks.

The old men were on the verge of surrender and the receipt of their money. Gino will not happen to him like that. He will deal with it with great calm in Sicilian manner and not in American fashion. The main share of art treasures is thus lost to all. The bum is in now in German and American Muses and look of visitor amazement pull over and have no idea. About the normal value, the other morning they have already forgotten what they have seen at all. He Gino lives with this art, only this art is his life. He can bite himself in the rear of the bad mistakes of the Amis in this matter. How well would these treasures have done in his home, parts of the Bernstein room and these infinite. Treasure that were not registered so far to which no one was entitled. Gino sets off on the way to the nearby Pizzeria in Arenberg in the red rooster. One real Italian pizzeria with a pizza that also tastes like pizza. The best pizza he has ever eaten in Germany. The host sits down at Gino and tells him the building that is as old as Arenberg. Here this house was the connection in the world. Here was the station of the coaches. The horse-carts for the journeys through the Westerwald over Montabaur into the world. Gino likes these old stories as much as his art.

After the good time he goes to the cult pub of Arenberg in the Klönsack. This pub is simple and really old, so according to its taste. Gino is quite loaded when he leaves the Klönsack. He arrives at the hotel of the nuns over the church and the Holy Garden. But first he had to talk to all the figures in the sacred garden. Everywhere he could meet Jesus. Mary, and some apostles. He had long conversations with everyone, so it was way past midnight when he came to his hotel room. He skin on his bed fully dressed. No once more maybe the shoes he gets off his feet. Only his statues of the sacred garden accompany him to sleep, no art but Mary and Jesus dominate his sleep as a truly strictly Catholic. The Soko Koblenz has now got some air of the art-screw and art-murder with the many dead comes so slowly from their heads. This art screw led her through half the world and gave her a lot of excitement. They are glad that everything can now be completed happily. Although the journeys through the USA were already a huge experience. Now they only wait for the return of the art treasures from the USA, they all have little. Reference to this art in the Soko, it means for them only work and danger. Nevertheless.

They hope that the German authorities will be able to bring this art back again. "It is strange," says Gerd, the head of SOKO, that these works of art are now being worked up here in Koblenz and then in the Bundeswehr barracks ". "I do not find that funny after the deal with the container theft in the police barracks, because they want to be safe. I wonder why this art is still here in Koblenz, art that is so valuable and interesting for so many rich people all over the world ". , You're right Bernd, I have also wondered why you've made these parts not directly to Berlin. The local museums tear this art but all under the nail. " "Yes, men, where you are right, you are right. Koblenz will once again not get hold of these old treasures ". The door to the Soko office opens and the police council appears in the doorway, in the excitement he has even forgotten to knock. But he does not do it anyway. "You guys will not believe it, we are invited by the Berlin Senate to the museum island, and we are the first to see this art here in five days to go to Berlin. As a reward for our work for saving this big part of art. " So the Soko has not reckoned, rewards are rare for police work.

For as good work as this was done in Koblenz. The commissioners are very happy about this invitation; at least something has now given them this fight. But they do not know, because this is struggle for art is not yet over for them. They have no idea that the Mafia one of their leaders already stretches their feelers according to their art in the barracks. The boss and art lover Gino has been in Koblenz for days. But they the Soko are also freed from these problems. The Bundeswehr got this problem charged. Empty barracks was redesigned to the Art storage and more than 10 experts are cleaning and spoiling these exhibits. These things, which are here for the time being, are directly on the Museum Island. For this reason, they have to be prepared. Gino worried about his old established Mafia friends all plans of the barracks. He photographs like a champ and also procured photos of the indoor unit of the barracks. In it, he works and he always needs sex, his girlfriend from the bar is more and more with him in the hotel. He has given her there as his secretary who helps him to satisfy his hobby. He does not want to stand out in a monastery of the nuns. In addition to his plans and the drawings, he is always intertwined with the pretty girl at the screw.

,, Moni, without you I get absolutely no clear head, I need you as artists need their muse, so you're the Dormant pole of my thoughts. " "What are you working so hard with the many pictures". "Yes, my darling, you are one of my joys and the art of the other part". Gino puts his pictures on the side, which at the moment show no art but should make him clear the way to his art. He now dedicates himself once again to his art of love and emotions. He treats Moni as soulful as his art, he lives it as it does a real Sicilian men. With much feeling and love tendernes and strength, after such love scene that always takes an hour or required Moni getting some air and tranquility. Now she decides to go to the wonderful garden. In the beautiful and well stocked herb garden and then go into the pleasant coolness of the sacred garden. A very nice old garden from time of 1860-80 full of memories of religious history. Memories of Jesus his mother, Joseph and all the Apostles and more. In front of each figure of Jesus, she pauses for a few minutes to sincerely pray. She leaves Gino alone longer, she knows that he can love like a possessed man and can work like a possessed man. He also works like a possessed, draws himself looks at photos and plans.

These intermediate games with Moni. Which is a wonderful woman driving him to the highest performance. His work for the liberation of art also benefits from his addiction to sex and to art. The plan for the liberation of art from the hands of the military Coming forward speedily. Gino knows that he does not have much time that it will not take long before this art is in Berlin. There is only one way to get art from the barracks or steal it on the long route. For Gino this is no steal, no theft, this art does not belong in any museum. This art belongs to his house of art in Naples. He has two possibilities to get possession of this art. There is an old manhole in the barracks which has been poured and has to be re-excavated. Or just a frontal attack no one expects. Its people have long since been formed in Koblenz and are ready for an attack on the barracks. It has been found that a digging of the old tunnel would be too difficult and would take much too long. If they had reached the barracks, the art treasures have long been in Berlin. So only the frontal attack on the barracks remains, which should be well camouflaged as an attack of an IS group. He learns by Moni the one in the barracks already doing the art treasures to be made ready for transport to Berlin.

Moni is in league with one of the officers on duty. So Gino also has his fingers in the armed forces, in the site management. So Moni good is that now only becomes a true art looted by him, in the recovery of his art. Better could be said if his plan worked out. He's after the next round of sex with Moni the bright idea. It can merge the two plans when he starts the attack when the transport starts. It makes sense to do so because everything is safe then loaded. It must be done when the truck is in the barracks. Gate exit the Bundeswehr. this old tunnel for which he was once good. This tunnel is now the Great distraction in the attack. Gino plan everything down to the last detail and prepare everything. Many wheels are now turned in Koblenz and Frankfurt. Gino is sure that he takes these treasures from Koblenz to Naples. The work on the treasures in the Koblenz barracks have been completed. The big truck of Schenker drives up the building, just feet away from the door of the barracks. All treasures are carefully loaded in the truck. Gino look at this from a safe distance to, just not now arouse any suspicion. He has been recognized with his men that some guards are here already arrived. It is very surprising that here by the federal government which this treasure.

Will include when it arrives in Berlin. These Competent men have no information about the already made thefts and traveling the other art treasures. You have no idea how many tricks art dealers work. You have no idea, because the commissioned art dealer earn a lot, a lot of money and they sure take no account of any human life. Long gone when it comes to such treasures. Neither the local police and the federal police have no idea of this transport. The truck has only two men escort and drive to the gate. The young soldier controls only the papers and gives the signal for the free ride. At this moment there is a huge explosion in the middle of the barracks complex. It is moving into the barracks. But even at the gate of the barracks so happens a lot. The guards standing there, two young soldiers are overwhelmed in no time, and the men of the private security company who are sitting in the truck as fast as they are entered flown out of the cab out and packed in seconds Hand strong and land in a small bus which has placed transversely in front of the gate. The truck starts moving and quickly disappears from the scene and left the barracks detailed terrain in minutes.

Sirens of the fire brigade and ambulance sirens of the race up to the barracks. Everything in the barracks focuses on the explosion. No one comes to the idea that at the gate something happened. The truck with the artworks and has left the two soldiers standing there as before, still and stiff with a rifle slung over his shoulder. The fire brigade and the ambulance is opened the barrier and back properly sealed. Everything is fine, three men and two vehicles leave the entrance to the barracks Follow the big truck Schenker transports. But strangely, these go over dirt roads and tanks roads on the Horchheimer that is shared altitude, on the old military site. There waiting 5 mall van. More than 10 men circle the Schenker trucks, the large door is flung open and in less than 1 hour, everything is transferred from the giant trucks in the five vans. The guards and the driver Schenker are brought blindfolded from the van in which they have been invited to the barracks. They are shipped in the box Schenker LKW.s and it is closed. Gino is the middle of everything and whose eyes shine Roberto has stopped wanted the three folding. No, ,, Roberto, I know you would like this but do there have been enough deaths to this art. The men did not see anything.

And can, t tell us. Drive the truck into a coverage and covers it off. So that it is not detected as quickly. Until you noticed what happened. We are already with the treasure in Italy, now from people, everyone drives the route that I have given. Within another hour throughout Koblenz is not a car in the Mafia. It takes notice to the changing of the guard until, as s the two soldiers there only dolls are in uniform. That the officer on duty bound in the guardhouse are. The fire brigade and the armed forces have long been established that there is something explodes which is completely harmless. It takes another hour until you know what it's all gone by this action. You know at once that this treasure they have cleaned so and have restored to shine. This action has been considered only this treasure and the truck. The police will be informed immediately and the military police chase going on around this truck can, t have gone far is found again. Gerd the police chief nearly falls out around when he hears this treasure was stolen again, from the barracks of the Bundeswehr. The commissioners of Soko meet with their police advice up at the barracks. ,, This can, t true, this treasure is stolen again. It may not be possible those damn rich and their art dealer.

Since we have some locked away and already some new back. Superintendent advice actually us does that here nothing more. That's a matter for the Federal Police .The should be looking for the robbers, a s big truck . The Schenker of must be but easy to find. " ,, Mr. Inspector, her team is because you have accompanied this art theft from the beginning ". ,, accompanied, yes sir Police Council, accompanied the right word. Ok if it wants the leadership then we place equal loss.",, Well done sir Commissioner, you can register here to the barracks Focus. We already work with the federal police all motorways and main roads in their sights, I think they should focus on the barracks now. " ,, Well, I see my commissioners the soldiers that matter to question. "Quickly, the commissioners have determined how clever the men proceeded again. You have Distracted soldiers with the explosion in the ancient tunnel. A tunnel already was no longer known. No more than a crawl tunnel was destined probably for waste disposal. In the evening, the commissioners meet to discuss the situation in Klönsack in Arenberg. Of the federal police no message still comes from the truck, which must be gone without a trace.

Just how easy dive as a truck. " Mani the host overheard serve the beer. ,, And when the truck drives on none at all road when this is hidden somewhere in the woods and was transferred to other vehicles. " " Mani, nailed and it's the guys are so K lever proceeded who thought further. where it was clear that they never come with this truck to Italy. The have reloaded very early to nowhere, a truck was spotted. "Mani gets involved again, because he knows up here on this side of the Rhine from best. ,, I would the truck say had it not far from Horchheim. To the Schmittenhöhe , there is the old training ground of the Bundeswehr. I'm there can be a truck easily hide ". ,, a good thought Mani, although I live on this side of the Rhine but up there I never go, it is I the one time Schmittemhöhe come. there, free pens for cattle and wild horses should be developed. I was there only once as a civilian so the event was for all-wheel friends in this have I got even in the pouring rain inside. Marianne, Sally and I have fled; it was there all hell broke loose." Gerd reaches for his mobile and calls his advice to police. ,, Councillor, I have a guess where we will find the truck. " ,, Where Mr. Schöder, where, they say it? ".

,, We could imagine that the truck on Schmittemhöhe is hidden. " Gerd hear on the phone as the Council slaps with the flat hand on his fore head. ,, Clear, Schöder, that's the idea, we have wasted a whole day. Today, nothing works but morning the armed forces. And a hundred will scour the whole area. I'll organize everything already starts at five o'clock. " Gerd knows his police council, an energy bolt, which it manages to send the police and the armed forces with more than 30 off-road vehicles on the search. Already at 9:00 the message comes to the Commissioners the course on the Schmittemhöhe. Please wait there. The truck is found and the truck the guards and the driver are included but safely. Just in case an emergency doctor and an ambulance comes, but the men have only minor injuries and only need a coffee. The commissioners coax even all the men have satisfied out of them. When they almost want to give up the interrogation, the driver is still an interesting reference. He can see through the double doors of the tailgate of the truck, s only then if they were driving through a pothole that followed them several small buses. Only for a few seconds he could see through a small gap. It was still light enough and.

He could see that these cars were all in the same colour, red in a dark. ,, man that's something from the state's Commissioner Schöder the search for red minibuses to get out and cancelled the truck manhunt. The KTU has already been released and examined the truck and the environment. All tracks are saved. Luckily it has not rained in the night and it can secure good tire tracks. ,, Do you Bernd, this is our lucky almost all crimes leave traces. Two hours later, they know the type of vehicle fitted with these tires. The Fiat Group has equipped almost all of his pickup truck with these tires, now the commissioners know. With which vehicles are carried away the treasures. These data immediately run in the hunt with one .Now the Soko is also safe, since these art treasures are to Italy. They dig out everything that has to do with Italian art market and also meet with Gino Fabreze. You know about him, that he should be one of the secret Mafia bosses. But as is so in Italy, which are also all covered and no one ever dares to suspicion Voice. ,, Gerd boosts wanted to after the Fiat vans. When once they are in Italy, they have only a slight chance ever to get the treasures again. The motorcade has not divided and that is their undoing.

The column was discovered on the German-Swiss border. The vehicles have been sighted in Müllheim about 40 kilometres from Basel. The local police already under surveillance the vehicles from a safe distance. You are in a somewhat secluded hotel. Gino is also in his boys, he leads from here the passage to Italy. The cars are covered with Italian advertising and so changed. All drivers are gathered around Gino. ,, men from here you will individually covering different drive nan border crossings. You for an Italian plumbing company if you are asked. The advertising on your car says this also. I am assuming that their problem-beyond the borders comes. I'll see you in Italy again. I have to recheck each minibus. Gino goes into each bus and sucks this mass of art into itself. He has this treasure well distributed among these five buses. He feels as good as never before in his life, he has the power stage as an art collector achieved even without the art in the containers and boxes are now available in the US. Be of whom have colleagues Hendriks and Franco Bruno is not much. Gino is confident that this be sometime at the end of its process chain behind bars. He Gino Fabreze has its smaller part c levered handled.

He bathes in each of minibuses in his art and small other parts this art in his luck, this fits great into its existing collection one. He bathes much longer than intended in his art, and still has no idea that this will be his last enjoyment of his art. The Soko Koblenz is located only 10 minutes from Müllheim. The LKA Baden Wuerttemberg has already. Set its SEC (special police in to the way and is already only 2 km far from the hotel. You want to wait until the buses away from the hotel to endanger any guests. Gino has hired for his men in suite rooms in which they can make fresh for the final stretch of the journey and strengthen. All this is the time to Gino he had to make it to Italy. Every second of wasted time increases the Police the chance of safe the time. Four civilian officials have long been at the hotel in order to hedge Gino can, t escape. For stays one more day in this hotel and then will fly the next day Basel to Naples. The Soko Koblenz is already close to the SEC from Baden Würtemberg landed. None 3 mails from the hotel with the Gangster. The Soko is immediately informed about everything and is very satisfied with the circumspection is traded with here. They could now also make contact with the police in Italy and received confirmation.

The now tangible evidence showing that Gino Fabreze one of the highest Mafia bosses in Italy. They also confirm that probably these drivers and security guards, two men in each car are very dangerous and they have almost certainly heavy weapons in their cars from a car rental from Naples Are the all velvet Gino Fabreze belongs.

The action is led by a wise police advice from Freiburg, everything he arranges like the Soko from Koblenz which is now equipped with bullet-proof vests. Everything seems to be set in motion. ,, We need with access to wait until everyone in this forest is safe. We forward close the road and then standing right behind them with armoured vehicles already well camouflaged on site. Which are within seconds in their places. We have from the forest from both sides in control none of the mafia men will escape. " The vehicle Colon starts to move, connected by radio, the men in the woods is informed for the attack on this Colon. Gino retires to his hotel and is full of joy, his heart seems to burst. But this joy lasts only minutes, she goes to him when he was arrested, still at his gun without a chance to come. The arrest of Mafia bosses goes off without bloodshed. But in the forest bloody play action.

From the sec and the police had no idea. That this so normal looks, buses have armoured windows and doors. Startled keep the drivers as they suddenly two armoured vehicles blocking the drive. Behind them, two vehicles have built-threatening, there is no back and forth more. The police loudspeaker it demands loud and clear on in German and Italian language.To the task. But none of the passengers in the cars would come under life sentence out of the mess. They know what their cars can, which are armoured in the cab and have all-wheel drive. For a moment the whole increased Colon then break them out in all directions off the road into the forest. Countless gifts from machine guns hit the cabins with no visible success.Two of the vehicles get stuck straight into a ditch. The vehicles have the break on the other side more luck. They come through but then get stuck in trees is very tight. You need to get out of their vehicles. You now know to escape possibly their chance. Their cabins are armoured but their location areas are not. One is not to prevent damage to this shooting the artworks. The SEC has moved and is now trying in turn to get the bandits from the secured cabins.

With heavy weapons they have but they can`t go to the buses approach, they know that they could damage the precious works. Now back who widely surrounded the wood the other forces partly to the vehicles approach. Some of the security guards can free themselves from the cabins and now crawling with their weapons cross the forest. It's like an war with thinking partisans Gerd everything from a safe location monitoring. The SEC can`t proceed. As usual hard unfortunately because of the need to protect the works of art. The police and the bandits of the Mafia provide a very targeted firefight. Man to man, they crawl that gives them Piecewise cover in the forest through the bushes. Everywhere the splinters flying off the tree trunks when a sheaf of shredded a tree trunk from a submachine gun. Branches flying high in the air and fall reeling from the force of the bullets on the floor. The gangsters are completely unsecured and give but not to lie, despite many calls, the guns away. They are all Mafia nationals, they will die or life sentence behind bars. Now all curse this job and her boss, which is securely seated somewhere in the warm and beloved cap his coffee or drinking Gino and they can die here because of this stupid looted art.

They stole in an adventurous action. The men get great anger at this charge they can now burn here. They begin on the vehicles to shoot and shoot only wild in an infinite rage at the cars and everything that moves. You are so confused anger that they bombard also Mutually. The head of the SEC sees the danger that the art of the Gangster. Sven is destroyed for their anger out and blows to attack all gangsters. It takes almost an hour until all are overwhelmed. The end result four dead gangsters and three seriously injured and five slightly injured. When SEK fortunately only 3 Easy injured policemen. Your protective clothing has proven itself once again, only this has made it possible for them to action against the mafia men to go. Gino actually already sitting with a coffee in Freiburg. Before the magistrate and is indented here only once until the extradition request by is. Italy expects a very high penalty him not life imprisonment for his work at the Mafia and for organizing the so much suffering to Europe and so many people bring. The men from Berlin who fear for their art are also arrived and the art is from the minibuses that have already been taken with winds from the fire department and the technical relief organization.

Back on the road and were unloaded under the eyes of the police and examined. Everything is still in a top condition and can be loaded directly into 2 Larger vans which are now full police get support. The Soko Koblenz travel back by train and is infinitely glad that this drama has now but still found the mill shaft in Koblenz be good end. How often do the art thieves have these items be mutually and the authorities in Germany and the United States stolen. Ronny gets told on his next visit in Koblenz this story. Even for this is Unbelievable. Gerd ,, I have seen all of these works of art, I do not want a single one in my house. " Gerd, laughing out loud, just the same, I've thought of that, nothing, not a piece of it I want. Then paid to have to sell it to crazy collector.

We have this crazy now well enough to know me it is a mystery how there can be people who want to have such a waste at home. Want to own and even have need because it is in their souls. For this murder take practically worship in buying only those things. ,, Well my dear Bernd, that we are different controlled and consider these things what they really are and is. Art is a business that is artificially constructed for the rich. In this case, we have now had 12 dead.

But the art will learn from nothing. "*,, That my dear boss and colleague, that is the art. Art is like religion it blinds people and blinded them. " ,, My God colleagues when you so to hear you might feel you are atheists and Art objectors ". ,, Can this not be in this world. " ,, Love colleague, we have to constantly deal with the reality of this world. Most criminal cases there are about money and art that fellow to have little to try to get more by any means. People to vie I have squandered their money in S inn and mindless things instead. Of their excess money to help those who need help urgently. Behind this background, everything passes me probably want for the arts. For this, the criminal acquisitions were allowed to experience it now with 12 deaths to a high degree itself. ,, If love men and women of SOKO, we now go our artworks by Koblenz enjoy. A thick knuckle with sauerkraut and beer. But I could you consider that always, for these 15, sometimes even murders.

๋

publishing company
Engelbert Rausch ISBN 978-3-946925-23-1
56736 Koblenz /Germany
Pfarrer Kraus Straße 83
Author Wolf Arenberg

A gripping thriller about rediscovered old NAZI Art Plus some parts of the Amber Room. Young soldiers, former against aircraft gun have brought these treasures on behalf of high-Nazis to Koblenz in the mill creek bay. There the treasures were lifted only 2016th This has attracted art thieves and dealers from around the world. The five old men had very little of the treasures. Some of them were in the age nor murderers.

The first of the eight DEAD was a curious nun from the convent in Arenberg. The rest was spread out over the whole world. The art treasures were moved and brought back. The FBI, Interpol and in particular the Soko Koblenz was engaged in this case a long time.

follow the next novels killed German corner.